THE
WANTING
SEED

Anthony Burgess

The Norton Library

W·W·NORTON & COMPANY·INC·

NEW YORK

The title of this novel is the refrain from
the folk-song 'The Wanton Seed', collected
in James Reeves's *The Everlasting Circle*.

W. W. Norton & Company, Inc. also publishes *The Norton
Anthology of English Literature*, edited by M. H. Abrams et al;
The Norton Anthology of Poetry, edited by Arthur M. Eastman
et al; *World Masterpieces*, edited by Maynard Mack et al; *The
Norton Reader*, edited by Arthur M. Eastman et al; *The Norton
Facsimile of the First Folio of Shakespeare*, prepared by Charlton
Hinman; *The Norton Anthology of Modern Poetry*, edited by
Richard Ellmann and Robert O'Clair; and the *Norton Critical
Editions*.

Library of Congress Catalog Card No. 63-15877

ISBN 0 393 0808 8

Printed in the United States of America
2 3 4 5 6 7 8 9 0

Part One

Part One

One

THIS was the day before the night when the knives of official disappointment struck.

Beatrice-Joanna Foxe snuffled a bereaved mother's grief as the little corpse, in its yellow plastic casket, was handed over to the two men from the Ministry of Agriculture (Phosphorus Reclamation Department). They were cheerful creatures, coal-faced and with shining dentures, and one of them sang a song which had recently become popular. Much burbled on the television by epicene willowy youths, it sounded incongruous coming from this virile West Indian deep bass throat. Macabre, too.

> 'My adorable Fred:
> He's so, so sweet,
> From the crown of his head
> To the soles of his feet.
> He's my meat.'

The name of the tiny cadaver had been not Fred but Roger. Beatrice-Joanna sobbed, but the man went on singing, having no feeling of his business, custom having made it in him a property of easiness.

'There we are, then,' said Dr Acheson heartily, a fat gelding of an Anglo-Saxon. 'Another dollop of phos-

3

phorus pentoxide for dear old Mother Earth. Rather less than half a kilo, I'd say. Still, every little helps.' The singer had now become a whistler. Whistling, he nodded, handing over a receipt. 'And if you'll just step into my office, Mrs Foxe,' smiled Dr Acheson, 'I'll give you your copy of the death certificate. Take it to the Ministry of Infertility, and they'll pay you your condolence. In cash.'

'All I want,' she sniffed, 'is my son back again.'

'You'll get over that,' said Dr Acheson cheerfully. 'Everyone does.' He watched benevolently the two black men carry the casket down the corridor towards the lift. Twenty-one storeys below, their van waited. 'And think,' he added. 'Think of this in national terms, in global terms. One mouth less to feed. One more half-kilo of phosphorus pentoxide to nourish the earth. In a sense, you know, Mrs Foxe, you'll be getting your son back again.' He led the way into his tiny office. 'Ah, Miss Herschhorn,' he said to his secretary, 'the death certificate, please.' Miss Herschhorn, a Teutonico-Chinese, rapidly quacked the details into her audiograph; a printed card slid out of a slot; Dr Acheson stamped his signature – flowing, womanly. 'There you are, Mrs Foxe,' he said. 'And do try to see all this rationally.'

'What I do see,' she said with asperity, 'is that you could have saved him if you'd wanted to. But you didn't think it was worth while. One more mouth to feed, more useful to the State as phosphorus. Oh, you're all so heartless.' She cried again. Miss Herschhorn, a plain thin girl with dog's eyes and very lank straight black hair, made a *moue* at Dr Acheson. They were, apparently, used to this sort of thing.

'He was in a very bad way,' said Dr Acheson gently.

'We did our best, Dognose we did. But that sort of meningeal infection just gallops, you know, just gallops. Besides,' he said reproachfully, 'you didn't bring him to us early enough.'

'I know, I know. I blame myself.' Her tiny nosewipe was soaked. 'But I think he could have been saved. And my husband thinks the same. But you just don't seem to care about human life any more. Any of you. Oh, my poor boy.'

'We do care about human life,' said Dr Acheson, stern. 'We care about stability. We care about not letting the earth get overrun. We care about everybody getting enough to eat. I think,' he said, more kindly, 'you ought to go straight home and rest. Show that certificate to the Dispensary on the way out and ask them to give you a couple of pacifiers. There, there.' He patted her on the shoulder. 'You must try to be sensible. Try to be modern. An intelligent woman like you. Leave mother-hood to the lower orders, as nature intended. Now, of course,' he smiled, 'according to the rules, that's what you're supposed to do. You've had your recommended ration. No more motherhood for you. Try to stop feeling like a mother.' He patted her again and then turned a pat into a slap of finality, saying, 'Now, if you'll forgive me –'

'Never,' said Beatrice-Joanna. 'I'll never forgive you, any of you.'

'Good afternoon, Mrs Foxe.' Miss Herschhorn had switched on a tiny speech-machine; this was reciting – in the manic tone of a synthetic voice – Dr Acheson's afternoon appointments. Dr Acheson's fat rump was turned rudely to Beatrice-Joanna. It was all over: her son on his way to be resolved into phosphorus pentoxide, she just a damned snivelling nuisance. She held her head up and marched into the corridor, marched towards the lift. She was a handsome woman of twenty-nine, handsome in the old way, a way no longer approved in a woman of her class. The straight graceless waistless black dress could not disguise the moving opulence of her haunches, nor could the splendid curve of her bosom be altogether flattened by its constraining bodice. Her cider-coloured hair was worn, according to the fashion, straight and fringed; her face was dusted with plain white powder; she wore no perfume, perfume being for men only – still, and despite the natural pallor of her grief, she seemed to glow and flame with health and, what was to be disapproved strongly, the threat of fecundity. There was something atavistic in Beatrice-Joanna: she instinctively shuddered now at the sight of two white-coated women radiographers who, leaving their department at the other end of the corridor, sauntered towards the lift, smiling fondly at each other, gazing into each other's eyes, fingers intertwined. That sort of thing was now encouraged – anything to divert sex from its natural end – and all over the country blared posters put out by the Ministry of Infertility, showing, in ironical nursery colours, an embracing pair of one sex or the other with the legend *It's Sapiens to be Homo*. The Homosex Institute even ran night-classes.

Beatrice-Joanna looked with distaste, entering the lift, on the embracing giggling pair. The two women, both Caucasian types, were classically complementary – fluffy kitten answered stocky bullfrog. Beatrice-Joanna nearly retched, her back to the kissing. At the fifteenth floor

6

the lift picked up a foppish steatopygous young man, stylish in well-cut jacket without lapels, tight calf-length trousers, flowery round-necked shirt. He turned sharp eyes of distaste on the two lovers, moving his shoulders pettishly, pouting with equal disgust at the full womanly presence of Beatrice-Joanna. He began, with swift expert strokes, to make up his face, simpering, as his lips kissed the lipstick, at his reflection in the lift-mirror. The lovers giggled at him, or at Beatrice-Joanna. 'What a world,' she thought, as they dropped. But, she reconsidered, glancing covertly but more keenly at him, perhaps this was a clever façade. Perhaps he, like her brother-in-law Derek, her lover Derek, was perpetually acting a public part, owing his position, his chance of promotion, to the gross lie. But, she couldn't help thinking yet again, having thought this often, there must be something fundamentally unsound about a man who could even act like that. She herself, she was sure, could never pretend, never go through the soggy motions of inverted love, even if her life depended on it. The world was mad; where would it all end? As the lift reached ground-level she tucked her handbag under her arm, held her head high again and prepared to plunge bravely into the mad world outside. For some reason the lift-doors refused to open ('Really,' tutted the big-bottomed exquisite, shaking them) and, in that instant of automatic fear of being trapped, her sick imagination converted the lift-cabin into a yellow casket full of potential phosphorus pentoxide. 'Oh,' she sobbed quietly, 'poor little boy.'

'Really.' The young dandy, bright with cyclamen lipstick, twittered at her tears. The lift-doors unjammed and opened. A poster on the vestibule wall showed a pair of male friends embracing. *Love your Fellow-Men,* ran the legend. The female friends giggled at Beatrice-Joanna. 'To hell with you,' she said, wiping her eyes, 'to hell with the lot of you. You're unclean, that's what you are, unclean.' The young man swayed, tut-tutted, undulated off. The bullfrog lesbian held protective arms round her friend, hostile eyes on Beatrice-Joanna. 'I'll give her unclean,' she said hoarsely. 'I'll rub her face in the dirt, that's what I'll do.' 'Oh, Freda,' adored the other, 'you're so brave.'

Two

WHILE Beatrice-Joanna was going down, her husband Tristram Foxe was ascending. He was humming up to the thirty-second floor of the South London (Channel) Unitary School (Boys) Division Four. A sixty-strong Fifth Form (Stream 10) awaited him. He was to give a lesson in Modern History. On the rear wall of the lift, half-hidden by the bulk of Jordan, an art-master, was a map of Great Britain, a new one, a new school issue. Interesting. Greater London, bounded by sea to south and east, had eaten further into Northern Province and Western Province: the new northern limit was a line running from Lowestoft to Birmingham; to the west the boundary dropped from Birmingham to Bournemouth. Intending migrants from the Provinces to Greater London had, it was said, no need to move; they merely had to wait. The Provinces themselves still showed their ancient county divisions, but, owing to diaspora, immigration and miscegenation, the old national designations of 'Wales' and 'Scotland' no longer had any precise significance.

Beck, who taught mathematics to the junior forms, was saying to Jordan, 'They ought to wipe out one or the other. Compromise, that's always been our trouble, the liberal vice of compromise. Seven septs to a guinea, ten tanners to a crown, eight tosheroons to a quid. The poor young devils don't know where they are. We can't bear to throw anything away, that's our big national sin –' Tristram got off, leaving old bald Beck to continue his invective. He marched to the Fifth Form classroom, entered, blinked at his boys. May light shone from the seaward window on their blank faces, on the blank walls. He started his lesson.

'– The gradual subsumption of the two main opposing political ideologies under essentially theologico-mythical concepts.' Tristram was not a good teacher. He went too fast for his pupils, used words they found hard to spell, tended to mumble. Obediently the class tried to take down his words in their notebooks. 'Pelagianism,' he said, 'was once known as a heresy. It was even called the British Heresy. Can anybody tell me Pelagius's other name?'

'Morgan,' said a boy called Morgan, a spotty boy.

'Correct. Both names mean "man of the sea".' The boy behind Morgan whistled a kind of hornpipe through his teeth, digging Morgan in the back. 'Stop that,' said Morgan.

'Yes,' continued Tristram. 'Pelagius was of the race

9

that at one time inhabited Western Province. He was what, in the old religious days, used to be called a monk. A monk.' Tristram rose vigorously from his desk and yellowed this word, as if he were fearful that his pupils would not be able to spell it, on the blueboard. Then he sat down again. 'He denied the doctrine of Original Sin and said that man was capable of working out his own salvation.' The boys looked very blank. 'Never mind about that for the moment,' said Tristram kindly. 'What you have to remember is that all this suggests human perfectibility. Pelagianism was thus seen to be at the heart of liberalism and its derived doctrines, especially Socialism and Communism. Am I going too fast?'

'Yes, sir.' Barks and squeals from sixty breaking voices.

'Right.' Tristram had a mild face, blank as the boys', and his eyes gleamed feverishly from behind their contact-lenses. His hair had a negroid kink; his cuticles half-hid blue half-moons. He was thirty-five and had been a schoolmaster for nearly fourteen years. He earned just over two hundred guineas a month but was hoping, since Newick's death, to be promoted to the headship of the Social Studies Department. That would mean a substantial increase in salary, which would mean a bigger flat, a better start in the world for young Roger. Roger, he then remembered, was dead. 'Right,' he repeated, like a sergeant-instructor of the days before Perpetual Peace had set in. 'Augustine, on the other hand, had insisted on man's inherent sinfulness and the need for his redemption through divine grace. This was seen to be at the bottom of Conservatism and other *laissez-faire* and non-progressive political beliefs.' He beamed at his class. 'The opposed thesis, you see,' he said, encouragingly. 'The whole thing is quite simple, really.'

'I don't get it, sir,' boomed a big bold boy named Abney-Hastings.

'Well, you see,' said Tristram amiably, 'the old Conservatives expected no good out of man. Man was regarded as naturally acquisitive, wanting more and more possessions for himself, an unco-operative and selfish creature, not much concerned about the progress of the community. Sin is really only another word for selfishness, gentlemen. Remember that.' He leaned forward, his hands joined, sliding his forearms into the yellow chalk-powder that covered the desk like windblown sand. 'What would you do with a selfish person?' he asked. 'Tell me that.'

'Knock him about a bit,' said a very fair boy called Ibrahim ibn Abdullah.

'No.' Tristram shook his head. 'No Augustinian would do that sort of thing. If you expect the worst from a person, you can't ever be disappointed. Only the disappointed resort to violence. The pessimist, which is another way of saying the Augustinian, takes a sort of gloomy pleasure in observing the depths to which human behaviour can sink. The more sin he sees, the more his belief in Original Sin is confirmed. Everyone likes to have his deepest convictions confirmed: that is one of the most abiding of human satisfactions.' Tristram suddenly seemed to grow bored with this trite exposition. He surveyed his sixty, row by row, as if seeking the diversion of bad behaviour; but all sat still and attentive, good as gold, as if bent on confirming

the Pelagian thesis. The microradio on Tristram's wrist
buzzed thrice. He lifted it to his ear. A gnat-song like
the voice of conscience said, *'Please see the Principal at
the end of the present period'* – a tiny plopping of
plosives. Good. This would be it, then, this would be it.
Soon he would be standing in poor dead Newick's place,
the salary perhaps back-dated. He now literally stood,
his hands clutching in advocate-style his jacket where,
in the days of lapels, the lapels would have been. He
resumed with renewed vigour.

'Nowadays,' he said, 'we have no political parties. The
old dichotomy, we recognize, subsists in ourselves and
requires no naïve projection into sects or factions. We
are both God and the Devil, though not at the same
time. Only Mr Livedog can be that, and Mr Livedog,
of course, is a mere fictional symbol.' All the boys
smiled. They all loved *The Adventures of Mr Livedog*
in the *Cosmicomic*. Mr Livedog was a big funny
fubsy demiurge who, *sufflaminandus* like Shakespeare,
spawned unwanted life all over the earth. Overpopula-
tion was his doing. In none of his adventures, however,
did he ever win: Mr Homo, his human boss, always
brought him to heel. 'The theology subsisting in our
opposed doctrines of Pelagianism and Augustinianism
has no longer any validity. We use these mythical
symbols because they are peculiarly suited to our age,
an age relying more and more on the perceptual, the
pictorial, the pictographic. Pettman!' Tristram shouted,
with sudden joy. 'You're eating something. Eating in
class. That won't do, will it?'

'I'm not, sir,' said Pettman, 'please, sir.' He was a boy
of purplish Dravidian colouring with strong Red Indian

features. 'It's this tooth, sir. I have to keep sucking it, sir, to stop it aching, sir.'

'A boy of your age should not have teeth,' said Tristram. 'Teeth are atavistic.' He paused. He had said that often to Beatrice-Joanna, who had a particularly fine natural set, top and bottom. In the early days of their marriage she had taken pleasure in biting his ear-lobes. 'Do stop that, darling. Ow, dear, that hurts.' And then little Roger. Poor little Roger. He sighed, then pushed on with his lesson.

Three

BEATRICE-JOANNA decided that, despite her tangle of nerves and the hammering at her occiput, she didn't want a pacifier from the Dispensary. She didn't want anything further from the State Health Service, thank you very much. She filled her lungs with air as if about to dive, then thrust her way into the jam of people packing the vast hospital vestibule. With its mixture of pigments, cephalic indices, noses and lips, it looked like some monstrous international airport lounge. She pushed to the steps and stood there awhile, drinking the clean street air. The age of private transport was all but over; only official vans, limousines and microbuses crawled the street crammed with pedestrians. She gazed up. Buildings of uncountable storeys lunged at the May sky, duck-egg blue with a nacreous film. Pied and peeled. Blue-beating and hoary-glow height. The procession of seasons was one abiding fact, an eternal recurrence, the circle. But in this modern world the circle had become an emblem of the static, the limited globe, the prison. Up there, at least twenty storeys high, on the façade of the Demographic Institute, stood a bas-relief circle with a straight line tangential to it. It symbolized the wished-for conquest of the population problem: that tangent, instead of stretching from everlasting to everlasting, equalled in length the circumference of the circle. Stasis. A balance of global population and global food supply. Her brain approved, but her body, the body of a be-reaved mother, shouted no, no. It all meant a denial of so many things; life, in the name of reason, was being blasphemed against. The breath of the sea struck her left cheek.

She walked due south down the great London street, the nobility of its sheer giddy loftiness of masonry and metal redeeming the vulgarity of the signs and slogans. *Glowgold Sunsyrup. National Stereotelly. Syntheglot.* She was pushing against the crowds, crowds all moving northward. There were, she observed, more uniforms than usual: policemen and policewomen in grey – awk-ward, many of them, as if they were new recruits. She walked on. At the end of the street, like a vision of sanity, glinted the sea. This was Brighton, London's administrative centre, if a coastline could be called a centre. Beatrice-Joanna strode as briskly as the tide of the north-moving crowd would let her towards the cool green water. Its vista, taken from this narrow giddy ravine, always promised normality, a width of freedom, but the actual arrival at the sea's edge always brought disappointment. Every hundred yards or so stood a stout

sea-pier loaded with office-blocks or hives of flats, pushing out towards France. Still, the clean salt breath was
there, and greedily she drank it in. She held an intuitive
conviction that, if there were a God, He inhabited the
sea. The sea spelled life, whispered or shouted fertility;
that voice could never be completely stilled. If only, she
felt crazily, poor Roger's body could have been thrown
into those tigrine waters, swept out to be gnawed by
fish, rather than changed coldly to chemicals and
silently fed to the earth. She had a mad intuitive notion
that the earth was dying, that the sea would soon be
the final repository of life. 'Vast sea gifted with delirium,
panther skin and mantle pierced with thousands and
thousands of idols of the sun –' She had read that somewhere, a translation from one of the auxiliary languages
of Europe. The sea drunk with its own blue flesh, a
hydra, biting its tail. 'Sea,' she said quietly, for this
promenade was as crowded as the street she had just
left, 'sea, help us. We're sick, O sea. Restore us to health,
restore us to life.'

'I beg your pardon?' It was an oldish man, Anglo-
Saxon, upright, ruddy, mottled, grey-moustached; in a
military age he would have been taken at once for a
retired soldier. 'Did you address – ?'

'Sorry.' Blushing beneath her bone-white powder,
Beatrice-Joanna walked rapidly away, turning instinctively towards the east. Her eyes were drawn upwards to
the tremendous bronze statue that stood defiant, a mile
in the air, at the summit of Government Building, the
figure of a bearded man, classically robed, glaring at
the sun. At night he was floodlit. A cynosure to ships,
man of the sea, Pelagius. But Beatrice-Joanna could

remember a time when he had been Augustine. And, so it was said, he had been at other times the King, the Prime Minister, a popular bearded guitarist, Eliot (a long-dead singer of infertility), the Minister of Pisciculture, captain of the Hertfordshire Men's Sacred Game eleven, and – most often and satisfactorily – the great unknown, the magical Anonymous.

Next to Government Building, fronting the fecund sea without shame, stood the squatter, humbler building of twenty-five storeys only which housed the Ministry of Infertility. Above its portico was the inevitable circle with its chastely kissing tangent, also a large bas-relief of a naked sexless figure breaking eggs. Beatrice-Joanna thought she might as well draw her (so cynically named) condolence. It would give her a reason for entering the building, an excuse for hanging about in the vestibule. It was quite possible that she might see *him*, leaving work. He was, she knew, this week on the A Shift. Before crossing the promenade she looked on the busy crowds with almost new eyes, perhaps the sea's eyes. This was the British people; rather, to be more accurate, this was the people that inhabited the British Islands – Eurasian, Euro-African, Euro-Polynesian predominated, the frank light shining on damson, gold, even puce; her own English peach, masked with white flour, was growing rarer. Ethnic divisions were no longer important; the world was split into language-groups. Was it, she thought in an instant almost of prophetic power, to be left to her and the few indisputable Anglo-Saxons like her to restore sanity and dignity to the mongrel world? Her race, she seemed to remember, had done it before.

Four

'ONE achievement of the Anglo-Saxon race,' said Tristram, 'was parliamentary government, which eventually meant government by party. Later, when it was found that the work of government could be carried on more expeditiously without debate and without the opposition that party government entailed, the nature of the *cycle* began to be recognized.' He went to the blueboard and yellow-chalked a large clumsy ring. 'Now,' he said, swivelling his head to look at his pupils, 'here is how the cycle works.' He marked off three arcs. 'We have a Pelagian phase. Then we have an intermediate phase.' His chalk thickened one arc, then another. 'This leads into an Augustinian phase.' More thickening, and the chalk was back where it had started. 'Pelphase, Interphase, Gusphase, Pelphase, Interphase, Gusphase, and so on, for ever and ever. A sort of perpetual waltz. We must now consider what motive power makes the wheel turn.' He faced his class seriously, beating one palm against the other to clean the chalk off. 'In the first place, let us remind ourselves what Pelagianism stands for. A government functioning in its Pelagian phase commits itself to the belief that man is perfectible, that perfection can be achieved by his own efforts, and that the journey towards perfection is along a straight road. Man wants to be perfect. He wants to be good. The citizens of a community want to co-operate with their rulers, and so there is no real need to have devices of coercion, sanctions, which will force them to co-operate.

Laws are necessary, of course, for no single individual, however good and co-operative, can have precise knowledge of the total needs of the community. Laws point the way to an emergent pattern of social perfection – they are guides. But, because of the fundamental thesis that the citizen's desire is to behave like a good social animal, not like a selfish beast of the waste wood, it is assumed that the laws will be obeyed. Thus, the Pelagian state does not think it necessary to erect an elaborate punitive apparatus. Disobey the law and you will be told not to do it again or fined a couple of crowns. Your failure to obey does not spring from Original Sin, it's not an essential part of the human fabric. It's a mere flaw, something that will be shed somewhere along the road to final human perfection. Is that clear?' Many of the pupils nodded; they were past caring whether they understood or not. 'Well, then, in the Pelagian phase or Pelphase, the great liberal dream seems capable of fulfilment. The sinful acquisitive urge is lacking, brute desires are kept under rational control. The private capitalist, for instance, a figure of top-hatted greed, has no place in a Pelagian society. Hence the State controls the means of production, the State is the only boss. But the will of the State is the will of the citizen, hence the citizen is working for himself. No happier form of existence can be envisaged. Remember, however,' said Tristram, in a thrilling near-whisper, 'remember that the aspiration is always some way ahead of the reality. What destroys the dream? What destroys it, eh?' He suddenly big-drummed the desk, shouting in crescendo, 'Disappointment. *Disappointment*. DISAPPOINTMENT.' He beamed. 'The governors,' he said, in a reasonable tone, 'become disappointed when they find that men are not as good as they thought they were. Lapped in their dream of perfection, they are horrified when the seal is broken and they see people as they really are. It becomes necessary to try and force the citizens into goodness. The laws are reasserted, a system of enforcement of those laws is crudely and hastily knocked together. Disappointment opens up a vista of chaos. There is irrationality, there is panic. When the reason goes, the brute steps in. Brutality!' cried Tristram. The class was at last interested. 'Beatings-up. Secret police. Torture in brightly lighted cellars. Condemnation without trial. Finger-nails pulled out with pincers. The rack. The cold-water treatment. The gouging-out of eyes. The firing-squad in the cold dawn. And all this because of disappointment. The Interphase.' He smiled very kindly at his class. His class was agog for more mention of brutality. Their eyes glinted, they goggled with open mouths.

'What, sir,' asked Bellingham, 'is the cold-water treatment?'

Five

BEATRICE-JOANNA, the waste of life-giving cold water behind her, entered the open mouth of the Ministry, a mouth that smelled as though it had been thoroughly rinsed with disinfectant. She jostled her way to an office flaunting the word CONDOLENCES. A great number of bereaved mothers were waiting at the counter, some – those who spoke with the accents of irresponsibility – in festal dress as for a day out, clutching death certificates like passports to a good time. There was the smell of cheap spirit – alc, as it was called – and Beatrice-Joanna saw the coarse skins and blear eyes of inveterate alc-drinkers. The day of the pawning of the flat-iron was over; the State condoned infanticide.

'Got sort of sufflicated in the bedclothes. Only three weeks old to the day he was, too.'

'Scalded, mine was. Pulled the kettle right on top of him.' The speaker smiled with a sort of pride, as though the child had done something clever.

'Fell out of the window, he did. Playing, he was.'

'Money comes in handy.'

'Oh, yes, it does that.'

A handsome Nigerian girl took the death certificate from Beatrice-Joanna and went off to a central cash-desk. 'God bless you, miss,' said a harridan who, from the look of her, seemed well past child-bearing age. She folded the notes the Euro-African clerk gave her. 'God bless you, miss.' Clumsily counting her coins, she waddled off happily. The clerk smiled at the old-fashioned locution; God was not much mentioned these days.

'Here you are, Mrs Foxe.' The handsome Nigerian had returned. 'Six guineas, three septs.' How this amount had been arrived at Beatrice-Joanna did not trouble to ask. With a flush of guilt she couldn't explain, she swept the money hurriedly into her bag. The three-shilling piece called a sept shone at her in triplicate, sliding into her coin-purse – King Charles VI as triplets, smiling quizzically to the left. The King and Queen were not subject to the same generative laws as ordinary people: three princesses had been killed last year, all in the same air crash; the succession had to be secured.

Don't have any More, said the poster. Beatrice-Joanna pushed her angry way out. She stood in the vestibule, feeling desperately lonely. White-coated workers rushed, busy and brisk as spermatozoa, into the department of Contraceptive Research. The lifts rose and fell, to and from the many floors of the Propaganda Department. Beatrice-Joanna waited. Men and half-men all about her, twittering and sibilating. Then she saw, as she had thought she might at this precise hour, her brother-in-law Derek, her furtive lover Derek, brief-case under his arm, talking animatedly with a flash of rings to a foppish colleague, making point after point on unfolding flashing fingers. Seeing the superb mime of orthodox homosexual behaviour (secondary or social aspects) she could not quell entirely the spark of contempt that arose in her loins. She could hear the snorting emphasis of his speech; his movements had a dancer's grace. Nobody knew, nobody except her, what a satyr lay couched behind the epicene exterior. He was, it was said by many, likely to rise very high in the hierarchy of the Ministry. If, she reflected with an instant's malice, if only his colleagues knew, if only his superiors knew. She could ruin him if she wanted to. Could she? Of course she couldn't. Derek was not the sort of man who would let himself be ruined.

She stood there, waiting, her hands folded in front of her. Derek Foxe said good-bye to his colleague ('Such a *very* good suggestion, my dear. I promise you, tomorrow we must really *hammer it out*.') and patted him in valedictory archness thrice on the left buttock. Then he saw Beatrice-Joanna, looked warily about him, and came over. His eyes gave nothing away. 'Hallo,' he said, writhing with grace. 'What news?'

'He died this morning. He's now –' She took a hold on herself '– now in the hands of the Ministry of Agriculture.'

'My dear.' That was spoken in a lover's tone, a man to a woman. He glanced furtively about him again, then whispered, 'We'd best not be seen together. Can I come round?' She hesitated, then nodded. 'What time does my dear brother get home today?' he asked.

'Not till seven.'

'I'll be along. I have to be careful.' He smiled queenlily at a passing colleague, a man with Disraeli-like ringlets. 'Some queer things are going on,' he said. 'I think I'm being watched.'

'You're always careful, aren't you?' she said, somewhat loudly. 'Always too damned careful.'

'Oh, do be quiet,' he whispered. 'Look,' he said, slightly agitated. 'Do you see that man there?'

'Which man?' The vestibule was thick with them.

'That little one with the moustache. Do you see him? That's Loosely. I'm sure he's watching me.' She saw who he meant: a small friendless-looking man with his wrist to his ear as though checking that his watch was going, actually listening to his microradio, standing aloof on the periphery of the crowd. 'You go off home, my dear,' said Derek Foxe. 'I'll be along in about an hour.'

'Say it,' commanded Beatrice-Joanna. 'Say it before I go.'

'I love you,' he mouthed, as through a window. Dirty words from a man to a woman in that place of anti-love. His face contorted as though he were chewing alum.

Six

'BUT,' went on Tristram, 'the Interphase cannot, of course, last for ever.' He contorted his face to a mask of shock. 'Shock,' he said. 'The governors become shocked at their own excesses. They find that they have been thinking in heretical terms – the sinfulness of man rather than his inherent goodness. They relax their sanctions and the result is complete chaos. But, by this time, disappointment cannot sink any deeper. Disappointment can no longer shock the state into repressive action, and a kind of philosophical pessimism supervenes. In other words, we drift into the Augustinian phase, the Gusphase. The orthodox view presents man as a sinful creature from whom no good at all may be expected. A different dream, gentlemen, a dream which, again, outstrips the reality. It eventually appears that human social behaviour is rather better than any Augustinian pessimist has a right to expect, and so a sort of optimism begins to emerge. And so Pelagianism is reinstated. We are back in the Pelphase again. The wheel has come full circle. Any questions?'

'What do they gouge eyes out with, sir?' asked Billy Chan.

Bells shrilled, gongs clanged, an artificial voice yelled

over the speakers, 'Change, change, all, all change. Fifty seconds to change. Count-down now begins. Fifty – forty-nine – forty-eight –' Tristram mouthed a good afternoon inaudible under the racket and walked out into the corridor. Boys dashed to lessons in concrete music, astrophysics, language control. The count-down went rhythmically on: 'Thirty-nine – thirty-eight –' Tristram walked to a staff lift and pressed the button. Lights showed that the cabin was already shooting down from the top floor (big-windowed art-rooms there; art-master Jordan quick, as always, off the mark). 43 – 42 – 41 – 40, flashed the indicator. 'Nineteen – eighteen – seventeen –' The cretic rhythm of the count-down had changed to trochaic. The lift stopped and Tristram entered. Jordan was telling Mowbray, a colleague, about new movements in painting; names like Zvegintzoy, Abrahams, F. A. Cheel were dealt like dull cards. 'Plasmatical assonance,' intoned Jordan. In some things the world had not changed at all. 'Three – two – one – zero.' The voice had stopped, but each floor (18 – 17 – 16 – 15) that rose before the eyes of Tristram showed boys not yet in their new classrooms, some not even scurrying. The Pelphase. Nobody tried to enforce the rules. The work got done. More or less. 4 – 3 – 2 – 1. Ground floor. Tristram left the lift.

Seven

BEATRICE-JOANNA entered the lift in Spurgin Building on

Rossiter Avenue. 1 – 2 – 3 – 4. She rose to the fortieth floor, where their tiny flat waited, empty of a son. In half an hour or so Derek would arrive, the comfort of whose arms she desperately needed. Was not Tristram then equipped to give of the same commodity? It was not the same, no. The flesh has its own peculiar logic. There had been a time when it had been pleasant, thrilling, ecstatically exciting, to be touched by Tristram. That had long gone – gone, to be precise, shortly after Roger's birth, as though Tristram's sole function had been to beget him. Love? She still, she thought, loved Tristram. He was kind, honest, gentle, generous, considerate, calm, witty sometimes. But it was Tristram in the living-room she loved, not Tristram in bed. Did she love Derek? She did not answer the question for a moment. 26 – 27 – 28. She thought it was strange that their flesh should be the same. But Tristram's had become carrion; that of his elder brother was fire and ice, paradisaical fruit, inexpressibly delicious and exciting. She was in love with Derek, she decided, but she did not think she loved him. 30 – 31 – 32. She loved, she decided, Tristram, but was not in love with him. So, so far hence in time, a woman contrived to think with (as it was in the beginning) her instincts, (is now) her complicated nerves, and (ever shall be) her inner organs (world without end) 39 – 40. (Amen.)

Courageously Beatrice-Joanna turned the key of the flatlet and walked in to the familiar smell of *Anaphro* (an air-freshener devised by chemists of the Ministry where her lover worked, piped throughout the block from an engine in the basement) and the hum of the refrigerator. Even though she had no real standards of comparison, she was always, on each entrance, struck afresh and aghast by the exiguity of the living-space (standard for people of their income-group) – the box of a bedroom, kitchen-coffin, bathroom almost to be worked into like a dress. Two fair strides would see her across the living-room, and the strides were only possible because all the furnishings hid in ceiling and walls, to be released, when wanted, at the touch of a switch. Beatrice-Joanna bade a chair come out, and an angular unlovely sit-unit grudgingly appeared. She was weary, she sat, sighing. The *Daily Newsdisc* still shone, like a black flat sun, on its wall-spindle. She conjured its artificial voice, sexless, expressionless. 'The strike at the National Synthelac Works continues. Appeals to the workers to return have proved of no avail. The strike-leaders are unwilling to compromise on their demand for a basic increase of one crown three tanners a day. Dock-workers at Southampton are, as a gesture of sympathy with the strikers, refusing to handle imported synthelac.' Beatrice-Joanna moved the needle on to the Woman's Band. A genuinely female voice – strident with a vinegar enthusiasm – spoke of the further reduction of the bust-line. She switched off. Her nerves still danced, her occiput still rocked from repeated hammer-cracks. She took off her clothes and bathed in the basin that was called a bath. She dusted her body with plain white scentless powder and donned a dressing-gown woven of some new long-chain synthetic polymeric amide. Then she went to the wall-panel of buttons and switches and made a pair of metal arms gently lower a plastic cupboard from a recess in the ceiling. She opened the cupboard and, from a brown bottle, shook out two tablets. She washed these down with water in a paper cup, thrust the empty cup into a hole in the wall. This launched it on a journey whose destination was the basement furnace. Then she waited.

Derek was late. She grew impatient. Her nerves zithered still, her head thumped. She began to have premonitions of death, doom; then, dragging in reason like some alien constrictive metal, she told herself that these premonitions were a hangover from events already past and irrevocable. She took two more tablets and sent another cup to fiery atomization. Then, at last, there came a knock at the door.

Eight

TRISTRAM knocked at the Principal's secretary's door, said that his name was Foxe and that the Principal wished to see him. Buttons were pressed; lights flashed over lintels; Tristram was bade enter. 'Come in, Brother Foxe,' cried Joscelyne. He looked rather like a fox himself, certainly not Franciscan. He was bald, twitched and had a good degree from the University of Pasadena. He himself, however, came from Sutton, West Virginia, and, though he was too foxily modest to talk much about it, was closely related to the High Commissioner for North American Territories. Nevertheless, he had obtained this post of Principal on sheer merit. That, and a life of blameless sexlessness. 'Sit down, Brother Foxe,' said Joscelyne. 'Sit right down. Have a caff.' He hospitably motioned towards the dish of caffeine tablets on his blotter. Tristram shook his head, smiling. 'Give you a lift when it's needed most,' said Joscelyne, taking two. Then he sat down at his desk. The afternoon sea-light shone on a long nose, a blue muzzle, the mouth large and mobile, the face prematurely lined. 'I tapped your lesson,' he said, nodding first towards the switchboard on the white wall, then to the ceiling-speaker. 'Do you think the kids take in much of that stuff?'

'They're not supposed to understand it too well,' said Tristram. 'Just a general impression, you know. It's in the syllabus but never comes up in the exam.'

'Yah, yah, I guess so.' Joscelyne was not really interested. He was fingering a grey-backed dossier, Tristram's: Tristram saw FOXE upside down on its cover. 'Poor old Newick,' said Joscelyne. 'He was pretty good. Now he's phosphorus pentoxide some place in Western Province. But I guess his soul goes marching on,' he said vaguely. And then, with speed, he added, 'Here in the school, I mean.'

'Yes, yes, of course. In the school.'

'Yah. Now,' said Joscelyne, 'you were all lined up to take his place. I've been reading through your dossier today –' *Were*. Tristram swallowed a bolus of surprise. *Were*, he said, *were*. '– Quite a book. You've done pretty good work here, I can see that. And you're senior in the department. You should have just walked into the job.' He leaned back, put thumb-tip to thumb-tip, then – little, ring, middle, index – let finger-tip meet finger-tip. He twitched meanwhile. 'You realize,' he said, 'that it's not up to me who fills these vacancies. It's up to the Board. All I can do is recommend. Yah, recommend.

28

Now, I know this sounds crazy, but what gets a man a job these days is not pry-merrily qualifications. No. It isn't how many degrees he's got or how good he is at whatever it is he does. It's – and I'm using the term in its most general sense – his family background. Yah.'

'But,' began Tristram, 'my family –'

Joscelyne held up a traffic-stopping hand. 'I don't mean whether your family was up in the world,' he said. 'I mean how much of it there is. Or was.' He twitched. 'It's a matter of arithmetic, not of eugenics or social status. Now I know as well as you do, Brother Foxe, that all this is absurd. But there it is.' His right hand suddenly took flight, hovered, then dropped to the desk like a paper-weight. 'The records,' he said, pronouncing the word 'wreckerds', 'the records here say – the records say – yah, here it is: they say you come of a family of four. You have a sister in China (she's on the Global Demographic Survey, right?) and a brother in, of all places, Springfield, Ohio. I know Springfield well. And then, of course, there's Derek Foxe here, homo and highly placed. Now you, Brother Foxe, are married. And you have one kid.' He looked up at Tristram sadly.

'Not any more. He died in hospital this morning.' Tristram's lower lip jutted, quivering.

'Dead, eh? Well.' Condolences nowadays were purely financial. 'Young, wasn't he? Very young. Not much P_2O_5 there. Well, his being dead doesn't alter the position as far as you're concerned.' Joscelyne clasped his hands tight as if about to pray away the fact of Tristram's fatherhood. 'One birth per family. Alive or dead. Singleton, twins, triplets. It makes no difference. Now,' he said, 'you've broken no law. You've not done a thing you theoretically shouldn't have. You're entitled to marry if you want to, you're entitled to one birth in the family, though, of course, the best people just don't. Just don't.'

'Damn it,' said Tristram, 'damn it all, somebody's got to keep the race going. There'd be no human race left if some of us didn't have children.' He was angry. 'And what do you mean by "the best people"?' he asked. 'People like my brother Derek? That power-struck little nancy, crawling, yes, literally crawling up the –'

'Calmo,' said Joscelyne, 'calmo.' He had only just returned from an educational conference in Rome, that popeless city. 'You were just going to say something very opprobrious then. "Nancy" is a very contemptuous term. The homos, remember, virtually run this country and, for that matter, the whole of the English-Speaking Union.' He lowered his eyebrows, gazing at Tristram with foxy sorrow. 'My uncle, the High Commissioner, he's homo. I was nearly homo myself once. Let's keep emotion out of this,' he said. 'It's unseemly, that's what it is, yah, unseemly. Just let's try to *parlare* about this *calmamente*, huh?' He smiled, trying to make the smile look homespun and cracker-barrel. 'You know as well as I do that the job of breeding's best left to the lower orders. Remember that the very term proletariat comes from Latin *proletarius*, meaning those that serve the State with their offspring or *proles*. You and me, we're supposed to be above that sort of thing, huh?' He sat back in his chair, smiling, tapping the desk with his ink-pencil – O, for some reason, in Morse. 'One birth per family, that's the rule or recommendation or whatever you like to call it, but the proletariat breaks that rule all

30

the time. The race is in no danger of dying. Just the opposite, I'd say. I hear rumours from high places, but never mind, never mind. The fact is that your old man and your old lady broke the rule very nastily, very nastily indeed. Yah. He was what? – something in the Ministry of Agriculture, wasn't he? According to this dossier he was. Well, it was just a little bit cynical, I'd say, helping to increase the national food supply with one hand and getting four kids with the other.' He saw that this was rather a grotesque antithesis but he shrugged it off. 'And that's not forgotten, you know, Brother Foxe, not forgotten. The sins of the fathers, as they used to say.'

'We'll all help the Ministry of Agriculture some day,' sulked Tristram. 'Quite a nice lump of phosphorous pentoxide, the four of us.'

'Your wife, too,' said Joscelyne, rustling the many sheets of the dossier. 'She's got a sister in Northern Province. Married to an agricultural officer. Two children there.' He tutted. 'A kind of aura of fertility surrounds you, Brother Foxe. Anyway, as far as this post of departmental head is concerned, it's pretty evident that, all things being equal, the Board will want to appoint a candidate with a cleaner family wreckerd.' This pronunciation became a focus of irritation to Tristram. 'Let's see. Let's look at the other candidates.' Joscelyne leaned forward, elbows on the desk, and began to tick them off on his fingers. 'Wiltshire's homo. Cruttenden's unmarried. Cowell's married with one kid, so he's out. Crum-Ewing's gone the whole hog, he's a *castrato*, a pretty strong candidate. Fiddian's just nothing. Ralph's homo –'

'All right,' said Tristram. 'I accept my sentence. I just stay where I am and see somebody younger – it's bound to be somebody younger; it always is – promoted over my head. Just because of my *wreckerd*,' he added bitterly.

'Yah, that's it,' said Joscelyne. 'I'm glad you're taking it this way. You see how a lot of these top-brass are going to look at it. Heredity, that's the word, heredity. A family pattern of deliberate fertility, that's it. Yah. Like being a hereditary criminal. Things are very tricky these days. In confidence, fella, you watch your step. Watch your wife. Don't start having any more kids. Don't start getting irresponsible like the proletariat. One false step like that and you'd be out. Yah, out.' He made the gesture of cutting his own throat. 'Lots of promising young men coming up. Men with the right ideas. I'd hate to lose you, Brother Foxe.'

Nine

'Dearest one.'

'Darling, darling, darling.' They embraced hungrily, the door still open. 'Yumyumyumyumyum.' Derek disengaged himself and kicked it shut.

'Must be careful,' he said. 'I wouldn't put it past Loosley to follow me here.'

'Well, what's the harm?' said Beatrice-Joanna. 'You can visit your brother if you wish to, can't you?'

'Don't be silly. Loosley's thorough, I'll say that for the

little swine. He'll have found out what Tristram's working-hours are.' Derek went over to the window. He came back from it immediately, smiling at his own foolishness. So many storeys up, so many indistinguishable crawling ants on the deep street. 'Perhaps I'm getting a bit too nervy,' he said. 'It's only that – well, things are happening. I've got to see the Minister this evening. It looks as though I'm in for a big job.'

'What sort of job?'

'A job that means, I'm afraid, we shan't be seeing quite so much of each other. Not for a time, anyway. A job with a uniform. Tailors came in this morning, measuring. Big things are happening.' Derek had shed his public skin of dandified epicene. He looked male, tough.

'So,' said Beatrice-Joanna. 'You're getting a job that's going to be more important than seeing me. Is that it?' She had thought, on his entering the flat and taking her in his arms, of urging, in a mad instant, that they run away together, to live for ever on coconuts and love among the banyans. But then her woman's desire for the best of both worlds had supervened. 'I sometimes wonder,' she said, 'whether you really mean what you say. About love and so on.'

'Oh, darling, darling,' he said impatiently. 'But listen.' He was in no mood for dalliance. 'Some things are happening which are far more important than love. Matters of life and death.'

Just like a man. 'Nonsense,' she said promptly.

'Purges, if you know what those are. Changes in the Government. The unemployed being drafted into the police force. Oh, big things, big things.'

33

Beatrice-Joanna started to snivel, to make herself look very weak, defenceless, small. 'It's been such an awful day,' she said. 'I've been so miserable. I've been so lonely.'

'Dearest one. It's beastly of me.' He took her in his arms again. 'I'm so sorry. I think only of myself.' Content, she went on snivelling. He kissed her cheek, neck, brow, buried his lips in hair the colour of cider. She smelt of soap, he of all the perfumes of Arabia. Embraced, they four-legged their way clumsily into the bedroom, as in some blind dance undisciplined by music. The switch had long been touched which sent the bed swinging – in an arc like Tristram's chalked Pelphase – to the floor. Derek swiftly undressed, disclosing a spare body knobbed and striated with muscle, and then the dead eye of the television screen on the ceiling was able to watch the writhing of a male body – crust-brown, delicate russet – and a female – nacreous, touched subtly with blue and carmine – in the exordia of an act which was technically both adulterous and incestuous.

'Did you,' panted Derek, 'remember to –?' There was now no possible ideal observer who could think of Mrs Shandy and, thinking, grin.

'Yes, yes.' She had taken tablets; everything was quite safe. It was only when the point of no return had been reached that she remembered that the tablets she had swallowed were analgesic, not contraceptive. Routine let one down sometimes. Then it was too late and she didn't care.

Ten

'GET on with it,' said Tristram, frowning unwontedly. 'Read it up on your own.' The seventh stream of the Fourth Form offered him wide eyes and mouths. 'I'm going home,' he said. 'I've had enough for one day. To-morrow there will be a test on the matter contained between Pages 267 and 274 – inclusive – of your textbook. The Chronic Nuclear Scare and the Coming of Perpetual Peace. Dunlop,' he said sharply. 'Dunlop.' The boy had a rubbery face, but, in this age of total nationalization, his name was neither appropriate nor inappropriate. 'Nose-picking is an unseemly habit, Dunlop,' he said. The class tittered. 'Get on with it,' repeated Tristram at the door, 'and a very good day to you. Or early evening,' he amended, glancing out at the rose marine sky. Curious that the English tongue had never evolved a valedictory form fitting this time of day. A sort of Interphase. Pelagian day, Augustinian night. Tristram walked boldly out of the classroom, down the corridor to the lift, then sped down and out of the mammoth building itself. Nobody hindered his leaving. Teachers just did not desert their classes before the final bell; ergo, Tristram was still, in some mystical way, at work.

He swam strongly through the crowds on Earp Road (tides simultaneously flowing in and out) and then turned left into Dallas Street. And there, just by the turning into McGibbon Avenue, he saw something which, for no immediate reason he could assign to the sensation, chilled him. On the road, blocking the sparse traffic, watched by crowds that kept their decent distance, was a company of men in the grey uniform of the police – three platoons with platoon commanders – standing at ease. Most of them grinned awkwardly, shuffled; recruits, Tristram divined, new recruits, but each already armed with a squat dull-shining carbine. Their trousers tapered to black elasticated bands which hugged the uppers of deep-soled boots; their waisted tunics were curiously archaic with their collars, brassy collar-dogs glinting on them, and with the collars went black ties. The men were capped in grey cheese-cutters; a police badge shone dead above the frontal lobes.

'Finding jobs for them,' said a man next to Tristram – an unshaven man in rusty black, a roll of fat on his chin though his body was meagre. 'The out-of-work, they are. Were,' he corrected himself. 'About time the Government did something about them. That's my brother-in-law there, see, second from the end of the first row.' He pointed, vicariously proud. 'Giving them jobs,' he repeated. He was evidently a lonely man, glad of the chance to talk to anybody.

'Why?' asked Tristram. 'What's it all about?' But he knew; this was the end of the Pelphase: people were going to be made to be good. He felt a certain panic on his own account. Perhaps he ought to be getting back to the school. Perhaps nobody would know anything about it if he went back right away. It was foolish of him, he'd never done anything like that before. Perhaps he ought to ring up Joscelyne and say he'd left before time because he wasn't feeling well –

'Keep some of them in order,' said the fat-chinned

thin man promptly. 'Too many of these young hooligans round the streets at night. Not strict enough with them, they're not. Teachers don't have any control over them any more.'

'Some of those young recruits,' said Tristram carefully, 'look suspiciously like young hooligans.'

'Are you calling my brother-in-law a hooligan? Best lad who ever breathed, he is, and been unemployed near fourteen months. He's no hooligan, mister.'

An officer now took post before the company. Smart, his pants moulded to his bottom, silver bars on his epaulettes agleam in the sun, a gun holstered in rich leather-substitute on his hip, he called in an unexpectedly manly voice: '*Campniiiiigh* –' The company stiffened, as if for a blow. '*Shn.*' The snarl was hurled like a pebble; the men came to attention raggedly. '*To your jewtahhhhz, diiiii* –' (The syllable wavered between two allophones) '*– zmiss.*' Some turned left, some right, some waited to see what the others were doing. Laughter and jeering claps from the crowd. And now the street was full of wandering knots of self-conscious policemen.

Tristram, feeling somewhat sick, made for Earnshaw Mansions. In a cellar under that thick dry tower was a drinking-shop called the Montague. The only intoxicant available these days was a pungent distillation from vegetable and fruit-peel. It was called alc, and only the lowest-class stomach could take it neat. Tristram put down a tosheroon on the counter and was served with a glass of this vicious viscous spirit, well diluted in orangeade. There was nothing else to drink: hop-fields, the ancient centres of viticulture – these had gone the way of the grazing-plains and the tobacco-lands of

Virginia and Turkey; all now supported more esculent crops. A near-vegetarian world, non-smoking, teetotal except for alc. Tristram gravely toasted it and, after another tosheroon's worth of orange fire, felt himself sufficiently reconciled to it. Promotion dead, Roger dead. To hell with Joscelyne. He panned his head almost genially round the close little drinking-hole. Homos, some of them bearded, twittered among themselves in the dark corner; the bar-drinkers were mostly hetero and gloomy. The greasy fat-bottomed barman waddled to a musicator in the wall, put a tanner in the slot, and let loose, like an animal, a grating kind of concrete music – spoons rattling in tin basins, a speech made by the Minister of Pisciculture, a lavatory cistern filling up, a revving engine: all recorded backwards, augmented or diminished, thoroughly mixed. The man next to Tristram said, 'Bloody awful.' He said this to the alc-casks, not moving his head and hardly moving his lips, as if, though the remark had had to be made, he did not want it to be picked up as a pretext for drawing him into conversation. One of the bearded homos now began to recite:

'My dead tree. Give me back my dead dead tree.
Rain, rain, go away. Let the earth be still
Dry. Kick the gods back into the cakey earth,
Making a hole, for that purpose, with a drill.'

'Bloody nonsense,' said the man, more loudly. Then he swung his head, slowly and warily, from side to side, examining Tristram on his right and the drinker on his left with care, as if one were a sculpture of the other and the likeness had to be checked. 'Know what I was?'

he said. Tristram wondered. A saturnine man with eyes in charcoal caves, reddish beak, sulky Stuart mouth. 'Give me another of those,' he said to the barman, plonking his money down. '*Thought* you wouldn't be able to tell,' he said in triumph, turning to Tristram. 'Well,' he said, and he downed raw alc with a smack and a sigh, 'I was a priest. Do you know what that is?'

'A sort of monk,' said Tristram. 'Something to do with religion.' He gave this man a mouthful of awe, as though he were Pelagius himself. 'But,' he objected, 'there aren't any priests any more. There haven't been priests for hundreds of years.'

The man held out his hands, fingers spread, as though testing himself for the shakes. 'These,' he said, 'have performed the daily miracle.' More reasonably, 'There've been a few,' he said. 'One or two pockets of resistance in the Provinces. People who don't hold with all this liberal muck. Pelagius,' he said, 'was a heretic. Man needs divine grace.' He returned to his hands, examining them clinically, as if for some minute spot which would announce the onset of disease. 'More of this stuff,' he told the barman, now using his hands to search in his pockets for money. 'Yes,' he told Tristram. 'There are priests still, though I'm no longer one of them. Thrown out,' he whispered. 'Unfrocked. Oh, God, God, God.' He became histrionic. One or two of the homos tittered, hearing the divine name. 'But they can never take away this power, never, never.'

'Cecil, you old cow!'

'Oh, my dear, just look what *she's* wearing!'

The heteros also turned to look, but with less enthusiasm. A trio of police recruits had come in, smiling wide. One of them performed a small step-dance, ending with a palsied salute. Another pretended to spray the room with his carbine. Remote, cold, abstract, the concrete music went on. The homos laughed, whinnied, embraced.

'It wasn't for that sort of thing I was unfrocked,' said the man. 'It was for real love, the real thing, not this blasphemous mockery.' He nodded gloomily in the direction of the gay group of police and civilians. 'She was very young, only seventeen. Oh, God, God. But,' he said strongly, 'they can't take away this divine power.' He again gazed at his hands, this time like Macbeth. 'Bread and wine,' he said, 'into the body and blood – But there's no wine any more. And the Pope,' he said 'an old, old, old man on St Helena. And me,' he said, without false modesty, 'a blasted clerk in the Ministry of Fuel and Power.'

One of the homo policemen had inserted a tanner in the musicator. A dance-tune plopped out suddenly, as though a bag of ripe plums had burst – a combo of abstract tape-noises with a slow gut-shaking beat deep beneath. One of the policemen began to dance with a bearded civilian. It was graceful, Tristram had to admit that, intricate and graceful. But the unfrocked priest was disgusted. 'Bloody exhibition,' he said, and, as one of the non-dancing homos turned up the volume of the music, he shouted loud and without warning, '*Shut that blasted row!*'

The homos gazed with mild interest, the dancers open-mouthed at him, still rocking gently in each other's arms. '*You* shut it,' said the barman. 'We don't want any trouble here.'

'Unnatural lot of bastards,' said the priest. Tristram admired the priestly language. 'The sin of Sodom. God ought to strike the lot of you dead.'

'You old spoilsport,' one snorted at him. 'Where's your manners?' And then the police were upon him. It was swift, balletic, laughing; not violence as Tristram had read of violence in the past; it seemed more tickling than hitting. But, in no more than a count-out of five, the unfrocked priest was leaning against the bar, trying to draw up breath from a great way down, blood all over his mouth. 'Are you his friend?' one of the police said to Tristram. Tristram was shocked to see that this one wore black lipstick to match his tie.

'No,' said Tristram. 'I've never seen him before. Never seen him before in my life. I was just going anyway.' He finished his alc-and-orange and started to leave.

'And then the cock crew,' grunted the unfrocked priest. 'This is my blood,' he said, wiping his mouth. He was too tipsy to have felt any pain.

Eleven

WHEN they lay panting more slowly, detumescence magically synchronically achieved, his arm under her relaxed body, she wondered if perhaps after all she hadn't meant that to happen. She said nothing to Derek; this was her own affair. She felt rather remote, detached from Derek, as a poet may feel – after a sonnet – detached from the pen that wrote it. The foreign word

41

Urmutter swam up from her unconscious, and she wondered what it meant.

He was the first to surface from the parachronic, asking, man being a chronic animal, lazily, 'What would the time be now?'

She didn't answer. 'I can't understand,' she said instead. 'All this hypocrisy and deceit. Why do people have to pretend they're something they're not? It's all a ghastly farce.' She spoke sharply but still as from some timeless state. 'You love love,' she said. 'You love love more than any man I've ever known. And yet you treat it as something to be ashamed of.'

He sighed profoundly. 'Dichotomy,' he said, throwing the word languidly at her, like a ball stuffed with duck's down. 'Remember the human dichotomy.'

'What about –' she yawned '– the human whatever-it-is?'

'The division. Contradictions. Instincts tell us one thing and reason tells us another. That could be tragic if we allowed it to be. But it's better to see it as comic. We were right,' he said elliptically, 'to throw God out and install Mr Livedog in his place. God's a tragic conception.'

'I don't know what you're talking about.'

'Never mind.' He caught her yawn belatedly, showing snowy plastic crowns. 'The conflicting claims of line and circle. You're all line, that's your trouble.'

'I'm circular. I'm globular. Look.'

'Physically, yes. Mentally, no. You're still a creature of instinct, after all these years of education and slogans and subliminal film propaganda. You don't give a damn about the state of the world, the state of the State. I do.'

'Why should I? I've got my own life to live.'

'You'd have no life at all to live if it weren't for people like me. The State is each of its members. Supposing,' he said seriously, 'nobody worried about the birth-rate. Supposing we didn't get concerned about the straight line travelling on and on and on. We'd literally starve. Dognose we've little enough to eat as it is. We've managed to achieve a sort of stasis, thanks to my department and similar government departments all over the world, but that can't last much longer, not the way things are going.'

'What do you mean?'

'It's the old story. Liberalism prevails, and liberalism means laxness. We leave it to education and propaganda and free contraceptives, abortion clinics and condolences. We encourage non-productive forms of sexual activity. We like to kid ourselves that people are good enough and wise enough to be aware of their responsibilities. But what happens? There was the case, only a few weeks ago, of a couple in Western Province who'd had six children. *Six.* I ask you. And all alive, too. A very old-fashioned couple – God-followers. They talked about fulfilling God's will and all that nonsense. One of our officials had a word with them, tried to make them see sense. Imagine – eight bodies in a flat smaller than this. But they wouldn't see sense. Apparently they had a copy of the Bible – Dognose where they'd got it from. Have you ever seen one of those?'

'No.'

'Well, it's an old religious book full of smut. The big sin is to waste your seed, and if God loves you He fills your house with kids. The language is very old-fashioned, too. Anyway, they kept appealing to this all the time, talking about fertility and barren fig trees getting cursed and so on.' Derek shuddered with genuine horror. 'They were quite a young couple, too.'

'What happened to them?'

'What *could* happen? They were told there was a law limiting offspring to one birth only, dead or alive, but they said it was a wicked law. If God didn't intend man to be fruitful, they said, why did He implant the instinct for increase in him? They were told that God was an outmoded concept, but they wouldn't take that. They were told they had a duty to their neighbours, and they conceded that, but they couldn't see how limitation of family constituted a duty. A very difficult case.'

'And nothing happened to them?'

'Nothing much. They were fined. They were warned against having any more kids. They were given contraceptive pills and ordered to attend the local birth-control clinic for instruction. But they seemed quite unrepentant. And there are a lot of people like that, all over the world – China, India, the East Indies. That's what's so frightening. That's why there's going to be a change. The world population figures are hair-raising. We're several millions on the wrong side. All through trusting people. You wait, you'll see our rations reduced in a day or so. What *is* the time?' he asked again. It was not an urgent question; he could, if he'd wanted, have removed his arm from under her warm lax body, leaned out to the far corner of the tiny room, and picked up his wrist micro-radio, which had a watch-face in its back. But he was too lazy to move.

'I should think it's about five-thirty,' said Beatrice-

Joanna. 'You can check with the telly, if you like.' His free arm was able, quite comfortably, to click the switch by the bedhead. A light curtain came down over the window, shutting out just enough of the day, and in a second or so synthetic music came gurgling and wailing gently from the ceiling. Unblown, unplucked, unbeaten music, like that heard distractedly by alc-drinking Tristram at that very moment. Here were oscillating valves, tap-water, ships' sirens, thunder, marching feet, vocalizations into a throat-mike – crabbed and inverted to create a brief symphony designed to please rather than excite. The screen above their heads glowed whitely, then erupted into a coloured stereoscopic image of the statue that crowned Government Building. The stone eyes, above a baroque beard, a nose strong to break the wind, glared out defiantly; clouds moved behind as if in a hurry; the sky was the colour of school ink.

'There he is,' said Derek, 'whoever he is – our patron saint. St Pelagius, St Augustine, or St Anonymous – which? We shall know tonight.'

The saint's image faded. Then bloomed an imposing ecclesiastical interior – venerable grey nave, ogee arches. From the altar marched down two plump male figures dressed snowily like hospital housemen. 'The Sacred Game,' announced a voice. 'Cheltenham Ladies against West Bromwich Males. Cheltenham Ladies have won the toss and elected to bat first.' The plump white figures came down to inspect the wicket in the nave. Derek switched off. The stereoscopic image lost a dimension, then died.

'It's just after six, then,' said Derek. 'I'd better be going.' He eased his numb arm from under his mistress's shoulder-blades, then swung himself off the bed.

'There's plenty of time,' yawned Beatrice-Joanna.

'Not any more.' Derek drew on his narrow trousers. He strapped his microradio to his wrist, glancing at the watch-face. 'Twenty past,' he said. Then, 'The Sacred Game, indeed. The last ritual of civilized Western Man.' He snorted. 'Look,' he said, 'we'd better not see each other for a week or so. Whatever you do, don't come looking for me in the Ministry. I'll get in touch with you somehow. Somehow,' he said vaguely, muffled by his shirt. 'Would you be an angel,' he said, putting on the homosexual mask with his jacket, 'and just peep out and see if there's anybody on the corridor? I don't want to be seen leaving.'

'All right.' Beatrice-Joanna sighed, got off the bed, put on her dressing-gown, and went to the door. She looked left and right, like a child practising kerb-drill, came back in and said, 'Nobody there.'

'Thank Dog for that.' He pronounced the final plosive too sibilantly, petulantly.

'There's no need to put on that homo act with me, Derek.'

'Every good actor,' he minced, 'starts acting in the wings.' He gave her a butterfly kiss on the left cheek. 'Good-bye, dearest.'

'Good-bye.' He undulated down the corridor towards the lift, the satyr in him put to sleep till next time, whenever that would be.

Twelve

STILL somewhat shaken, despite two more glasses of alc in a drinking-cellar nearer home, Tristram entered Spurgin Building. Even here, in the large vestibule, there were laughing grey uniforms. He didn't like it, he didn't like it one bit. Waiting at the lift-gates were neighbours of the fortieth floor – Wace, Durtnell and Visser; Mrs Hamper and young Jack Phoenix; Miss Wallis, Miss Runting, Arthur Spragg; Phipps, Walker-Meredith, Fred Hamp, the octogenarian Mr Earthrowl. The lift-indicators flashed yellow: 47 – 46 – 45. 'I saw a rather terrible thing,' said Tristram to old Mr Earthrowl. 'Eh?' said Mr Earthrowl. 38 – 37 – 36. 'A special emergency regulation,' said Phipps of the Ministry of Labour. 'They've all been ordered back to work.' Young Jack Phoenix yawned; Tristram noticed, for the first time, black hairs on his cheekbones. 22 – 21 – 20 – 19. 'Police on the docks,' Durtnell was saying. 'Only way to deal with the bastards. Rough stuff. Should have done it years ago.' He looked with approval at the grey police, black-tied as if in mourning for Pelagianism, light carbines under their arms. 12 – 11 – 10. In imagination Tristram punched a homo or castro on his sweet plump face. 3 – 2 – 1 – G. And there was the face, neither sweet nor plump, of his brother Derek. Both looked astonished at each other.

'What,' asked Tristram, 'in Dogsname are you doing here?'

'Oh, Tristram,' minced Derek, alveolizing the name

47

to an insincere caress. 'So there you are.'

'Yes. Have you been looking for me or something?'

'That's it, my dear. To tell you how terribly sorry I am. Poor, poor little boy.'

The lift was filling fast. 'Is this official commiseration? I always understood your department rejoiced over deaths.' He frowned, puzzled.

'This is me, your brother,' said Derek. '*Not* an official of the M of I.' He spoke rather stiffly. 'I came to offer my –' He nearly said 'condolences', but that, he realized in time, would have sounded cynical. 'A fraternal visit,' he said. 'I've seen your *wife*' (the slight pause before the word, the unnatural stressing – these made it rather obscene) 'and she told me you were still at work, so I – Anyhow, I'm terribly, terribly sorry. We must,' he valedicted vaguely, 'get together some evening. Dinner, or something. Now I must fly. An appointment with the Minister.' And he was off, his bottom wagging. Tristram crushed himself into the lift, hard against Spragg and Miss Wallis, still frowning. What was going on? The door slid to, the lift began to rise. Miss Wallis, a pallid dumpling with a nose that shone as if wet, breathed on Tristram a ghost of reconstituted dehydrated potatoes. Why had Derek deigned to pay their flat a visit? They disliked each other, and not solely because the State had always, as an aspect of the policy of discrediting the whole notion of family, encouraged fraternal enmity. There had always been jealousy, resentment of the preferential cosseting given to Tristram, his father's favourite – a warm place in his dad's bed on holiday mornings; the top of his breakfast egg; the superior toys on New Year's Day. The other brother and the sister had shrugged good-humouredly at this, but not Derek. Derek had expressed his jealousy in sly kicks, lies, mud spattered on Tristram's Sunday space-suit, acts of vandalism on his toys. And the final channel between them had been dug in adolescence – Derek's sexual inversion and Tristram's undisguised nausea at this. Moreover, despite inferior educational chances, Derek had got on far, far better than his brother – snarls of envy, thumbed noses of triumph. So, what malevolent motive had brought him here today? Tristram instinctively associated the visit with the new régime, the opening of the Interphase. Perhaps there had been swift telephone messages to and from Joscelyne and the Ministry of Infertility (search his flat for heterodox lecture-notes; question his wife about his views on Population Control). Tristram, in slight panic, leafed through memories of lessons he had given – that ironic laudation of the Mormons in Utah; that eloquent digression on *The Golden Bough* (forbidden reading); a possible sneer at the homo hierarchy after a particularly bad school luncheon. It was most unfortunate that he should have chosen to leave the school premises without permission, he thought yet again, on this day of all days. And then the brave spirit rose within his stomach as the lift stopped at the fortieth floor. The alc cried, 'To hell with them!'

Tristram made for his flat. Outside the door he paused, wiping out the automatic expectation of a child's cry of greeting. He went in. Beatrice-Joanna sat in her dressing-gown, doing nothing. She got up quickly, very surprised, on seeing her husband home so early. Tristram noticed, the bedroom door being open, a crumpled bed, bed of a fever-patient.

'Have you had a visitor?' he asked.

'A visitor? What visitor?'

'I saw my dear brother down below. He said he'd been here, looking for me.'

'Oh, him.' She let out a good deal of breath. 'I thought you meant, you know – a visitor.'

Tristram sniffed through the all-pervading scent of Anaphro, as if after something fishy. 'What did he want?'

'Why are you home so early?' asked Beatrice-Joanna. 'Didn't you feel well or something?'

'What I was told made me very unwell. I don't get my promotion. My father's philoprogenitiveness disqualifies me. And my own heterosexuality.' He wandered, hands behind him, into the bedroom.

'I didn't have time to tidy up,' she said, coming in to straighten the bedclothes. 'I was at the hospital. I haven't been back long.'

'We seem to have had a disturbed night,' he said. He left the bedroom. 'Yes,' he continued. 'The job's going to some little homo squirt like Derek. I suppose I should have expected it.'

'We're going through a rotten period, aren't we?' she said. She stood limply an instant, forlorn-looking, holding the end of a rumpled sheet. 'No luck at all.'

'You still haven't told me what Derek was after.'

'It wasn't at all clear. He was looking for you.' A close squeak, she was thinking; a very narrow shave. 'It was a bit of a surprise, seeing him,' she improvised.

'The liar,' he said. 'I thought it wouldn't be just to commiserate with us. How would he know about Roger, anyway? How would he have found out? I bet he only knew because you told him.'

'He knew,' she invented. 'He'd seen it at the Ministry. The daily death figures, or something. Will you eat now? I'm not a bit hungry.' She left the bed, came into the living-room, and made the tiny refrigerator, like some Polar god, descend from the ceiling.

'He's after something,' said Tristram. 'That's certain. I'll have to watch my step.' And then, the alc helping, 'Why the hell should I? Blast the lot of them. People like Derek running the country.' He summoned a chair from the wall. Beatrice-Joanna capped this by making a table rise from the floor. 'I feel anti-social,' said Tristram, 'deliriously anti-social. Who are they to tell us how to run our lives? And, oh,' he said, 'I don't like what's happening at all. There are a lot of police about. Armed.' He neglected to tell her what had happened to the unfrocked priest in the bar. She didn't approve of his drinking.

Beatrice-Joanna served him with a cutlet of reconstituted vegetable dehydrate, cold. He ate with fair appetite. Then she gave him a slice of synthelac pudding. 'Have a nut?' she offered, when he'd finished. A nut was a nutrition-unit, creation of the Ministry of Synthetic Food. She leaned over him, reaching for these from a wall-cupboard, and he caught a glimpse of her rich nakedness under the dressing-gown. 'God damn and blast them all,' he said, 'and it's God I mean.' He got up and tried to take her in his arms.

'No, please, don't,' she begged. It was no good; she couldn't bear his touch. She struggled. 'I'm not feeling at all well,' she said. 'I'm upset.' She began to snivel. He desisted.

'Oh, well,' he said. 'Oh, very well.' He bit at his left little finger-nail with his plastic teeth, standing by the window, awkward. 'I'm sorry I did that. I just didn't think.' She gathered the paper plates from the table and shot them into the firehole in the wall. 'Ah, hell,' he said with sudden violence. 'They've turned normal decent sex into a crime. And you don't want it any more. Just as well, I suppose.' He sighed. 'I can see that I'll have to join the volunteer geldings if I even want to keep my job.'

At that moment Beatrice-Joanna had a sharp revisitation of a sensation that, just for a blinding second, had buffeted her cortex when lying under Derek on that crumpled fever-bed. A sort of eucharistic moment of high-pitched trumpets and a crack of light like that (so it is said) seen at the instant of severing the optic nerve. And a tiny voice, peculiarly penetrating, squealing, 'Yes yes yes.' If everybody was talking about being careful, perhaps she'd better be careful, too. Not all that careful, of course. Only careful enough for Tristram not to know. Contraceptive devices had been known to fail. She said: 'I'm sorry, darling. I didn't mean that.' She put her arms round his neck. 'Now, if you like.' If only it could be done under an anaesthetic. Still, it wouldn't last long.

Tristram kissed her hungrily. '*I'll* take the tablets,' he said, 'not you.' Ever since the birth of Roger – on the admittedly and blessedly few occasions of his seeking his conjugal rights – he had always insisted on taking the precautions himself. For he had not really wanted Roger. 'I'll take three,' he said. 'Just to be on the safe side.' The tiny voice within had a miniature chuckle at that.

Thirteen

BEATRICE-JOANNA and Tristram, preoccupied in their several ways, did not see and hear the Prime Minister's announcement on television. But in millions of other homes – generally on the bedroom ceiling, there being insufficient space elsewhere – the stereoscopic image of the pouched, bulbous, classical scholar's face of the Right Hon. Robert Starling glowed and scolded like a fretful lamp. It spoke of the desperate dangers that England, that the English-Speaking Union, that the great globe itself would soon be running into unless certain strong repressive measures were, albeit regretfully, taken. This was war. War against irresponsibility, against those elements that were sabotaging – and such sabotage was clearly intolerable – the engines of state, against the wholesale flouting of reasonable and liberal laws, especially that law which, for the community's good, sought to limit the growth of population. All over the planet, said the luminous face with gravity, the leaders of state would be speaking – tonight or tomorrow – in similar urgent terms to their various peoples; the whole world was declaring war on itself. The severest punishments for continued irresponsibility (hurting the punishers more than the punished, it was implied); planetary survival dependent on the balance of population and a scientifically calculated minimal food supply; tighten belts; win through; evil things they would be fighting; pull together; long live the King.

Beatrice-Joanna and Tristram also missed some exciting stereoscopic film-shots of the summary settling of the strike at the National Synthelac Works – the police, nicknamed greyboys, using truncheons and carbines, laughing the while; a splash of chromatic brains on the camera lens.

They also missed a later announcement about the formation of a corps called the Population Police, its proposed Metropolitan Commissioner well-known to them both – brother, betrayer, lover.

Part Two

Part Two

One

An eight-hour shift system operated in all the State Utilities. But the schools and colleges split the day (every day, vacations being staggered) into four shifts of six hours each. Nearly two months after the opening of the Interphase, Tristram Foxe sat at midnight breakfast (shift starting at one) with a full summer moon slanting in. He was trying to eat a sort of paper cereal moistened with synthelac, and – though hungry at all hours these days, the rations having been cut considerably – he found it very difficult to spoon down the wet fibrous horror: it was somehow like having to eat one's words. As he munched an endless mouthful, the synthetic voice of the *Daily Newsdisc* (23.00 edition) squealed like a cartoon mouse, what time the organ itself wheeled slow and shiny black on the wall-spindle. '. . . Unprecedently low herring catches, explicable only in terms of inexplicable failure to breed, Ministry of Pisciculture reports –' Tristram reached out his left hand and switched off. Birth control among fish, eh? Tristram reeled an instant in a sudden race-memory – a sort of round flat fish overlapping the plate, crisp brown with a sharpish sauce. But all fish caught these days were crunched up by machines, converted into manure or mashed into the all-purpose nutrition-block (to be served as soup, cutlets, bread or pudding) which the Ministry of Natural Food issued as the main part of the weekly ration.

The living-room now being emptied of the manic voice and its ghastly journalese, Tristram could hear more clearly his wife being sick in the bathroom. Poor girl, she was regularly sick on rising these days. Perhaps it was the food. Enough to make anyone sick. He got up from the table and looked in on her. She was pale and tired-looking, limp as though the vomiting had wrung her out. 'I should go to the hospital if I were you,' he said kindly. 'See what's the matter.'

'I'm all right.'

'You don't seem all right to me.' He turned over his wrist microradio; the watch-face on the back said past twelve-thirty. 'I must fly.' He kissed her damp forehead. 'Look after yourself, dear. Do go and see somebody at the hospital.'

'It's nothing. Just a tummy upset.' And indeed she began, as if for his benefit, to look much better.

Tristram left (just a tummy upset) and joined the group waiting at the lift. Old Mr Earthrowl, Phipps, Arthur Spragg, Miss Runting – race-blocks like nutrition-blocks: Europe, Africa, Asia mashed together, salted by Polynesia – off to their jobs in the ministries and the national factories; Allsopp and the bearded Abazoff, Darking and Hamidun, Mrs Gow whose husband had been taken off three weeks before – ready for the shift that would end two hours later than Tristram's own. Mr Earthrowl was saying, in a wavering ancient voice, 'It's not right at all, the way I see it, having these coppers watching you all the time. Wasn't like that in my young days. If you wanted a smoke in the lavatory you went for a smoke, and no questions asked. But not now, oh, no. Breathing down your neck, these coppers are, all the time. Not right, way I look at it.' He continued his grumbling, the bearded Abazoff nodding the while, as they got into the lift – an old man, harmless and not very bright, driver of a large screw into the back of the television cabinet that, in endless multiplication, crawled towards and past him on a conveyor-belt. In the lift, Tristram said quietly to Mrs Gow:

'Any news?'

She looked up at him, a long-faced woman of forty-odd, her skin dry and smoked like that of a gipsy. 'Not a word. It's my belief that they've shot him. *Shot him,*' she suddenly cried aloud. Fellow-passengers pretended not to hear.

'Nonsense.' Tristram patted her thin arm. 'He didn't commit any real crime. He'll be back soon, you'll see.'

'It was his own fault,' said Mrs Gow. 'Drinking that there alc. Shooting his mouth off. I always told him he'd go too far one of these days.'

'There, there,' said Tristram, continuing to pat. The truth was that Gow hadn't technically shot his mouth off at all; he'd merely rasped a brief rude noise at a knot of policemen outside one of the rougher drinking-shops, somewhere off Guthrie Road. He'd been carted off amid great hilarity, and no more had been seen of him. It was best to keep off alc these days, best to leave alc to the greyboys.

4 – 3 – 2 – 1 – G. Tristram shuffled out of the lift. Moonshot plummy night waited outside in the packed street. And in the vestibule were members of the Poppol or Population Police – black uniform, cap with shiny

59

peak, badge and collar-dogs ashine with a bursting bomb which proved, on closer inspection, to be a breaking egg. Unarmed, less given to summary violence than the greyboys, smart, polite, they were mostly a credit to their commissioner. Tristram, joining the I-had-not-thought-death-had-undone-so-many workward crowd, uttered the word 'brother' aloud to the night-running Channel and its silver sky. The term had taken on purely pejorative connotations for him, which was not fair on poor inoffensive George, eldest of the three, hard at work on an agricultural station near Springfield, Ohio. George had recently sent one of his rare letters, dully factual about experiments with new fertilizers, puzzled about a strange wheat-blight seeping east through Iowa, Illinois and Indiana. Good solid old George.

Tristram entered the good solid old skyscraper which was the South London (Channel) Unitary School (Boys) Division Four. The Delta Shift was streaming out, and one of Joscelyne's three deputies, an open-mouthed grey-coxcombed man named Cory, stood in the great vestibule, watching. The Alpha Shift darted and needled into lifts, up stairs, down corridors. Tristram's first lesson was on the second floor – Elementary Historical Geography for the twentieth stream of the First Form. The artificial voice counted: '– Eighteen – seventeen –' Was it only his imagination, or was that creation of the National Syntheglot Corporation sterner, more iron-like, than it used to be?' '– Three – two – one.' He was late. He shot up in a staff-lift and panted into the class-room. One had to be careful these days.

Fifty-odd boys of various colour-mixtures greeted him

in a single polite 'Good morning'. Morning, eh? Night sat firmly on outside; the moon, great and frightening female symbol, sat over the night. Tristram said:

'Homework. Homework on your desks, please.' The tinkle of metal fasteners as the boys undid their satchels, then the flap of exercise-books, the rustle as they turned to the page where they had drawn their map of the world. Tristram strolled round, hands clasped behind, cursorily examining. The great crowded globe on Mercator's Projection, the two great empires – Enspun (English-Speaking Union) and Ruspun (Russian-Speaking Union) – crudely copied by lolling tonguetip-protruding boys. The Annexe Islands for population overflow, still building on the major oceans. A peaceful world that had forgotten the arts of self-destruction, peaceful and worried. 'Careless,' said Tristram, his forefinger on Cottam's drawing. 'You've put Australia too far south. You've forgotten to put in Ireland.' 'Sir,' said Cottam. And here was a boy – Hynard – who had not done his homework, a scared-looking boy, dark moons under his eyes. 'What,' asked Tristram, 'is the meaning of this?'

'I wasn't able to, sir,' said Hynard, his lower lip shaking. 'They moved me to the Hostel, sir. I hadn't time, sir.'

'Oh. The Hostel.' This was something new, an institution for orphans, temporary and permanent. 'What happened?'

'They took them away, sir, my dad and mum. They said they'd done wrong.'

'What had they done?'

The boy hung his head. An awareness of crime, not

61

taboo, kept him red and silent. Tristram said, kindly:

'Your mother has just had a baby, is that it?'

'Going to,' mumbled the boy. 'They took them away. They had to pack everything up. And then they took me to the Hostel.'

A great anger suffused Tristram. It was (and he realized this with shame) really a factitious anger, a pedantic anger. He saw himself in the Principal's office, ranting: 'The State regards the education of these children as important, which presumably means that they regard homework as important, and here the State comes sticking in its ugly hypocritical snout and stops one of my pupils from doing his homework. For Dog-sake let's know where we stand.' The weak fretfulness of a man invoking principle. He knew, of course, what the answer would be: first things first, the first thing being survival. He sighed, patted the boy's head, then went back to the front of the class. 'This morning,' he said, 'we're going to draw a map of the Sahara Reclamation Area. Take out your pencils.' Morning indeed. Night, that sea of school ink, flowed strongly away outside.

Two

BEATRICE-JOANNA sat writing a letter. She wrote in pencil, unhandily through desuetude, using the paper-saving logograms she had learned at school. Two months, and she had seen both nothing and too much of Derek. Too much of the public television image – Derek as black-uniformed reasonably exhorting Commissioner of the Population Police; nothing of Derek the lover, wearing a more becoming uniform of nakedness and desire. There was no censorship of letters, and she felt she could write freely. She wrote: 'Darling, I suppose I ought to be proud of the great name you're making for yourself, and you certainly look lovely in your new clothes. But I can't help wishing things were as they were before, when we could lie together loving each other, and not a care in the world except making sure that nobody knew what was going on between us. I refuse to believe that those lovely times are over. I miss you so much. I miss your arms around me and your lips on mine and –' She deleted this ampersand; some things were too precious to give to cold logograms. '– and your lips on mine. Oh, darling, sometimes I wake in the night or afternoon or morning or whenever it is we go to bed, according to the shift he's working, and want to cry out with desire for you.' She crammed her left fist in her mouth as if to stifle such a cry. 'Oh, dearest one, I love you, love you, love you. I long for your arms around me and your lips –' She saw that she had already said that, so she crossed it out; but the crossing-out made it appear that she had thought better of wanting his arms, lips and so on. She shrugged and went on. 'Couldn't you get in touch with me somehow? I know it's too risky for you to write to me, as Tristram would be sure to see the letter in the block letter-rack, but surely you could somehow give me a sign to show you still love me? And you do still love me, don't you, dearest?' He could send her a token. In the old days, the days of Shakespeare and steam radio, lovers had sent their mistresses flowers.

Now, of course, what flowers there were were all rendered esculent. He could send a packet of dehydrated cowslip broth, but that would mean cutting into his meagre rations. She longed for something romantic and daring, some big heretical gesture. In inspiration she wrote, 'When next you are on the telly please, if you love me still, bring in some special word, just for me. Bring in the word "love" or the word "desire". Then I'll know that you go on loving me as I go on loving you. There is no news, life goes on as it always does, very dull and dreary.' That was a lie: there was, she thought, a very definite item of news, but that had to be kept to herself. The straight line within her, the eternal and life-giving lance, wanted to say 'Rejoice', but the circle counselled caution; more than that, it span in a self-made breeze of apprehension. She refused to worry; things would work out all right. She signed the letter, 'Your eternally adoring Beatrice-Joanna.'

She addressed the letter to Commissioner D. Foxe, Population Police HQ, Infertility Building, Brighton, London, feeling a slight tremor as she wrote 'Infertility', that word which contained its opposite. She added in big bold logograms 'PRIVATE AND CONFIDEN-TIAL'. Then she went on the long vertical journey to the post-box by Earnshaw Mansions. It was a lovely July night, high moon riding, stars, earth-satellites wheeling, a night for love. Five young greyboys, lit by a street-lamp, were laughingly beating up a bewildered-looking old man who appeared, from his lack of response to the slaps and truncheonings, anaesthetized by alc. He seemed also, a Neronian Nazarene set upon by tittering lions, to be singing a hymn. 'You ought to be ashamed,' rebuked Beatrice-Joanna fiercely, 'downright ashamed. A poor old man like that.'

'You mind your own business,' said one of the grey policemen peevishly. '*Woman.*' he added with scorn. Their victim was allowed to crawl away, still singing. Very much a woman, minding her own business, socially and biologically, she shrugged and posted her letter.

Three

A LETTER for Tristram in the staff-room letter-rack, a letter from his sister Emma. It was four-thirty, hour of the half-hour luncheon break, but the bell had still to go. Dawn was coming up deliciously over the sea far beneath the staff-room window. Tristram fingered the letter with its garish Chinese stamp, its superscription *Air Mail* in ideograms and Cyrillic, smiling at yet another example of family telepathy. It was always happening like this – a letter from George in the West followed a day or so after by one from Emma in the East. Neither of them, significantly, ever wrote to Derek. Tristram read, still smiling, standing among his colleagues: '. . . The work goes on. I flew last week from Chengkiang to Hingi to Changchai to Tuyun to Shihtsien – exhausting. It's still almost standing room only here, but really frightening measures are being taken by the Central Government since the recent change in policy began. A mass execution of offenders against the Increase in Family laws took place in Chungking only ten days ago. This seemed to a lot of us to be going too far –' Typical of her, that understatement; Tristram caught an image of her prim forty-five-year-old face, the thin prim lips saying it. '– But it does seem to be having a salutary effect on some who, despite everything, still cherish as a life's ambition becoming an honourable ancestor to be worshipped by a milling mound of progeny. Such people are likely to become ancestors sooner than they expect. Curiously, ironically, there looks like being something of a famine in Fukien Province where the rice-crops – for some reason unknown – have failed . . .' Tristram frowned and wondered. George's report about the wheat-blight, the news about herring catches, now this. There awoke in him a faint nagging suspicion about something, he couldn't tell what.

'And how,' said a young mincing niggling voice, 'is our dear Tristram today?' It was Geoffrey Wiltshire, the new head of the Social Studies Department, literally a blue-eyed boy, so fair as almost to look white-headed. Tristram, who was trying not to hate him too much, gave a lemony smile and said, 'Well.'

'I tuned in to your Sixth Form lesson,' said Wiltshire. 'I know you won't mind my saying this, my dear dear Tristram.' He brought a whiff of perfume and two sets of twittering lashes close to his colleague. 'Saying that, in effect, you were teaching something you should *not* have been teaching.'

'I don't recollect.' Tristram tried to master his breath-ing.

'I, on the other hand, recollect rather perfectly. You said something like this: art, you said, cannot flourish in a society like ours, because, you seemed to say, art is the product of – I think this is the term you used – *paternity lust*. Wait,' he said, 'wait,' to Tristram's open mouth. 'You also said that the materials of the arts were, in effect, fertility symbols. Now, apart from the fact, my still dear Tristram, apart from the fact that one is at a complete loss to know how exactly this fits into the syllabus, you were quite gratuitously – and you can't deny this – quite gratuitously teaching something which is, however you look at it, to say the least heretical.' The bell rang for luncheon. Wiltshire put his arm round Tristram as they all processed to the staff dining-hall.

'But,' said Tristram, fighting his anger, 'damn it all, it's true. All art is an aspect of sexuality –'

'Nobody, my dear Tristram, denies that that, to some extent, is perfectly true.'

'But it goes deeper. Great art, the art of the past, is a kind of glorification of increase. I mean, take even drama for instance. I mean, tragedy and comedy had their origin in fertility ceremonies. The sacrificial goat – that's *tragos* in Greek – and the village Priapic festivals which crystallized into comic drama. I mean – and,' spluttered Tristram, 'take architecture –'

'We shall take no more.' Wiltshire stopped, dropped his arm from around Tristram's shoulder, and wagged a forefinger at Tristram's eyes, as though to disperse the smoke in them. 'We shall have no more of that, shall we, dear Tristram? Do, please, please, be careful. Everybody's really quite fond of you, you know.'

'I don't quite see what that has to do with anything –'

'It has a *lot* to do with *everything*. Now, just be a good boy –' he was at least seven years younger than

Tristram '– and stick to the syllabus. You can't go very far wrong if you do that.'

Tristram said nothing, pushing the lid down hard on his boiling temper. But, entering the steamy dining-hall, he deliberately stalked away from Wiltshire, seeking a table where sat Visser, Adair, Butcher (a very ancient trade-name), Freathy and Haskell-Sprott. These were harmless men who taught harmless subjects – simple skills into which controversy could never enter. 'You look,' said Mongol-eyed Adair, 'pretty sick.'

'I feel pretty sick,' said Tristram. Haskell-Sprott, at the head of the mess, spooned out very thin vegetable stew, saying:

'This'll make you sicker.'

'– Little bastards have been better behaved since we've had a chance to be tough with them,' Visser was saying. He mimed violent boxing. 'Take young Mildred, for example – queer name, Mildred, a girl's name, though that's the lad's surname, of course – take him. Late again today, so what do I do? I let the toughs get at him – you know, Brisker and Couchman and that lot. They roughed him up something beautiful. Just two minutes of that, that's all. He couldn't get up from the floor.'

'You've got to have discipline,' agreed Butcher through a mouthful of stew.

'I say,' said Adair to Tristram, 'you *do* look pretty sick.'

'As long as he hasn't got morning sickness,' leered the joker Freathy.

Tristram put down his spoon. 'What did you say then?'

68

'A joke,' said Freathy. 'I meant no harm.'

'You said something about morning sickness.'

'Forget it. Just my fun.'

'But that's impossible,' said Tristram. 'That couldn't be possible.'

'If I were you,' said Adair, 'I should go and have a lie down. You don't look at all well.'

'Absolutely impossible,' said Tristram.

'If you don't want your stew,' said Freathy, dripping with greed, 'I'd be very much obliged –' And he slid Tristram's plate towards himself.

'That's not fair,' said Butcher. 'It should be shared out. That's sheer damned gutsiness.' They tugged, slopping the stew.

'I think I'd better go home,' said Tristram.

'You do that,' said Adair. 'You might be sickening for something. Something catching.' Tristram got up and tottered over to tell Wiltshire. Butcher had won the stew and was sucking it down in triumph.

'Gulosity,' said Haskell-Sprott tolerantly. 'That's the word.'

Four

'But how could it have happened?' cried Tristram. 'How? How? How?' Two paces to the window, two paces back to the wall, his hands agitatedly clasped behind him.

'Nothing's one hundred per cent sure,' said Beatrice-

Joanna, sitting placidly. 'There might have been sabotage at the Contraceptive Works.'

'Nonsense. Absolute and utter bloody nonsense. That's a frivolous sort of remark,' cried Tristram, turning on her. 'That's typical of your whole attitude.'

'Are you sure,' said Beatrice-Joanna, 'that you actually took your tablets on that memorable occasion?'

'Of course I'm sure. I wouldn't dream of taking a risk like that.'

'No, of course you wouldn't.' She swayed her head, reciting in sing-song: 'Take a tablet instead of a risk.' She smiled up at him. 'That would have made a good slogan, wouldn't it? But, of course, we don't have slogans to make us good any more. We have the big stick.'

'It's completely beyond my understanding,' said Tristram. 'Unless –' He beetled down at her. 'But you wouldn't do that, would you? You wouldn't be so wicked and evil and sinful as to do that.' Augustinian words. He grasped her by the wrist. 'Is there anybody else?' he asked. 'Tell me the truth. I promise not to be angry,' he said angrily.

'Oh, don't be stupid,' she said very quietly. 'Even if I wanted to be unfaithful, who could I be unfaithful with? We don't go anywhere, we don't know anyone. And,' she said with heat, 'I object strongly to your saying that. To your thinking that. I've been faithful to you ever since the day we got married, and a fat lot of thanks or appreciation I've ever had for my fidelity.'

'I must have taken the tablets,' said Tristram, thinking hard back. 'I remember when it was. It was the day when poor young Roger –'

'Yes, yes, yes.'

'– And I'd just had my dinner and, if I remember rightly, it was you who suggested –'

'Oh, no, Tristram. It wasn't me. It certainly wasn't me.'

'– And I have a distinct recollection that I pulled the medicine cupboard down from the ceiling and that I –'

'You'd been drinking, Tristram. You smelt *terribly* of alc.' Tristram hung his head an instant. 'Are you sure you took the *right* tablets? I didn't check that with you. You always know best, don't you dear?' Her natural teeth gleamed in sarcasm. 'Anyhow, there it is. Perhaps it was a sudden accession of *paternity lust*.'

'Where did you get that expression from?' he blazed at her. 'Who told you those words?'

'You did,' she said sighing. 'It's an expression you sometimes use.' He stared at her. 'There must,' she added, 'be quite a lot of the heretic in you. In your unconscious, anyway. You say things in your sleep, you know. You wake me up with your snoring and then, assured of an audience, you talk. You're quite as bad as I am, in your way.'

'Well.' He looked round vaguely for somewhere to sit down. Beatrice-Joanna made another chair come purring out of the wall. 'Thanks,' he said distractedly. 'However it happened,' he said, sitting, 'you'll have to get rid of it. You'll have to take something. You won't want to leave it till you have to go to the Abortion Centre. That'll be shameful. That'll be almost as bad as breaking the law. Carelessness,' he muttered. 'No self-control.'

'Oh, I don't know.' She was too cool about the whole thing. 'Things may not be as bad as you think. I mean,

71

people have been having children in excess of the ration and nothing much has happened to them. I'm entitled to a child,' she said more warmly. 'The State killed Roger. The State let him die.'

'Ah, nonsense. We've been over all that before. What you don't seem to realize in your stupidity is that things have changed. *Things have changed.*' He emphasized this by punching her on the knee, once for each word. 'Look,' he said. 'The days of asking are over. The State doesn't ask any more. The State orders, the State compels. Do you realize that in China people have actually been put to death for disobeying the birth-control laws? Executed. Hanged or shot – I'm not sure which. It's in a letter I got from Emma.'

'This isn't China,' she said. 'We're more civilized here.'

'Ah, arrant bloody nonsense. It's going to be the same everywhere. The parents of one of my pupils were carted off by the Population Police – do you realize that? It happened only last night. And, as far as I can gather, they hadn't even had the baby yet. She just happened to be pregnant, as far as I can gather. Good Dog, woman, it won't be long before they'll be coming round with mice in a cage, testing urine for pregnancy.'

'How do they do that?' she asked, interested.

'You're incorrigible, that's what you are.' He got up again. Beatrice-Joanna let his chair whine back to the wall, giving him room to pace. 'Thanks. Now, look,' he said, 'just think of our position. If anybody found out we'd been careless, even without the results of the carelessness going any further, if anybody found out that –'

'How could anybody find out that?'

'Oh, I don't know. Somebody might hear you, in the morning, when you get up, that is,' he said delicately. 'There's Mrs Pettitt next door. There are spies around, you know. Where you have police you always have spies. Narks, they call them. Or you might say something to somebody – accidentally, I mean. I might as well tell you that I don't like the way things are going at the school. That little swine Wiltshire keeps plugging in on my lessons. Look,' he said, 'I'm going out now. I'm going to the chemist's. I'm going to get you some quinine tablets. And some castor oil.'

'I don't like them. I hate the taste of both of them. Give it a bit longer, will you? Just give it a bit longer. Everything may be all right.'

'There you go again. Let me try and get it into your thick skull,' said Tristram, 'that we're living in dangerous times. The Population Police have a lot of power. They can be very very nasty.'

'I don't think they'd ever do me any harm,' she said complacently.

'Why not? Why wouldn't they?'

'I've just got a feeling, that's all.' Careful, careful. 'I just have a sort of intuition about it, that's all.' Then, 'Oh,' she cried powerfully, 'I'm sick to death of the whole business. If God made us what we are, why should we have to worry about what the State tells us to do? God's stronger and wiser than the State, isn't He?'

'There is no God.' Tristram looked at her curiously. 'Where have you been getting these ideas from? Who's been talking to you?'

'Nobody's been talking to me. I see nobody, except when I go out to buy rations. When I talk, I talk to

73

myself. Or to the sea. Sometimes I talk to the sea.'

'What is all this? What exactly is going on? Do you feel all right?'

'Except for being hungry all the time,' said Beatrice-Joanna, 'I feel very well. Very well indeed.'

Tristram went to the window and gazed up at the patch of sky visible between topless towers. 'I wonder sometimes,' he said, 'if perhaps there is a God after all. Somebody up there,' he mumbled, musing, 'controlling everything. I wonder sometimes. But,' he said, turning in a small show of sudden panic, 'don't tell anybody I said that. I didn't say there *was* a God. I just said I wondered sometimes, that's all.'

'You don't trust me very much, do you?'

'I don't trust anyone. Forgive me, but I might as well be honest with you. I just daren't trust anybody at all. I don't seem able even to trust myself, do I?' Then he went out into the pearly morning to buy quinine in one State Druggist's, castor oil in another. In the first shop he talked loudly about malaria, even mentioning an educational trip he had once taken down the Amazon; in the second he simulated a convincing costive look.

Five

IF no God, there must be at least a pattern-making demiurge. So Tristram was later to think, when he had leisure and inclination for thinking. The next day (though only the calendar really accepted such a term, the shift-system cutting across natural time like a global air-journey) the next day Tristram knew he was being followed. A neat blob of black in the crowds behind him, keeping its distance, seen fully – as Tristram turned into Rostron Place – as a comely small man with a moustache, Poppol egg bursting in the sun on his cap-badge, three glinting stars on each epaulette. Tristram became aware of the gelatinous sensations of nightmare – limbs melting, shallow breath, hopelessness. But, when a lorry and trailer loaded with equipment for the Ministry of Synthetic Food timidly began to poke into Adkins Street from Rostron Place, Tristram had enough strength and will-to-survive to dash round to its off-side, so that many red tons of pipes and cauldrons interposed themselves between himself and his pursuer. Not that it made any difference, he realized, feeling hopeless and foolish; they would get him if they really wanted him. He took the second turning to the left – Hanania Street. There stretched, along the whole bottom storey of Reppel Building, the Metropole, haunt of high officials, no place for a humble schoolmaster unsure of his position. Clacking the few septs, tanners and tosheroons in his left-hand trouser-pocket, he entered.

Ring of glasses, broad backs and girlish shoulders in grey and black uniforms, voices of policy. ('RB stroke 371 is perfectly clear about it.') Tristram crawled to an empty table and awaited a waiter. ('Allocation of raw materials should be worked out in inter-departmental conference.') A waiter came, black as the ace of spades in a cream jacket. 'With what, sir?' he asked. 'With orange,' said Tristram, his eyes on the swinging doors. A couple of grey-uniformed exquisites entered, expiring with laughter; an eye-glassed stern bald gelding with his boy secretary; a mannish woman with a big useless bust. Then Tristram saw his pursuer enter, saw with a kind of relief. The officer took off his cap, disclosing short straight oiled rust-coloured hair, and looked into the throng of drinkers; Tristram nearly waved to show where he was. But the officer noticed him soon enough and, smiling, came over. 'Mr Foxe? Mr *Tristram* Foxe?'

'Yes, as you very well know. You'd better sit down. Unless, of course, you want to take me off right away.' The black waiter brought Tristram's drink.

'Take you off?' The officer laughed. 'Oh, I see. Look,' he said to the waiter, 'I'll have one of those. Yes,' he said to Tristram, 'you are quite like your brother. Your brother Derek, that is. In appearance. For the rest, of course, I just don't know.'

'Don't play with me,' said Tristram. 'If you want to prefer a charge, then prefer it.' He even thrust forward his wrists, as if in a mime of cycling.

The officer laughed louder. 'Take a tip from me, Mr Foxe,' he said. 'If you've done something indictable, wait till it's found out. We've enough to cope with without people volunteering, do you see.' He put both hands supine on the table, as if to show that they were free of blood, and smiled pleasantly at Tristram. He seemed a decent sort of man, about Tristram's own age.

'Well,' said Tristram, 'if I may ask –' The officer swivelled his head as though to see whether anybody, whether listening or not, would be able to hear. But Tristram had humbly chosen a remote and isolated table. The officer nodded slightly in satisfaction. He said:

'I won't tell you my name. My rank you can see – captain. I work in the organization of which your brother is Commissioner, do you see. It's about your brother that I wish to speak. I take it that you're not too fond of your brother.'

'I'm not, as a matter of fact,' said Tristram. 'But I don't see what that's got to do with anything or anybody.' The waiter brought the captain's alc, and Tristram ordered another. 'This is on me,' said the captain. 'Bring two more. Doubles, make them.' Tristram raised his eyebrows. He said:

'If your intention's to make me drunk so that I'll say things I shouldn't say –'

'Such balderdash,' laughed the captain. 'You're a very suspicious type of man I'd say, do you see. You know that, I suppose. You know that you're a very suspicious type of man, I should imagine.'

'I am,' said Tristram. 'Circumstances are making all of us suspicious.'

'I would say,' said the captain, 'that your brother Derek has done very well for himself, wouldn't you agree? That, of course, is in spite of a lot of things. In spite of his family background, for instance. But being homo, do you see, wipes out all other sins, the sins of the fathers, for instance, do you see.'

'He's got on very well,' said Tristram. 'Derek is now a very big man.'

'Oh, but I'd say his position is not impregnable, not impregnable at all. And as for being a *big* man – well, bigness is a very relative thing, isn't it? Yes,' the captain agreed with himself, 'it is.' He leaned closer to Tristram and said, with seeming irrelevance, 'My rank in the

77

Ministry rightly entitled me to a majority at least, do you see, in the new corps. You behold me, however, with but three captain's pips. A man called Dann, much my junior, wears the crowns. Have you ever experienced that sort of thing, Mr Foxe? Have you ever, do you see, had the humiliating experience of seeing a junior man promoted over your head?'

'Oh, yes,' said Tristram. 'Oh, yes, indeed. Oh, very much yes, indeed.' The waiter brought two double alcs. 'Run out of orange,' he said. 'This here is blackcurrant. Hope you gentlemen will not mind.'

'I thought,' nodded the captain, 'you would understand.'

'It's through not being homo, of course,' said Tristram.

'I do believe,' said the captain in massive understatement, 'that that has something to do with it. Your brother would certainly be the last to deny how much he owes, do you see, to his pretty inverted sexual ways. But now you must tell me, Mr Foxe, about these pretty inverted sexual ways of his, you having known him all your life. Would you say they were genuine?'

'Genuine?' Tristram frowned. 'All too horribly genuine, I'd say. He started to play about in that way before he was sixteen. He never showed any interest in girls.'

'Never? Well. We revert now to your admission that you're a suspicious man, Mr Foxe. Have you ever been suspicious of your wife?' He smiled. 'That's a hard question to ask any husband, but I ask it in all good faith.'

'I don't quite see –' said Tristram. And then, 'Good Dog, what are you implying?'

'You begin to see,' nodded the captain. 'You're quite

quick at this sort of thing. This, do you see, is a matter of very great delicacy.'

'Are you trying to tell me,' said Tristram, incredulous, 'are you trying to insinuate that my wife – that my wife and my brother Derek –'

'I've watched him for some time now,' said the captain. 'He's known that I've watched him, but he doesn't seem to have cared very much. Pretending to be homosexual must, for a normally sexed man, be a very great strain, rather like trying to smile all the time. That your brother Derek has met your wife on various occasions I can vouch for. I can give dates. He has been to your flat many times. All this, of course, may have meant nothing. He may have been giving your wife Russian lessons.'

'The bitch,' said Tristram. 'The bastard.' He didn't know which one to turn on more. 'She never said. She never said a word about his going to the flat. But it all ties up now. Yes, I begin to see. I met him coming out. About two months ago.'

'Ah.' The captain nodded again. 'There was never any real proof of anything, though, do you see. In a court of law, when there used to be courts of law, all this would not be real evidence of misconduct. Your brother may have visited your flat regularly because he was fond of his nephew. He would not, of course, visit when you were there, knowing you had no love for him, nor, for that matter, he for you. And your wife would not want to mention his visits, do you see, for fear of your becoming angry. And when your child died, two months ago if I remember rightly, these visits ceased. Of course, the visits may have ceased for a quite different reason,

79

namely his elevation to the post he now holds.'

'You know a lot, don't you?' said Tristram bitterly.

'I have to know a lot,' said the captain. 'But, do you see, suspicion is not knowledge. Now I come to something important that I really know about your wife and your brother. Your wife has been writing to your brother. She has written what, in the old days, was known as a love-letter. Just one, no more, but, of course, very incriminating. She wrote the letter yesterday. In it she says how much she misses your brother and, inevitably, how much she loves him. There is a certain amount of erotic detail also – not too much, but a certain amount. It was foolish of her to write the letter, but it was even more foolish of your brother not to destroy the letter as soon as he'd read it.'

'So,' said Tristram growling, '*you* saw it, did you? The faithless bitch,' he added. And then, 'That explains everything. I knew I couldn't have made a mistake. I knew it. The deceiving treacherous little –' He meant both of them.

'Unfortunately,' said the captain, 'you only have my word for this business of the letter. Your wife will deny everything, I should imagine. But she will be waiting for your brother Derek's next little talk on the television, for in that next little talk she has requested a hidden message to herself. She has requested that he introduce somehow the word "love" or the word "desire". A pretty idea,' commented the captain. 'I take it, however, that you will not find it necessary to wait for that sort of confirmation. It may never occur, do you see. In any case, those two words, both or either, could occur quite naturally in a television talk of a patriotic nature (all television talks are patriotic now, are they not?). He could say something about love of country or everybody's desire, do you see, to do their bit to end the present emergency, such as it is. The point is, I take it, that you'll want to act almost at once.'

'Yes,' said Tristram. 'At once. She can leave. She can go. She can get out. I never want to see her again. She can have her child. She can have it wherever she likes. I shan't stop her.'

'You mean to say,' said the captain in awe, 'that your wife is pregnant?'

'It's not me,' said Tristram. 'I know that. I swear it's not me. It's Derek. The swine Derek.' He bashed the table and made the glasses dance to their own tune. 'Cuckolded,' he said, as in some sniggering Elizabethan play, 'by my own brother.'

The captain smoothed his rusty moustache with his left little finger, now one wing, now the other. 'I see,' he said. 'Officially, I have no knowledge of this. There is no proof, do you see, that you are not responsible. There is, as you yourself must admit, a possibility that the child – if the child is ever born, which, officially, of course, it must not be – that the child is yours. What I mean is, how, officially, does anybody know that you're telling the truth?'

Tristram looked narrowly at him. 'Do you believe me?'

'What I believe is neither here nor there,' said the captain. 'But you must admit that pinning this business on the Commissioner of the Population Police is going to be met with, do you see, incredulity. A liaison with a woman is a different matter. That is, for your high-placed brother, wickedness and foolishness. But to impregnate his *inamorata* – that would be a glorious kind of head-swimming idiocy too imbecilic to be true. Do you see? Do you see?' It was the first time he had used this tag as a genuine question.

'I'll get him,' vowed Tristram. 'Never fear, I'll get him, the swine.'

'We'll have another drink on that,' said the captain. The black waiter was near, banging his metal tray against his slightly flexed knee, humming tunelessly to the tinny drum-beat. The captain finger-snapped. 'Two more doubles,' he ordered.

'They're equally guilty,' said Tristram. 'What worse betrayal could there be than this? Betrayal by wife. Betrayal by brother. Oh, Dog, Dog, Dog.' He clapped his hands on his eyes and cheeks, shutting out the betraying world but letting his mouth tremble at it.

'He's the really guilty one,' said the captain. 'He's betrayed more than his brother. He's betrayed the State and his high position in the State. He's committed the foulest of crimes and the most stupid of crimes, do you see. Get him first, get him. Your wife has been merely a woman, and women haven't much sense of responsibility. He's the one, he. Get him.' The drinks came, funeral purple in colour.

'To think,' moaned Tristram, 'that I gave her love, trust – all that a man can give.' He sipped his alc and fruit-juice.

'To hell with that, do you see,' said the captain impatiently. 'You're the only one who can get him. What can I do, eh, in my position? Even if I'd kept that letter, even if I'd kept it, don't you think he would have known? Don't you think he'd get some of the thugs on to me? He's a dangerous man.'

'What can *I* do?' said Tristram tearfully. 'He's in a very high position.' This new glass was full of the stuff of snivelling. 'Taking advantage of his position, that's what he's been doing, to betray his own brother.' His mouth crumbling, wet oozed round his contact lenses. But, suddenly cracking his fist hard on the table, 'The bitch,' he exploded, showing his lower set. 'Wait till I see her, just wait.'

'Yes, yes, yes, that can indeed wait, do you see. Look, get him first, as I tell you. He's changed his flat, he's at 2095 Winthrop Mansions. Get him there, do him in, teach him a lesson. He lives alone, do you see.'

'Kill him, you mean?' said Tristram in wonder. 'Kill?'

'*Crime passionel*, they used to call it. Your wife can be made to confess, sooner or later, do you see. Get him, do him in.'

Tristram gleamed with unsteady suspicion. 'How far can I trust you?' he said. 'I'm not going to be used, I'm not going to be made to do somebody else's dirty work, do you see.' That tag was bound to infect him. 'You've said things about my wife. How do I know it's right, how do I know it's true? You've got no proof, you've shown me no proof.' He pushed his empty glass to the centre of the table. 'You keep your dirty drink, trying to make me drunk.' He started, with some small difficulty, to rise. 'I'm going home to have it out with my wife, that's what I'm going to do. Then we'll see. But I'm not doing any of your dirty work for you. I don't trust one of you, and that's flat. Plotting, that's what it is.'

'So you're still unconvinced,' said the captain. He began to feel in one of his tunic side-pockets.

'Yes, plotting. Struggle for power within the party – characteristic of the Interphase. Historian, that's what I am. I should have been Head of the Social Studies Department, if that homo swine hadn't –'

'All right, all right,' said the captain.

'Betrayed,' said Tristram dramatically. 'Betrayed by homos.'

'If you go on like this,' said the captain, 'you'll get yourself arrested.'

'That's all you people can do, arrest people. Arrested development, ha ha.' And then, 'Betrayed.'

'Very well,' said the captain. 'If you want proof, here it is.' And he took a letter out of his pocket and held it up.

'Give it me,' said Tristram, clawing. 'Let me see it.'

'No,' said the captain. 'If you don't trust me, why should I trust you?'

'So,' said Tristram. 'So she did write to him. A filthy love letter. Wait till I see her. Wait till I see both of them.' He clanked an uncounted handful of septs and florins on to the table and, unseeing and very unsteady, began to leave.

'Him first,' said the captain. But Tristram was weaving his way out, blindly firm of purpose. The captain made a tragi-comic face and put the letter back in his pocket. It was a letter from an old friend, one Dick Turnbull, on holiday in the Schwarzwald. People didn't look these days, didn't listen, didn't remember. Still, that other letter did exist. Captain Loosley had quite definitely seen it on the Metropolitan Commissioner's desk. And, unfortunately, the Metropolitan Commissioner had – before sweeping it and other private correspondence, some of it abusive, into the hellhole in the wall – seen that he'd seen it.

Six

SAND-HOPPERS, mermaids' purses, sea gooseberries, cuttle bones, wrasse, blenny and bullhead, tern, gannet and herring gull. Beatrice-Joanna took a last breath of the sea and then went to the State Provisions Store (Rossiter Avenue branch) at the foot of the mountain of Spurgin Building. The rations had been cut yet again with neither warning nor apology from the twin ministries responsible. Beatrice-Joanna received and paid for two blocks of brown vegetable dehydrate (legumin), a large white tin of synthelac, compressed sheets of cereal, a blue bottle of 'nuts' or nutrition units. Unlike the other women shoppers, however, Beatrice-Joanna did not indulge in whines and threats (though these were muffled, there having been a small quickly quelled shoppers' riot three days before, the door today flanked by greyboys); she felt full of the sea, as of some huge satisfying round dish of wobbly blue-green marbled meat. She wondered vaguely, leaving the shop, what meat had tasted like. Her mouth recollected only the salt of live human skin in a purely amatory context – lobes, fingers, lips. 'He's my meat,' sang the song about adorable Fred. That, she supposed, was what was meant by the term sublimation.

It was thus in a full street, engaged in an innocent housewife's task, that she was suddenly confronted with the loud accusations of her husband. 'There you are,' he called, swaying with alc. He semaphored wildly at her, his feet seemingly glued to the pavement outside the entrance to the flats which made up the greater part of Spurgin Building. 'Caught in the act, eh? Caught coming back from it.' Many passers-by became interested. 'Pretending to go and do the shopping, eh? I know all, so you needn't pretend.' He ignored her string-bag of meagre groceries. 'I've been told everything, the lot.' He teetered, with balancing arms, as though on a high window-ledge. The little life inside Beatrice-Joanna shuddered as if threatened. 'Tristram,' she began to scold bravely, 'you've been on the alc again. Now get inside at once and into that lift –' 'Betrayed,' wailed Tristram. 'Going to have a baby. By my own blasted brother. Bitch, bitch. Well, have it. Go on, get out and have it. They all know, everybody knows.' Some passers-by tutted. 'Tristram,' said Beatrice-Joanna with spread lips. 'Don't call me Tristram,' said Tristram, as though that were not his name. 'Deceiving bitch.' 'Get inside,' ordered Beatrice-Joanna. 'There's been a mistake. This is not a public matter.' 'Isn't it?' said Tristram. 'Isn't it just? Go on, get out.' The whole crowded street, the sky, had become his own betrayed home, a cell of suffering. Beatrice-Joanna firmly tried to enter Spurgin Building. Tristram tried to prevent her with arms weaving like cilia.

Then noise could be heard coming from Froude Place. It was a procession of rough-looking men in overalls, loud with confused cries of disaffection. 'You see,' said

Tristram triumphantly. 'Everybody knows.' They all wore the crown and the NSW of the National Synthefabrik Works. Some carried banners of grievance – pieces of synthetic cloth tacked on to broom-handles, hastily cut bits of card on slender laths. The only true inscription was the logogram STRK; for the rest, there were crude drawings of human skeletons. 'It's all over between us,' said Tristram. 'You stupid idiot,' said Beatrice-Joanna, 'get inside. We don't want to be involved in this.' A wild-eyed workers' leader stood on the plinth of a street lamp, hugging the pillar with his left arm. 'Brothers,' he called, 'brothers. If they want a fair day's work they've got to bloody well feed us proper.'

'Hang old Jackson,' wavered an elderly worker. 'String him up.'

'Shove him in a stewpot,' called a Mongol with comic strabismus.

'Don't be a fool,' said Beatrice-Joanna in disquiet. 'I'm getting out of this if you're not.' She pushed Tristram violently out of her way. Her provisions went flying and Tristram himself staggered and fell. He began to cry. 'How could you, *how could you*, with my own brother?' She went grimly into Spurgin Building, leaving him to his sonata of reproach. Tristram got up from the pavement with difficulty, clutching the tin of synthelac. 'You stop shoving,' said a woman. 'Nowt to do with me. I want to get home.'

'They can threaten,' said the leader, 'till they're bloody well blue in the face. We have our rights and they can't take them away, and the withholding of labour's a lawful right in case of just grievance, and they can't bloody well deny it.' Roars. Tristram found himself wound round, stirred into the crowd of workers. A schoolgirl, also caught in it, began to cry. 'You do well to do that,' nodded a youngish man with pimples and a bad shave. 'Starved, the bloody lot of us, that's about it.' The cross-eyed Mongol turned to give Tristram his full face. A fly had settled on his porous nose; his eyes were well set for looking at it. He watched it fly away, wondering, as though it symbolized liberation. 'My name,' he said to Tristram, 'is Joe Blacklock.' Then, satisfied, he turned back to listening to his leader. The leader called, himself unfortunately plump as a table bird, 'Let them listen to the crying-out of the empty guts of the workers.' Roars. 'Solidarity,' yelled this solid man. More roars. Tristram was crushed, pushed. Then two greyboys from the State Provisions Store (Rossiter Avenue branch) appeared, armed only with truncheons. Manly-looking, they began vigorously to belabour. There was a great cry of pain and anger as they jerked at the right arm of the lamp-clutching leader. The leader flailed and protested. One of the police went down, crunched under boots. Blood appeared from nowhere on somebody's face, an earnest of earnest. 'Aaaaargh,' gargled the man next to Tristram. 'Do the bastards in.' The schoolgirl shrieked. 'Let her get out,' cried soberer Tristram. 'For Dogsake clear a way there.' The crushing crowd came on. The still upright greyboy was now at bay against the freestone wall of Spurgin Building. He cracked, his panting mouth open, at skulls and faces. An upper set was spewed out by someone, a Cheshire Cat grin in the air for an instant. Then whistles shrilled hollowly. 'More of the bastards,' throated a voice in Tristram's neck-nape. 'Make a bloody dash for it.'

'Solidarity,' cried the lost leader from somewhere among fists. The sirens of police cars rose and fell in *glissandi* of dismal tritones. The crowd tongued out in all directions like fire or stone-dinged water. The schoolgirl needled across the street with spider-legs, escaped into an alley. Tristram was still clutching, like a baby, the white tin of synthelac. Greyboys now held the street, some tough and stupid, others sweetly prettily smiling, all with carbines at the ready. An officer with two bright bars on each shoulder strutted, whistle in mouth like a baby's dummy, hand on holster. At each end of the street were crowds, watching. Placards and banners shifted to and fro uncertainly above shoulders, already looking sheepish and forlorn. There were black vans waiting, side-doors open, lorries with tail-boards down. A sergeant yelped something. There was a jostling at one place, the vexillae advanced. The whistled shining inspector unholstered his pistol. He peeped one silver blast, and a carbine spat at the air. 'Get the sods,' called a worker in torn overalls. A tentative thrust of a phalanx of crushed men gained momentum speedily, and a greyboy went down shrieking. The whistle now pierced like toothache. Carbines opened out frankly, and shot whined like puppies from the walls. 'Hands up,' ordered the inspector, whistle out of his mouth. Some workers were down, gaping and bleeding in the sun. 'Get 'em all in,' yelped the sergeant. 'Room for everyone, the little beauties.' Tristram dropped his tin of synthelac. 'Watch that one there,' cried the officer. 'Home-made bomb.'

'I'm not one of these,' Tristram tried to explain, hands clasped over his head. 'I was just going home. I'm a teacher. I object strongly. Take your dirty hands off.'

'Right,' said a bulky greyboy obligingly, and carbine-butted him fairly in the gut. Tristram sent out a delicate fountain of the purple juice that had diluted the alc. 'In.' He was prodded to a black lorry, his nasopharynx smarting with the taste of the brief vomit. 'My brother,' he protested. 'Commissioner of the Pop-poppoppop –' He couldn't stop popping. 'My wife's in there, let me at least speak to my wife.' 'In.' He fell up the rungs of the swinging tail-board. 'Speeeeak tuh mah wahf,' mocked a worker's voice. 'Haw haw.' The lorry was full of sweat and desperate breathing, as though all inside had been kindly rescued from some killing cross-country run. The tail-board clinked up with merry music of chains, a tarpaulin curtain came down. The workers cheered at the total darkness, and one or two squeaked in girly voices, 'Stop it, I'll tell my ma' and 'Oh, you *are* awful, Arthur.' An earnest breathing bulk next to Tristram said, 'They don't take it seriously, that's the trouble with a lot of these here. Let the side down, that's what they do.' A hollow voice with slack Northern vowels ventured a pleasantry: 'Would anybody lahk a fried egg samwidge?' 'Look,' almost wept Tristram to the odorous dark, 'I was just going in to have it out with my wife, that's all. It was nothing to do with me. It's unfair.' The serious voice at his side said, 'Course it's unfair. They never have been fair to the working man.' Another, hostile to Tristram's accent, growled, 'Shut it, see. We know your type. Watching you, I am,' which was manifestly impossible. Meanwhile, they roared along in convoy, as they could tell, and there was a sense of streets full of happy unarrested people. Tristram wanted to blubber. 'I take it,' said a new voice, 'that you don't want to associate yourself with our struggle, is that it, friend? The intellectuals have never been on the side of the workers. Sometimes they've let on to be, but only for purposes of betrayal.' 'I'm the one who's been betrayed,' cried Tristram. 'Betray his arse,' said someone. 'Treason of clerks,' came a bored voice. A harmonica began to play.

At length the lorry stopped, and there was a grinding finality of brakes, an opening and slamming of the doors of the driver's cabin. A noise of unslotting, a chainy rattle, and then great daylight blew in like a wind. 'Out,' said a carbined corporal, pock-marked Micronesian. 'Look here,' said Tristram, getting out, 'I want to register the strongest possible protest about this. I demand that I be allowed to telephone Commissioner Foxe, my brother. There's been a ghastly mistake.' 'In,' said a constable, and Tristram was shoved with the rest through a doorway. Forty-odd storeys dove into heaven over their heads. 'You lot in here,' said a sergeant. 'Thirty-five to a cell. Plenty of room for all, you horrible great antisocial things, you.' 'I protest,' protested Tristram. 'I'm not going in there,' going in. 'Ah, shut it,' said a worker. 'With pleasure,' said the sergeant. Three bolts slammed in on them and, for good measure, a key ground round in a rusty ward.

Seven

Beatrice-Joanna packed one bag only, there not being

much to pack. This was no age of possessions. She said good-bye to the bedroom, her eyes moistening at her last sight of the tiny wall-cot that had been Roger's. Then, in the living-room, she told out all her cash: five guinea-notes, thirty crowns, odd septs, florins and tanners. Enough. There was no time to let her sister know, but Mavis had often said, often written, 'Now, come any time. But don't bring that husband of yours with you. You know Shonny can't stand him.' Beatrice-Joanna smiled at the thought of Shonny, then cried, then pulled herself together. She also pulled the main switch and the hum of the refrigerator ceased. It was a dead flat now. Guilty? Why should she feel guilty? Tristram had told her to get out, and she was getting out. She wondered again who had told him, how many knew. Perhaps she would never see Tristram again. The small life within her said, 'Act, don't think. Move. I'm all that counts.' She would, she thought, be safe in Northern Province; *it* would be safe. She could think of no other obligation than to this, the single inch of protest, weighing thirty-odd grains, the cells dividing again and again in protest, blasts of protest – epi, meso, hypo. Tiny life protesting at monolithic death. Away.

It was starting to rain, so she put on her waterproof, a thin skin like a mist. There was dried blood on the pavement, needles of rain pricking it to make it flow, if only down the gutter. The rain came from the sea and stood for life. She walked briskly into Froude Square. The red-lit underground station entrance milled with people, red-lit like devils of the old mythical hell, silent, chunnering, giggling, sped singly or in pairs down the grumbling escalator. Beatrice-Joanna bought her ticket from a machine, dove down to the aseptic white cata-combs where winds rushed out of tunnels, and boarded a tube-train to Central London. It was a swift service and would get her there in less than half an hour. Next to her an old woman champed and champed, talking to herself, her eyes closed, saying aloud at intervals, 'Doris was a good girl, a good girl to her mother, but the other one –' Preston, Patcham, Pangdean. Passengers left, passengers boarded. Pyecombe. The old woman alighted, mumbling, 'Doris.' 'A pie was what they used to eat,' said a pale fat mother in powder-blue. Her child cried. 'Hungry, that's his trouble,' she said. And now the legs of the journey grew longer. Albourne. Hickstead. Bolney. Warninglid. At Warninglid a scholarly-looking man with a stringy neck boarded, sitting next to Beatrice-Joanna to read, puffing like a tortoise, *Dh Wks v Wlym Shkspr*. He unwrapped a synthechoc bar and began to chew, puffing. The child renewed his crying. Handcross. Pease Pottage. 'Pease pottage was something else they used to eat,' said the mother. Crawley, Horley, Salfords. Nothing edible there. Redhill. At Redhill the scholar alighted and three members of the Population Police came aboard. They were young men, subalterns, well set-up, their metal ashine and their black unmacu-lated by hairs, scurf or food-droppings. They examined the women passengers insolently, as with eyes expert at burrowing to illegal pregnancies. Beatrice-Joanna blushed, wishing the journey were over. Merstham, Caterham, Coulsdon. It soon would be. She pressed her hands over her belly as though its cellulating inmate were already leaping with audible joy. Purley, Croydon, Thornton Heath, Norwood. The police officers alighted.

And now the train went purring into the deep black heart of the immemorial city. Dulwich, Camberwell, Central London. And soon Beatrice-Joanna was on the local line to the North-West Terminus.

She was shocked at the number of grey and black police that infested the noisy station. She joined a queue in the booking-hall. Officers of both forces sat at long tables barring the way to the bank of booking-guichets. They were smart, pert, clipped.

'Identity-card, please.' She handed it over. 'Destination?'

'State Farm NW313, outside Preston.'

'Purpose of trip?'

She fell easily into the rhythm. 'Social visit.'

'Friends?'

'Sister.'

'I see. *Sister.*' A dirty word, that. 'Duration of visit?'

'I can't say. Look here, why do you want to know all this?'

'Duration of visit?'

'Oh, perhaps six months. Perhaps longer.' How much should she tell them? 'I'm leaving my husband, you see.'

'Hm. Hm. Check on this passenger, will you?' A constable-clerk copied from her identity-card on to a buff form, official. Meanwhile another young woman was in trouble. 'I tell you I'm *not* pregnant,' she kept saying. A gold-haired thin-lipped policewoman in black began to pull her to a door blazoned MEDICAL OFFICER. 'We'll soon see,' she said. 'We'll soon know all about that, shan't we, dear?'

'But I'm *not*,' cried the young woman. 'I tell you I'm *not.*'

94

'There,' said Beatrice-Joanna's interrogator, handing back her stamped carnet. He had a pleasant prefect's face on which grimness sat like a bogey-mask. 'Too many illeg pregs trying to escape to the provinces. *You* wouldn't be trying anything like that, would you? Your card says you've got one child, a son. Where is he now?'

'Dead.'

'I see. I see. Well, that's that then, isn't it? Off you go.' And Beatrice-Joanna went to book her single ticket to the north.

Police at the barriers, police patrolling the platform. A crowded train (nuclear-propelled). Beatrice-Joanna sat down, already exhausted, between a thin man so stiff that his skin seemed to be armour and a very small woman whose legs dangled like a very big doll's. Opposite was a check-suited man with a coarse comedian's face, sucking desperately at a false molar. A small girl, open-mouthed as with adenoid growths, surveyed Beatrice-Joanna from head to foot, foot to head, in a strict slow rhythm. A very fat young woman glowed like a deliberate lamp, her legs so tree-like that they seemed to be growing out of the floor of the compartment. Beatrice-Joanna closed her eyes. Almost at once a dream leaped on to her: a grey field under a thundery sky, cactus-like plants groaning and swaying, skeletal people collapsing with their black tongues hanging out, then herself involved – with some bulky male form that shut out the scene – in the act of copulation. Loud laughter broke out and she awoke fighting. The train was still in the station; her fellow-travellers stared at her with (except for the adenoidal girl) only a little curiosity. Then–as if that dream had been an obligatory rite before departure – they began to ease out, leaving the grey and black police behind.

Eight

'WHAT will they do to us?' asked Tristram. His eyes had grown used to the dark and could see that the man next to him was the cross-eyed Mongol who, ages ago in the rebellious street, had announced his name as Joe Blacklock. Of the other prisoners, some squatted like miners – there were no seats – and others propped up the walls. One old man, formerly phlegmatic, had become possessed of a fit of excitement and had gripped the bars, crying to the corridor, 'I left the stove on. Let me get home and turn it off. I'll come straight back, honest I will,' and now lay exhausted on the cold flags.

'Do to us?' said Joe Blacklock. 'There's nothing laid down, far as I know. Far as I know, they let some out and keep others in. That's right, isn't it, Frank?'

'Ringleaders gets what for,' said Frank, gaunt, tall, gormless. 'We all said to 'Arry it was waste of time. Shouldn't never have done it. Look where it's got us. Look where it'll get him.'

'Who?' asked Tristram. 'Where?'

'Strike-leader he calls himself. He'll do hard labour for a bit. Might be worse than that, what with things getting tougher all round.' He made a gun of his hand and levelled it at Tristram. 'As it might be yourself,' he said. 'Bang bang.'

'It was nothing to do with me,' said Tristram for the thirtieth time. 'I just got caught up in the crowd. It's all a mistake, I keep telling you.'

'That's right. You tell them that when they come for you.' Frank then went into the corner to micturate. The whole cell stank cosily of urine. A middle-aged man with grey chick-down on his dome, wild-looking like a lay-preacher, came over to Tristram and said:

'You'll convict yourself soon as you open your mouth, mister. Bless your heart and soul, they'll know you for an intellectual soon as you walk in there. I reckon you've been real brave in one way or another, sticking up for the workers. You'll get your reward when better times come, you mark my words.'

'But I wasn't,' almost wept Tristram. 'I didn't.'

'Ah,' said a voice in a corner, 'I heareth footsteps, verily I dost, methinks.' The corridor light was switched on, raw as an egg, and boots clomped towards the cell. From the floor the old man pleaded, 'I only want to turn it off. I won't be gone long.' The cell-bars, dead black against the new light, grinned frankly at them all. Two greyboys, young and thuggish, armed, grinned in between the grinning bars. The bolts shot out, the key ground round, the cell-door clanged open. 'Right,' said one of the greyboys, a lance-jack, shuffling a deck of identity cards. 'I'm giving these out, back, see? Them I give them to can skedaddle and are not to be naughty boys no more. Right. Aaron, Aldiss, Barber, Collins, Chung –' 'Now what the hell have *I* done wrong?' said Joe Blacklock. '– Davenport, Dilke, Mohamed Daud, Dodds, Endore, Evans –' The men came eagerly grabbing and were pushed out roughly to freedom. '– Fairbrother, Franklin, Gill, Hackney, Hamidin –' 'There must be some mistake,' cried Tristram. 'I'm an F.' '– Jones, Lindsay, Lowrie –' The cell was emptying fast. '– Mackintosh, Mayfield, Morgan, Norwood, O'Connor –' 'I'll be back,' said the old man, trembling, taking his card, 'as soon as I've turned it off. Thanks, lads.' '– Paget, Radzinowicz, Smith, Snyder, Taylor, Tucker, Ucuck, Vivian, Wilson, Wilson, Wilson. That's the lot. Who are you, chum?' asked the greyboy of Tristram. Tristram told him. 'Right, you're to stay here, you are.' 'I demand to see the man in charge,' demanded Tristram. 'I demand that I be allowed to contact my brother. Let me phone my wife. I shall write to the Home Secretary.' 'No harm in writing,' said the greyboy. 'Perhaps writing will keep you quiet. You do that, chum. You write.'

Nine

'WELL,' boomed Shonny, 'glory be to God in the highest, look who it is. My own little sister-in-law, God bless us and keep us, not looking a day older than when I saw her last, and that must be all of three years ago. Come in, come in, and highly welcome.' He peered suspiciously out, saying, 'I mean no harm to him, mind, but I hope you haven't brought that horrible man with you, seeing as there's something in the very look of the man that makes my hackles rise and sets my teeth on edge.' Beatrice-Joanna shook her head, smiling. Shonny was something out of the fabulous past – open, direct, honest, virile, with a burnt coarse humorous moon-face, surprised ice-blue eyes, a simian upper lip, a lower lip that drooped fleshily, big-bodied in sack-like farmer's garb. 'Mavis,' he called, 'Mavis,' and Mavis appeared in the tiny hallway – six years older than Beatrice-Joanna, with the same cider hair, speck-brown eyes and lavish limbs, bathycolpous.

'I didn't have time to let you know,' said Beatrice-Joanna, kissing her sister. 'I left in rather a hurry.'

'A good place to leave in a hurry,' said Shonny, picking up her bag, 'that great horrible metropolis, God send it bad dreams.'

'Poor little Roger,' said Mavis, her arm round her sister, leading her to the living-room. 'Such a shame.' The room was not much bigger than the one in the Foxe flat, but it seemed to breathe space and oxygen. Shonny said:

'Before we go any further, we'll have a drink of something.' He opened a trap-door to disclose a platoon of bottles. 'Something you'd never buy at twenty crowns the noggin in that benighted carcinoma you've left behind, God blast it.' He held up a bottle to the electric light. 'Plum wine of my own making,' he said. 'Wine-making's supposed to be forbiden like a lot of other wholesome and God-fearing things, but the hell with the lot of the little-souled law-making dung-beetles, Christ have mercy on them.' He poured. 'Take that in your right hand and say after me,' he ordered. They drank. 'Wait,' said Shonny. 'What is it we drink to?'

'A lot of things,' said Beatrice-Joanna. 'Life. Freedom. The sea. Us. Something I'll tell you about later.'

'We'll have a glass for each of those,' said Shonny. He beamed. 'Nice to have you with us,' he said.

Shonny was a Pancelt, one of the rare survivors of the Celtic Union that, in voluntary exodus, had left the British Isles and, wave after wave, settled in Armorica nearly a century before. In Shonny was a heartening stew of Manx, Glamorgan, Shetland, Ayrshire and County Cork, but this, as Shonny was hot in pointing out, could not be called miscegenation. Fergus, the Moses of the Union, had taught that the Celts were one people, their language one language, their religion fundamentally one. He had wrung the doctrine of the Messiah's second coming out of Catholicism, Calvinistic Methodism, Presbyterianism: church, kirk and chapel were one temple of the imminent Lord. Their mission was, in a world whose Pelagianism was really Indifferentism, to cherish the Christian flame, as once before in face of the Saxon hordes.

'We've been praying, you know,' said Shonny, pouring out more wine for the ladies, 'though, of course, that's illegal, too. They used to leave us alone in the old days, but now they've got these infernal police on the job, spying and arresting, just like in the ancient penal days of sacred memory. We've had mass here a couple of times. Father Shackel, God bless and help the poor man, was picked up in his own shop the other day by some of these simperers with guns and lipstick – Father Shackel's a seedsman by trade – and taken off we don't know where. And yet, and this the poor benighted imbeciles can't or won't realize, we've been offering the sacrifice for the State's own good. We're all going to starve, God bless us, if we don't pray for forgiveness for our blasphemous ways. Sinning against the light, denying life. The way things are going is being sent as a divine judgment on the lot of us.' He tossed off a beaker of plum wine and smacked his great meaty lips.

'They've kept on cutting the rations,' said Beatrice-Joanna. 'They don't say why. There've been demonstrations in the streets. Tristram got mixed up in one of those. He was drunk at the time. I think the police must have taken him off. I hope he's going to be all right.'

'Well,' said Shonny, 'I don't wish him any real harm. Drunk, was he? There may be some good in him after all.'

'And how long do you propose to stay with us?' asked Mavis.

'I suppose I might as well tell you now as later,' said Beatrice-Joanna. 'I hope you're not going to be shocked or anything. I'm pregnant.'

'Oh,' said Mavis.

'And,' said Beatrice-Joanna, 'I'm glad I'm pregnant. I *want* to have the baby.'

'We'll certainly drink to that,' roared Shonny. 'Damn the consequences, say I. A gesture, that's what it is, keeping the flame going, saying mass in the cellar. Good girl.' He poured more wine.

'You want to have the baby here?' said Mavis. 'It's dangerous. It's not something you can keep hidden for long. It's something you ought to think about very carefully, things being as they are these days.'

'It's the will of God,' cried Shonny. 'Go forth and multiply. So that little man of yours has still got some life in him, eh?'

'Tristram doesn't want it,' said Beatrice-Joanna. 'He told me to get out.'

'Does anybody know you've come here?' asked Mavis.

'I had to tell the police at Euston. I said I was just coming on a visit. I don't think they'll do anything about it. There's nothing wrong with coming on a visit.'

'A pretty long visit,' said Mavis. 'And there's the question of room. The children are away at the moment, staying with Shonny's Aunt Gertie in Cumnock. But when they come back –'

'Now, Mavis,' said Beatrice-Joanna, 'if you don't want me to stay, tell me straight. I don't want to be a burden and a nuisance.'

'You won't be either,' said Shonny. 'We can fix you up, if need be, in one of the outhouses. A greater mother than you gave birth in a –'

'Oh, stop that sentimentality,' scolded Mavis. 'That's the sort of thing that turns me against religion sometimes. If you're determined,' she said to her sister, 'really determined, well, we must just go ahead and hope for better times soon. I know how you feel, don't think I don't. Our family's always been very strong on motherhood. We must just hope for more sensible times to come again, that's all.'

'Thank you, Mavis,' said Beatrice-Joanna. 'I know there'll be a lot of problems – registration and rations and so on. There's time enough to think of those things.'

'You've come to the right place,' said Shonny. 'My veterinary training will come in very handy, God bless you. Many's the litter I've helped to bring into the world.'

'Animals?' said Beatrice-Joanna. 'You don't mean to say you have animals?'

'Battery hens,' said Shonny gloomily, 'and our old sow Bessie. Jack Beare over at Blackburn has a boar which he hires out. It's all supposed to be illegal, may the Holy Trinity curse them, but we have managed to eke out our shameful diet with a bit of pig-meat. Everything's in a shocking state,' he said, 'and nobody seems able to understand it at all. This blight that seems to be sweeping the world, and the hens won't lay, and Bessie's last farrow so sickly with some queer internal growth, vomiting worms and all, I had to put them out of their misery. There's a curse settling on us, God forgive us all, with our blaspheming against life and love.'

'Talking about love,' said Mavis, 'is it all over between you and Tristram?'

'I don't know,' said Beatrice-Joanna. 'I've tried to worry about him, but somehow I can't. It seems I've got to concentrate all my love now on something that hasn't even been born. I feel as though I'm being taken over and *used*. But I don't feel unhappy about it. Rather the opposite.'

'I always felt you married the wrong man,' said Mavis.

Ten

DEREK FOXE read for a second time the scrawled two sheets of toilet paper signed by his brother; read smiling. 'I am illegally incarcerated here and I am not allowed to see anybody. I call upon you as my brother to bring your influence to bear and have me released. The whole thing is shameful and unjust. If this simple brotherly appeal fails to move you, perhaps the following intimation will: to wit, I know now that you and my wife have been conducting a protracted liaison and that she is now carrying your child. How could you – you, my brother? Get me out of here at once, it is the least you can do and you owe it to me. You have my solemn assurance that I will not let this go any further if you give me the help I ask. If you do not, however, I shall be compelled to divulge *all* to the appropriate authorities. *Get me out of here.* Tristram.'

The letter was rubber-stamped all over like a passport: '*Seen*, Commandant Franklyn Road Temporary Detention Centre'; '*Seen*, Officer Commanding Brighton Police District'; '*Seen*, Officer Commanding 121 Police Circle'; '*Opened*, Poppol Central Registry'. Derek Foxe smiled, leaning back in his leather-substitute chair, smiled at the huge idiot moon of a clock on the wall opposite, at the bank of telephones, at the back of his flavicomous male secretary. Poor Tristram. Poor not-very-bright Tristram. Poor moronic Tristram who had, by the mere act of writing, already divulged all to all available authorities, appropriate and inappropriate. And it didn't, of course, matter. Unsupported libels and slanders whizzed all day long through the offices of the great, a sort of gnat-fritinancy, disregarded. Still, Tristram at large might be a nuisance. Tristram, horn-mad, with a gang of schoolboy thugs. Tristram with a sly knife waiting in the shadows. Tristram alc-demented with a pistol. It was better that Tristram remain caged for a while; it was a bore to have to contemplate being on guard against one's brother.

How about her? That was altogether different. Wait, wait – the next phase might not be too long coming. And poor stupid Captain Loosley? Leave him alone for the time being, idiot. Derek Foxe rang through to Police Headquarters and requested that Tristram Foxe be, on grounds of suspicion, kept indefinitely out of circulation. Then he went on with the draft of the television talk (five minutes after the 23.00 news on Sunday), warning and appealing to the women of Greater London. 'Love of country,' he wrote, 'is one of the purest kinds of love. Desire for one's country's welfare is a holy desire.' This sort of thing came easily to him.

Part Three

Part Three

One

A WET August and a parched September, but the sickness of the world's grain crops seemed to ride, like an aircraft, above the weather. It was a blight never known before, its configuration under the microscope not cognate with any other pattern of disease, and it proved resistant to all the poisons the Global Agricultural Authority could devise. But it was not only rice, maize, barley, oats and wheat that were affected: fruit fell off the trees and the hedges, stricken with a sort of gangrene; potatoes and other roots became messes of black and blue mud. And then there was the animal world: worms, coccidiosis, scaly leg, marble bone disease, fowl cholera, prolapse of the oviduct, vent gleet, curled toe paralysis, slipped hock disease – these were just a few of the maladies that struck the hen batteries and turned them into feathery morgues. Shoals of rotting fish corpses were washed ashore on the north-east coast during early October; the rivers stank.

The Right Hon. Robert Starling, Prime Minister, lay awake in an October night, tossing alone in his double bed, his catamite having been banished from it. His head was full of voices – voices of the experts who said they didn't know, they just didn't know; voices of the fanciful who blamed stowaway viruses in returned moon-rockets; panicky fruity voices of the last Enspun Premiers' Conference saying, 'We can get through this year, we can just about get through this year, but wait till next –' And one very privy voice whispered statistics and showed, against the blackness of the bedroom, horrific lantern slides. 'Here we see the last food riot in Cooch Behar, dealt with most summarily, four thousand shovelled into a common grave, plenty of phosphorus pentoxide there, eh? And now we have highly coloured famine in Gulbarga, Bangalore and Rajura: look closely, admire those rib-cages. We turn now to Nyasaland: starvation in Livingstonia and Mpika. Mogadishu in Somalia – that was great fun for the vultures. And now we cross the Atlantic –'

'No! No! No!' The Right Hon. Robert Starling shouted so loud that he awoke his little friend Abdul Wahab, a brown boy who slept on a truckle-bed in the Right Hon. Robert Starling's dressing-room. Abdul Wahab came running in, knotting a sarong round his middle. He switched on the light.

'What is it? What's the matter, Bobby?' The melting brown eyes were full of concern.

'Oh, nothing. Nothing we can do anything about. Go back to bed. I'm sorry I woke you.'

Abdul Wahab sat on the edge of the bouncy mattress and stroked the Prime Minister's forehead. 'There,' he said. 'There, there, there.'

'They all seem to think,' said the Prime Minister, 'that we're in this game for our own ends. They think I'm in love with power.' He closed his eyes gratefully to the cool stroking. 'They don't know, they just don't know the first thing about it.'

'Of course they don't.'

'It's all for their own good, everything we do is for their own good.'

'Of course it is.'

'How would they like to be in my position? How would they like to have the responsibility and the heart-break?'

'They wouldn't stand it for one minute.' Wahab went on soothing with his cool brown hand.

'You're a good boy, Wahab.'

'Oh, not really.' He simpered.

'Yes, you're a good boy. What are we going to do, Wahab, what are we going to do?'

'Everything will be all right, Bobby. You'll see.'

'No, everything won't be all right. I'm a liberal, I believe in man's ability to control the world about him. We don't just leave things to chance. The whole planet is dying, and you say everything will be all right.'

Abdul Wahab changed hands; his master was lying at a very awkward angle. 'I'm not very clever,' he said. 'I don't understand politics. But I always thought that the big trouble was having too many people in the world.'

'Yes, yes. That is our great problem.'

'But not now, surely? The population is being very quickly reduced, isn't that so? People are dying of not having enough to eat, aren't they?'

'You foolish boy. You very nice but very foolish boy. Don't you see, you foolish boy, that we could, if we wanted, kill off three-quarters of the world's population like that –' He snapped finger and thumb. '– Just like that? But government is not concerned with killing but with keeping people alive. We outlawed war, we made war a terrible dream of the past; we learned to predict earthquakes and conquer floods; we irrigated desert places and made the ice-caps blossom like a rose. That is progress, that is the fulfilment of part of our liberal aspirations. Do you understand what I'm saying, you foolish boy?'

Abdul Wahab tried to yawn with his mouth closed, smiling tight-lipped.

'We removed all the old natural checks on population,' said the Prime Minister. '*Natural checks* – what a cynical and sinister term. The history of man is the history of his control over his environment. True, we have often been let down. The greater part of mankind is not yet ready for the Pelagian ideal, but soon perhaps they may be. Perhaps very soon. Perhaps already they are learning. Learning through pain and privation. Ah, what a wicked world, a foolish world.' He sighed deeply. 'But what are we going to do? The shadow of famine stalks the world and we are caught in its clutches.' He frowned at that metaphor but let it pass. 'All our scientific knowledge and skill are set at nought by this menace.'

'I'm not very clever,' said Wahab again. 'My people used to do not very clever things when they thought the harvest might be bad or the fish fail to bite. They did perhaps very foolish things. One thing they used to do was to pray.'

'Pray?' said the Prime Minister. 'When we pray we admit defeat. There is no place for prayer in a liberal society. Moreover, there is nothing to pray to.'

'My people,' said stroking Wahab eagerly, 'had many

things to pray to. But mostly they prayed to what they called Allah.' He pronounced the name in the strict Arabic way, with a great curled l and a harsh snore at the end.

'Another name for God,' said the Prime Minister. 'God is the enemy. We have conquered God and tamed him into a comic cartoon character for children to laugh at. Mr Livedog. God was a dangerous idea in people's minds. We have rid the civilized world of that idea. Do go on stroking, you lazy boy.'

'And,' said Wahab, 'if praying was no good, then they used to kill something. That was meant to be a sort of present, you see. They used to call it *madzbuh*. If you wanted a really big favour then you offered up something very big, very important. You made a present of an important man, such as the Prime Minister.'

'If that is meant to be funny I don't consider it to be very funny,' huffed the Right Hon. Robert Starling. 'You can be a very facetious boy sometimes.'

'Or the King,' said Wahab, 'if you happened to have one.'

The Prime Minister thought about that. Then he said, 'You're full of the silliest ideas, you silly boy. And you're forgetting that, even if we did want to sacrifice the King, there's nothing to sacrifice him to.'

'Perhaps,' suggested Wahab, 'this thing has a sort of understanding. This thing, I mean, that's stalking the earth like a shadow with claws. You could pray to that.'

'That,' said the Prime Minister, huffily again, 'was a rather inept personification on my part. Inept figures of speech are the very stuff of political oratory.'

'What,' asked Wahab, 'is personification?'

'You pretend that something has life when it really hasn't. A kind of animism. Do you know that word, you ignorant boy?'

Wahab smiled. 'I'm very stupid,' he said, 'and I know very few words. Years and years ago my people used to pray to trees and rivers, pretending that these things could hear and understand. You would regard them as very foolish, being a great man and a Prime Minister, but I have heard you pray to the rain.'

'Nonsense.'

'I've heard you say, "Rain, rain, go away, come again another day." That was when you and I and Reginald and Gaveston Murphy were to go walking in Northern Province.'

'That was just a joke, just a bit of superstition. It didn't mean anything.'

'Nevertheless, you wanted it to stop raining. And now you want this thing to stop. Perhaps you ought to try a bit of superstition, as you call it. You certainly ought to try a bit of something. But,' added Wahab, 'don't listen to me. I'm just an ignorant boy and a foolish boy and a facetious boy.'

'Also a nice boy,' smiled the Prime Minister. 'I think I'll try and get some sleep now.'

'You don't want me to stay?'

'No, I want to sleep. Perhaps I'll dream of the solution to all our problems.'

'You're a great one for dreams,' said Abdul Wahab acutely. He kissed his finger-tips and shut his master's eyes with them. Then, before leaving the chamber, he put out the light and his tongue.

In the darkness the lantern-lecture began again.

'Here,' said the voice, 'we see a fine specimen of a diet riot, all the way from yellow Mozambique. The rice-store at Chovica was raided, with what results you here see. Black man's blood, red as your own. And now comes starvation in Northern Rhodesia, broken men at Broken Hill, Kabulwebulwe a lament in itself. Finally, for a *bonne bouche*, cannibalism in – guess where? You'll never guess, so I'll tell you. In Banff, Alberta. Incredible, isn't it? A very small carcase, as you see, a boy's rabbit-body. A few good stews out of that, though, and there's one lad who'll never go hungry again.'

Two

TRISTRAM was much thinner and he had a beard, very wiry. He had long been transferred from the Franklyn Road Temporary Detention Centre to the formidable Metropolitan Institute of Correction (Male) at Penton-ville, growing there – with his beard – daily more trucu-lent, frequently gorilla-shaking the bars of his cage, sullenly scratching scabrous graffiti on the walls, snarl-ing at the warders, a changed man. He wished Joscelyne were there and also that pretty boy Wiltshire: he would give them what for and think nothing of it. And as for Derek – A delirium of gouged-out eyeballs, castration with a bread-knife and other pretty fancies passed much of Tristram's waking time. Tristram's cell-mate was a veteran criminal of about sixty – pickpocket, forger, peterman – a man of grey dignity who smelled musty.

'If,' he said to Tristram this October dawn, 'if I'd had the benefit of book-learning like yourself, there's no knowing to what heights I mightn't have reached.' Tristram shook the bars and snarled. His cell-mate placidly went on mending his upper denture with a bit of putty he had swiped from one of the workshops. 'Well,' he said, 'despite the pleasure of your company this month and more, I can't say as how I shall be sorry to leave, especially as the weather looks to be keeping up a bit longer. Though without a doubt I shall be renewing the privilege of your acquaintance in the not too distant future.'

'Look, Mr Nesbit,' said Tristram, turning from the bars. 'For the last time. Please. It would be a service not only to me but to the entire community. Get him. Do him in. You've got his address.'

'Speaking for the last time myself, Mr Foxe, on this particular matter, I repeat again that I am in the criminal profession for gain and not for the pleasure of private vendettas or the like. In murder of the revengeful kind there is no money. Much as I'd like to oblige a friend, which I presume to consider that you are, it would go very much against my principles.'

'That's your last word?'

'Regretfully, Mr Foxe, as I have to say it, I have to definitely say it.'

'Well, then, Mr Nesbit, you're an unfeeling bastard.'

'Tut, Mr Foxe, such words is unseemly. You're a young man and still have your way to make so you won't resent a last bit of advice from an old codger like myself. Which is, to keep self-control. Without self-control you will achieve nothing. With self-control and keeping all personal feeling out of things allied to your book-learning, that way you should go far.' He thumbed the putty which wedded teeth to plastic palate and, seemingly satisfied, inserted the denture in his mouth. 'Better,' he said. 'That should serve. Always keep a smart appearance is my advice to young aspirants. As it might be yourself.'

The clanking of keys approached. A hatchet-faced pigeon-chested warder in worn blue opened the cell door. 'Right,' he said to Mr Nesbit, 'out, you.' Mr Nesbit got up from his plank-bunk, sighing.

'Where's bloody breakfast?' snarled Tristram. 'Breakfast is bloody late.'

'Breakfast is done away with,' said the warder, 'as from this morning.'

'That's bloody unfair,' shouted Tristram. 'That's bloody monstrous. I demand to see the bloody Governor.'

'I've told you before,' said the warder sternly. 'Keep a clean tongue in your head or things'll be made really hot for you, they will that.'

'Well,' said Mr Nesbit, extending a courtly hand, 'I take my leave, hoping for a resumption of a very pleasant acquaintanceship.'

'He talks proper, he does,' said the warder. 'You and your type'd do better to take example by him than go on blinding and bloodying all the time.' And he led Mr Nesbit out, clanging the door shut afterwards, grinding the key like a rebuke. Tristram took his iron spoon and savagely hacked a filthy word on the wall.

Just as he was finishing the oblique down-stroke of the last letter, the warder returned with a clank and grind. 'Here,' he said, 'is a new pal for you. One of *your*

sort, not a gentleman like the last one you had. In, you.'
It was a saturnine-looking man with eyes deep in charcoal caves, a vermilion beak, a small sulky Stuart mouth. The loose grey sack-garment of shame suited him, seeming to suggest the habit of a monk.

'Here,' said Tristram, 'I think we've met before.'

'Nice, isn't it?' said the warder. 'An old pals' reunion.' He left the cell, locked the door and grinned sardonically through the bars. Then he clanked off.

'We met,' said Tristram, 'in the Montague. The police beat you up a bit.'

'Did they? Did we?' said the man vaguely. 'So many things, so many people, so many affronts and buffetings. As to my Master, so to me.' He surveyed the cell with very dark eyes, nodding. Then he said, conversationally, 'If I forget thee, O Jerusalem, let my right hand lose her cunning, let my tongue cleave to the roof of my mouth if I remember not Jerusalem above my chief joy.'

'What are you in for?' asked Tristram.

'They caught me saying mass,' said the man. 'Unfrocked as I am, I still have the power. There has been a demand lately, a growing demand. Fear breeds faith, never doubt that. Quite a fair congregation can be assembled, believe me, these days.'

'Where?'

'It is a return to the catacombs,' said the man with satisfaction. 'Disused underground tunnels. Underground platforms. Even underground trains. Mass in motion, I call that. Yes,' he said, 'the fear is growing. Famine, that dread horseman, rides abroad. God asks an acceptable sacrifice, a placation of His anger. And, under one kind, wine being outlawed, it is offered to

Him. Ah,' he said, squinting at Tristram's graffiti, 'lapidary inscriptions, eh? Something to pass the time.' He was a very different man from the one Tristram remembered from that brief violent occasion in the Montague. He was tranquil, measured of speech, and he examined Tristram's carved obscenities as if they were in an unknown tongue. But 'Interesting,' he said. 'I see that you have inscribed the name of your Maker several times. You mark my words, everybody is coming back to God. You will see, we shall all see.'

'I used the word,' said Tristram brutally, 'as a gesture of defiance. It's just a dirty word, that's all.'

'Exactly,' said the unfrocked with quiet joy. 'All dirty words are fundamentally religious. They are all concerned with fertility and the processes of fertility and the organs of fertility. God, we are taught, is love.'

As if in derision of that statement, the big loudspeakers, set like doomsday trumpets at the imagined corners of each round tiered gallery, blasted a noise of eructation that fell into the empty belly of the well. 'Attention,' they said, and the word ('Attention -tension-ension-shun') bounced like a ball, the call of the farthest speakers overlapping the call of the nearest. 'Pay great attention. This is the Governor speaking.' It was the tired refined voice of ancient royalty. 'I am instructed by the Home Secretary to read out the following, which is being read out also at this moment in the schools, hospitals, offices and factories of the kingdom. It is a prayer devised by the Ministry of Propaganda.'

'Do you hear that?' danced the unfrocked priest in awed jubilation. 'God be praised, things are going our way. Alleluia.'

'Here it is,' said the tired voice. It coughed and then went into a hypnotic singsong. ' "It is conceivable that the forces of death which at present are ravaging the esculent life of this planet have intelligence, in which case we beseech them to leave off. If we have done wrong – allowing in our blindness natural impulse to overcome reason – we are, of course, heartily sorry. But we submit that we have already suffered sufficiently for this wrong and we firmly resolve never to sin again. Amen." ' The voice of the Governor collapsed into loud coughing and, before crackling out, muttered, 'Lot of damned nonsense.' The mutterings were at once taken up all around the gallery of cells.

Tristram's cell-mate looked ashen. 'God forgive us all,' he said, deeply shocked, crossing himself, 'they're going the other way. They're praying to the powers of evil, God help us.'

But Tristram was elated. 'Don't you see what this means?' he cried. 'It means the Interphase is coming to an end. The shortest on record. The State's reached the limit of despair. Sin, they're talking about sin. We'll be out soon, any day now.' He rubbed his hands. 'Oh, Derek, Derek,' he growled. 'I can hardly wait.'

Three

AUTUMN passed into winter, and that prayer, of course, was not answered. Nobody, of course, had ever seriously, of course, thought that it would be. As far as H.M.

Government was concerned, it was a mere sop to the irrational: nobody could now possibly say that H.M. Government had not tried everything.

'It all shows you, though,' said Shonny in December, 'how everything leads back to the Almighty.' He was far more optimistic than Tristram's cell-companion. 'Liberalism means conquest of environment and conquest of environment means science and science means a heliocentric outlook and a heliocentric outlook means an open mind about there being forms of intelligence other than human and —' He took a deep breath and swigged some plum wine '— and, well, you see, if you accept the possibility of that, then you concede the possibility of superhuman intelligence and so you get back to God.' He beamed at his sister-in-law. In the kitchen his wife was trying to make sense of the pitiful rations.

'Superhuman intelligence might be evil, though,' objected Beatrice-Joanna. 'That wouldn't be God, would it?'

'If you have evil,' said Shonny, 'you've got to have good.' He was unshakable. Beatrice-Joanna smiled her confidence in him. In another two months she would be relying on Shonny a great deal. The life inside her kicked; she was swollen but very well. There were many worries, though she was happy enough. Guilt about Tristram pricked her, she was exercised by the problems of keeping her long secret. When visitors came or farm-workers looked in, she had to dart to the lavatory, as fast as her bulk would allow. She had to take exercise furtively, after dark, walking with Mavis between ruined hedgerows, by fields of blasted wheat and barley. The children were good, long conditioned to not talking in school or out of it about the dangerous blasphemies of their parents; quiet about God, they were also quiet about their aunt's pregnancy. They were sensible hand-some country-looking children, though thinner than was right, Dymphna seven and Llewelyn nine. They sat today, Christmas a day or two off, cutting bits of cardboard into silhouettes of holly leaves, all the natural holly being stricken by the blight. 'We'll do our best for Christmas again,' said Shonny. 'I've plum wine still and a sufficiency of alc. And there are those four poor old hens sitting in the icebox. Time enough to contem-plate the uncontemplatable future when Christmas has come and gone.'

Dymphna, steering her scissors, her tongue-tip out with concentration, said, 'Dad.'

'Yes, my dear?'

'What's Christmas really about?' They were as much the children of the State as of their parents.

'You know what it's about. You know as well as I do what it's *all* about. Llewelyn, you tell her what it's about.'

'Oh,' said Llewelyn, cutting, 'this chap was born, you see. Then he was killed by being hung up on a tree, and then he was eaten.'

'Now, for a start,' said Shonny, 'He wasn't a chap.'

'A man, then,' said Llewelyn. 'But a man's a chap.'

'The Son of God,' said Shonny, banging the table. 'God and man. And He wasn't eaten when He was killed. He went straight up to heaven. Now, you're half-right about the eating, God bless your heart, but it's ourselves that do the eating. When we have mass we eat His body and drink His blood. But they're disguised – do you see, are you listening to what I'm telling you? – as bread and wine.'

'When He comes again,' said Llewelyn, snipping, 'will He be eaten properly?'

'What, now,' asked Shonny, 'would you be meaning by that strange statement?'

'Eaten,' said Llewelyn, 'like Jim Whittle was eaten.' He started cutting out a new leaf, intent on it. 'Will it be like that, Dad?'

'What's all this?' said Shonny, agitated. 'What's all this you're saying about somebody being eaten? Come on now, speak up, child.' He shook the boy's shoulder, but Llewelyn went on cutting calmly.

'He didn't come to school,' he said. 'His mother and dad cut him up and ate him.'

'How do you know this? Where did you get that outrageous story from? Who's been telling you these wicked things?'

'It's true, Dad,' said Dymphna. 'Is that all right?' she asked, showing her cardboard leaf.

'Never mind about that,' said her father impatiently. 'Tell me about this, come on now. Who's been telling this horrible tale to you?'

'It's not a horrible tale,' pouted Llewelyn. 'It's true. A lot of us went by their house coming home from school and it was true. They had a big pan sort of thing on the stove and it was bubbling away like anything. Some of the other kids went in and they saw.' Dymphna giggled.

'God forgive everybody,' said Shonny. 'This is a shocking and terrible thing, and all you can do is laugh about it. Tell me –' He shook both his children. '– Are you speaking the truth, now? Because, by the Holy Name, if you're just making a joke out of a horrible thing like that I promise you, by the Lord Jesus Christ, I'll give both of you the father and mother of a beating.'

'It's true,' wailed Llewelyn. 'We saw, we both did. She had a big spoon and she was putting it on two plates and it was all steaming hot and some of the other kids asked for some because they were hungry, but Dymphna and me were frightened because they said that Jim Whittle's father and mother are not right in the head, so we ran home quick but we were told to say nothing about it.'

'Who told you to say nothing about it?'

'They did. Some of the big boys did. Frank Bamber said he'd hit us if we told.'

'If you told what?'

Llewelyn hung his head. 'What Frank Bamber did.'

'What did he do?'

'He had a big piece in his hand, but he said he was hungry. But we were hungry too, but we didn't have any. We just ran home.' Dymphna giggled. Shonny let his hands drop. He said:

'God Almighty.'

'Because it was stealing, see, Dad,' said Llewelyn. 'Frank Bamber grabbed it in his hand and ran out and they shouted at him.'

Shonny looked green, Beatrice-Joanna felt it. 'What a horrible, horrible thing,' she panted.

'But if you eat this chap who's God,' said Llewelyn stoutly, 'how can it be horrible? If it's all right to eat God why is it horrible to eat Jim Whittle?'

'Because,' said Dymphna reasonably, 'if you eat God there's always plenty left. You can't eat God up because

124

God just goes on and on and on and God can't ever be finished. You silly clot,' she added and then went on cutting holly leaves.

Four

'A VISITOR for you,' said the warder to Tristram. 'But if you curse and blind at him as you have done at me, then you're really for it and no error, Mister Foulmouth. This way, sir,' he said to the corridor. A black-uniformed figure marched up, eggs bursting on its lapels. 'Neither of these will do you any harm, sir, so there's no call to be nervous. I'll come back in about ten minutes, sir.' And the warder went off.

'Look, I know you,' said Tristram, thin, weak, well-bearded.

The captain smiled. He took off his cap, disclosing short straight oiled rust-coloured hair and, still smiling, smoothed one wing of his moustache. 'You *should* know me,' he smiled. 'We had a very pleasant but, I fear, as it turned out, not very profitable drinking session together, do you see, at the Metropole, do you see, a couple of months ago.'

'Yes, I know you all right,' said Tristram fiercely. 'I never forget a face. That's where being a teacher comes in. Well, have you got an order for my release? Are the times of trial over at last?'

The unfrocked priest, who lately had insisted on being called the Blessed Ambrose Bayley, looked up light-headedly and said, 'Come, there's a mile of penitents out-side. Kneel down quickly and make your confession.' The captain grinned foolishly.

'I've merely come to tell you,' he said, 'where your wife is.'

Tristram looked sullen and blockish. 'Haven't got a wife,' he muttered. 'I put her away.'

'Nonsense, do you see,' said the captain. 'You most certainly have a wife, and at the moment, do you see, she's staying with her sister and brother-in-law near Preston. State Farm NW313 is the address.'

'So,' said Tristram evilly. 'So that's where the bitch is.'

'Yes,' said the captain, 'your wife is there, awaiting her illegal though legitimate, do you see, child.'

The unfrocked priest, weary of waiting for the captain to kneel down and begin, was now hearing, with much head-rolling and groaning, the confession of some-one unseen and unknown. 'A foul sin,' he said, 'fornica-tion. How many times?'

'At least,' said the captain, 'one presumes that. She has been left alone, do you see, she has remained un-molested by any of our people in that corner of Northern Province. I received the information of her whereabouts from our Travel Control Branch. Now,' he said, 'you may be wondering, do you see, why we do not pounce. Perhaps you have been wondering that.'

'Ah, bloody nonsense,' snarled Tristram. 'I don't wonder anything because I don't know anything. Stuck in here starving, no news of the outside world, no letters. Nobody comes to see me.' He was ready to revert to the old Tristram, to start to snivel, but he took a grip on himself and growled, 'I don't care, damn you. I don't care for any of the damned lot of you, get it?'

'Very well,' said the captain. 'Time is short, do you see. I want to know when, by your computation, she will be having the child.'

'What child? Who said anything about a child?' growled Tristram.

'Go in peace and God bless you,' said the Blessed Ambrose Bayley. And then, 'I forgive my tormentors. Through the light of these consuming flames I see the everlasting light of the hereafter.'

'Oh, come on now, do you see,' said the captain impatiently. 'You said she was to have a child. We can check easily enough, of course, do you see, that she's pregnant. What I want to know is, when is she to have the child? When did she, by your calculation, conceive?'

'No idea.' Tristram shook his head in gloom and apathy. 'No idea at all.'

The captain took from one of his tunic pockets something in rustling yellow paper. 'Perhaps you're hungry,' he said. 'Perhaps a little synthechoc would help.' He unwrapped the bar and held it out. The Blessed Ambrose Bayley was quicker than Tristram; he darted like a ray and snatched the bar, drooling. Tristram was on to him, and the two snarled, clawed, tore. Finally each got about half. Three seconds were enough to wolf the brown sticky stuff down. 'Come on now,' said the captain sharply. 'When was it?'

'En oz ot?' Tristram was licking round his palate and sucking his fingers. 'Oh, that,' he said at last. 'It must have been in May. I know when it was. It was at the beginning of the Interphase. Have you any more of that stuff?'

'What do you mean?' asked the captain patiently. 'What is the Interphase?'

'Of course,' said Tristram, 'you're not a historian, are you? Of the science of historiography you know nothing. You're just a hired thug with pockets crammed tight with synthechoc.' He belched and then looked sick. 'When all you hired thugs began to swagger through the streets. Give me more of that, blast you.' He then turned savagely on his cell-mate. 'That was mine and you ate it. It was meant for me, blast you.' He weakly belaboured the Blessed Ambrose Bayley who, hands joined and eyes swooning upwards, said, 'Father, forgive them, for they know not what they do.' Tristram gave up, panting.

'Good,' said the captain. 'Well, then, we know when to take action. You can look forward, do you see, to the final disgracing of your brother and the punishment of your wife.'

'What do you mean? What are you talking about? Punishment? What punishment? If it's my wife you're going to go for, you leave that bitch alone, do you hear? She's my wife, not yours. I'll deal with my wife in my own way.' He sank without shame into snivelling. 'Oh, Beattie, Beattie,' he whined, 'why don't you get me out of here?'

'You realize, of course,' said the captain, 'that you're in here because of your brother?'

'Less talk from you,' sneered Tristram, 'and more synthechoc, you gutsy hypocrite. Come on, hand over.'

'Sustenance, for the love of heaven,' fluted the Blessed

128

Ambrose Bayley. 'Do not forget the servitors of the Lord in the days of your fatness.' He fell on to his knees and clung to the captain's shins, nearly bringing him over.

'Warder!' called the captain.

'And,' said Tristram, 'you leave my child alone. It's *my* child, you infanticidal maniac.' He started. with feeble fists, to hammer on the captain like a door. '*My* child, you swine. My protest, my dirty word to the dirty world, you robber.' He began to frisk the captain for synthechoc with the quick long hands of a monkey.

'Warder!' called the captain, fighting him off.

The Blessed Ambrose Bayley relaxed his hold and crawled, dispirited, back to his bench-bunk. 'Five Our Fathers and five Hail Marys,' he said perfunctorily, 'today and tomorrow in honour of the Little Flower. Go in peace and God bless you.'

The warder came, saying cheerfully, 'Not given you any trouble, have they, sir? That's right.' Tristram's arms, too weak for further frisking, had dropped to his sides. 'Him,' pointed the warder. 'A proper little terror he was, when he first came here. Couldn't get no sense out of him, one of the real criminal class. Much tamer now, he is,' he said, with a touch of pride. Tristram slumped in his corner, muttering, '*My* child, *my* child, *my* child.' With those spondees in his ears, the captain, grinning nervously, left.

Five

LATE December, in Bridgwater, Somerset, Western Province, a middle-aged man named Thomas Wharton, going home from work shortly after midnight, was set upon by youths. These knifed him, stripped him, spitted him, basted him, carved him, served him – all openly and without shame in one of the squares of the town. A hungry crowd clamoured for hunks and slices, kept back – that the King's Peace might not be broken – by munching and dripping greyboys. In Thirsk, North Riding, three lads – Alfred Pickles, David Ogden and Jackie Priestley – were struck dead with a hammer in a dark ginnel and dragged into a terraced house by way of the backyard. The street was gay for two nights with the smoke of barbecues. In Stoke-on-Trent the carcase of a woman (later identified as Maria Bennett, spinster, aged twenty-eight) grinned up suddenly – several good clean cuttings off her – from under a bank of snow. In Gillingham, Kent, Greater London, a shady back-street eating-shop opened, grilling nightly, and members of both police forces seemed to patronize it. In certain unregenerate places on the Suffolk coast there were rumours of big crackling Christmas dinners.

In Glasgow, on Hogmanay, a bearded sect professing worship of Njal offered a multiple human sacrifice, reserving the entrails for the deified burnt advocate, the flesh for themselves. Kirkcaldy, less subtle, saw a number of private ceilidhs with meat sandwiches. The New Year commenced with stories of timid anthropophagy from

Maryport, Runcorn, Burslem, West Bromwich and Kidderminster. Then the metropolis flashed its own sudden canines: a man called Amis suffered savage amputation of an arm off Kingsway; S. R. Coke, journalist, was boiled in an old copper near Shepherd's Bush; Miss Joan Waine, a teacher, was fried in segments.

Those were the stories, anyway. There was no real way of checking the truth of them; they might well have been the delirious fantasies of extreme hunger. One story in particular was so incredible that it cast doubt on the others. It was reported from Brodick on the Isle of Arran that a vast communal nocturnal gorge of man-flesh had been followed by a heterosexual orgy in the ruddy light of the fat-spitting fires and that, the morning after, the root known as salsify was seen sprouting from the pressed earth. That could not, by any manner of means or stretch of the organ of credulity, possibly be believed.

Six

BEATRICE-JOANNA'S pains were starting.

'Poor old girl,' said Shonny. 'Poor, poor old lady.' He and his wife and sister-in-law were standing, this bright snappy forenoon in February, by the sty of Bessie, the ailing sow. Bessie, all the slack grey deadweight of her, lay snorting feebly, a great ruin of flesh, on her side. Her uppermost flank, curiously mottled, heaved as in a dream of hunting. Shonny's Panceltic eyes filled with tears. 'Worms a yard long,' he grieved, 'horrible live worms. Why should a worm have life and she none? Poor, poor, poor old lady.'

'Oh, stop it, Shonny,' Mavis sniffed. 'We've got to make ourselves hard-hearted. She's only a pig, after all.'

'Only a pig? *Only* a pig?' Shonny was indignant. 'She's grown up with the children, God bless the old girl. She's been a member of the family. She's given her piglings unstintingly that we might be decently fed. She shall, the Lord keep her soul, be given a Christian burial.'

Beatrice-Joanna could sympathize with his tears; she was, in many ways, closer to Shonny than Mavis was. But she had other things on her mind now. The pains had started. A fair balance today: death of a pig, birth of a man. She was not afraid, she had confidence in Shonny and Mavis, especially Shonny; her pregnancy had run a healthy conventional course, subject only to certain frustrations: a strong desire for pickled gherkins had had to go unsatisfied, an urge to rearrange the furniture of the farmhouse had been stamped on by Mavis. Sometimes in the night an overwhelming longing for the comforting arms not, strangely, of Derek but of –

Aaaargh.

'That makes two in twenty minutes,' said Mavis. 'You'd better come inside.'

'It's the contractions,' said Shonny with something like glee. 'It'll be some time tonight, praise the Lord.'

'A bit of a twinge,' said Beatrice-Joanna. 'Not much. Just a bit, that's all.'

'Right,' bubbled Shonny eagerly. 'The first thing you've got to have is an enema. Soap and water. You'll see to that, will you, Mavis? And she'd better have a good warm bath. Right. Thank the Lord we've plenty of hot water.' He rushed them into the house, leaving Bessie to suffer in loneliness, and started opening and slamming drawers. 'The ligatures,' he cried. 'I've got to make the ligatures.'

'There's plenty of time,' said Mavis. 'She's a human being, you know, not a beast of the field.'

'That's why I've got to make the ligatures,' blustered Shonny. 'Good God, woman, do you want her just to bite it off, like a she-cat?' He found linen thread and, singing a hymn in Panceltic, twisted ten-inch lengths for tying the umbilical cord, knotting them at the ends. Meanwhile Beatrice-Joanna was taken upstairs to the bathroom, and the hot-water pipes of the house sang full-throatedly, creaking and straining like a ship under way.

The pains grew more frequent. Shonny prepared the bed in the heated outhouse, spreading brown paper across its middle and smoothing a drawsheet over, singing all the time. The crops had failed and a faithful sow was dying, but a new life was preparing to thumb its nose – in the gesture once known as 'fat bacon' – at the forces of sterility. Suddenly, unbidden, two strange names – bearded names they seemed somehow – came into Shonny's head: Zondek and Aschheim. Who were they now? He remembered: they were the ancient devisers of a pregnancy test. A few drops of pregnant woman's urine would send a baby mouse speeding to sexual maturity. He had read that, reading up the duties which he was now beginning to perform. His heart, for some reason, lifted in tremendous elation. Of course, *there* was the big secret – all life was one, all life was one. But no time to think about that now.

Dymphna and Llewelyn came home from school. 'What's the matter, Dad? What's going on, Dad? What are you doing, Dad?'

'Your aunt's time is come. Don't bother me now. Go and play somewhere. No, wait, go and stay with poor old Bessie. Hold her trotter, poor old girl.'

Beatrice-Joanna now wanted to lie down. The amnion had ruptured in a rush, the amniotic waters had escaped. 'On your left side, girl,' ordered Shonny. 'Is it hurting? Poor old lady.' The pains were, in fact, growing much worse; Beatrice-Joanna began to hold her breath and to bear down strenuously. Shonny knotted a long towel to the bed-head, urging, 'Pull on that, girl. Pull hard. God bless you, it won't be long now.' Beatrice-Joanna pulled, groaning. 'Mavis,' said Shonny, 'this is going to be a longish job. Fetch me in a couple of bottles of plum wine and a glass.'

'There are only a couple of bottles left.'

'Fetch them in just the same like a good girl. There, there, my beauty,' he said to Beatrice-Joanna. 'You pull away there, bless you.' He checked that the old-fashioned swaddling clothes – knitted by the two sisters in the long winter evenings – were warming on the radiator. He had sterilized his ligatures; a pair of scissors was boiling in a pan; a tin bath shone on the floor; cotton wool waited to be teased into pledgets; there was a bolster-slip for a binder – all, in fact, was ready. 'God bless you, my dear,' he said to his wife as she reappeared with the bottles. 'This is going to be a great day.'

It was certainly a long day. For nearly two hours

Beatrice-Joanna struggled muscularly. She cried with the pains, and Shonny, swigging his plum wine and shouting encouragement, watched and waited, sweating as much as she. 'If only,' he muttered, 'we had an anaesthetic of some kind or another. Here, girl,' he said boldly, 'drink some of this,' and he proffered his bottle. But Mavis dragged his hand back.

'Look,' she cried. 'It's coming!'

Beatrice-Joanna shrieked. The head was being born: it had finished its difficult journey at last, leaving behind the bony tunnel of the pelvic girdle, pushing through the sheath to the air of a world that, now indifferent, would soon be hostile. After a brief pause the child's body pushed itself out. 'Perfect,' said Shonny, his eyes shining, wiping the child's shut eyes with a moist pledget, delicate and loving in his movements. The newborn yelled to greet the world. 'Lovely,' said Shonny. Then, when the pulse in the umbilical cord began to stop, he took two of his ligatures and skilfully made his ties, tight, tighter, tightest, forming two frontiers with a no-man's-land in the middle. Here, careful with his sterilized scissors, he snipped. The new bit of life, full of savagely gulped air, was now on its own. 'A boy,' said Mavis.

'A boy? So it is,' said Shonny. Free of its mother, it had ceased to be merely a thing. Shonny turned to watch for the thrust of the placenta while Mavis wrapped the child in a shawl and laid it, him, in a box by the radiator; the bath could come later. 'Good God,' said Shonny, watching. Beatrice-Joanna cried out, but not so loud as before. 'Another one,' called Shonny in awe. 'Twins, by God. A litter, by the Lord Jesus.'

135

Seven

'Out, you,' said the warder.

'And about time,' blustered Tristram, getting up from his bunk. 'About bloody time, you nasty thing. Give me something to eat, blast you, before I go.'

'Not you,' said the warder with relish. 'Him.' He pointed. 'You'll be with us a long time yet, Mister Dirty. It's him as has got to be released.'

The Blessed Ambrose Bayley, shaken by the warder, blinked and goggled his way out of the perpetual presence of God that had set in at the end of January. He was very weak.

'Traitor,' snarled Tristram. 'Stool-pigeon. Telling lies about me, that's what you've been doing. Buying your shameful freedom with lies.' To the warder he said, hopefully, his eyes fierce and large, 'Are you sure you haven't made a mistake? Are you quite sure it isn't me?'

'Him,' pointed the warder. 'Not you. Him. You're not a –' He squinted at the paper in his hand. '– Not a minister of the cloth, whatever that means, are you now? All them have to be released. But foul-mouths like you have to go on being here. Right?'

'It's flagrant bloody injustice,' yelled Tristram, 'that's what it is.' He fell on his knees before the warder, clasping his hands in prayer and hunching his shoulders as if he had just broken his neck. 'Please let me out instead of him. He's past it. He thinks he's dead already, burnt at the stake. He thinks he's well on the road to canonization. He just doesn't know what's going on. *Please.*'

'Him,' pointed the warder. 'His name's on this bit of paper. See – A. T. Bayley. You, Mister Swearer, have got to stay here. We'll find another pal for you, don't worry. Come on, old man,' he said gently to the Blessed Ambrose. 'You've got to get out there and report for orders to some bloke in Lambeth who's going to tell you what to do. Come on, now.' And he shook him somewhat roughly.

'Let me have his rations,' begged Tristram, still on his knees. 'That's the least you can do, damn and blast your eyes. I'm bloody starving, blast it, man.'

'We're all starving,' snarled the warder, 'and some of us have to work and not just lounge about all day. We're all trying to live on these here nuts and a couple of drops of this here synthelac, and they reckon those can't last much longer, things being the way they are. Do come on,' he said, shaking away at the Blessed Ambrose. But the Blessed Ambrose lay bright-eyed in a holy trance, hardly moving.

'Food,' grumbled Tristram, getting up with difficulty. 'Food, food, food.'

'I'll give you food,' scolded the warder, not meaning that at all. 'I'll send in one of these man-eaters as have been picked up, that's what I'll do. That's who your new cell-pal will be, one of those. He'll have your liver out, that he will, and cook it and eat it.'

'Cooked or raw,' moaned Tristram, 'makes no difference. Give it me, give it me.'

'Aaargh, you,' sneered the warder in disgust. 'Come on now, old man,' he said to the Blessed Ambrose in growing disquiet. 'Get up now, like a good fellow. You're going out. Out, out, out,' he went like a dog.

The Blessed Ambrose rose very shakily, leaning on the warder. '*Quia peccavi nimis,*' he wavered in a senile voice. Then he collapsed clumsily. The warder said, 'You look to me to be in a pretty bad way, you do that.' He hunkered, frowning over him as if he were a stopped-up drain. '*Quoniam adhuc,*' mumbled out of the Blessed Ambrose, supine on the flags.

Tristram, thinking he saw his chance, fell on to the warder, like, as he thought, a tower. The two rolled and panted all over the Blessed Ambrose. 'You would, would you, Mister Nasty?' growled the warder. The Blessed Ambrose Bayley moaned as the Blessed Margaret Clitheroe must, pressed by hundredweights, have, at York in 1586, moaned. 'You've done for yourself good and proper now,' gasped the warder, kneeling on Tristram and pounding him with his two fists. 'You've asked for this, you have, Mister Treacherous. You'll never get out of here alive, that you won't.' He cracked him on the mouth viciously, breaking his dentures. 'You've had this coming a long time, you have.' Tristram lay still, breathing desperately. The warder began, still panting, to drag the Blessed Ambrose Bayley to freedom. '*Mea culpa, mea culpa, mea maxima culpa,*' went this unfrocked man, banging his own chest thrice.

Eight

'GLORY be to God,' ejaculated Shonny. 'Mavis, come and see who's here. Llewelyn, Dymphna. Quick, quick, the lot of you.' For who should have walked into the house but Father Shackel, seedsman by trade who, many months before, had been taken off by lipsticked brutal greyboys. Father Shackel was in his early forties, with a very round cropped head, pronounced exophthalmia, and chronic rhinitis caused by a one-sided bulge on the septum. His ever-open mouth and wide eyes gave him a look of William Blake seeing fairies. He raised his right hand now in blessing.

'You're very thin,' said Mavis.

'Did you get tortured?' asked Llewelyn and Dymphna.

'When did they let you out?' cried Shonny.

'What I'd like most of all,' said Father Shackel, 'is a drink of something.' His speech was muffled and de-nasalized, as with an everlasting cold.

'There's a tiny drop of plum wine,' said Shonny, 'left over from the labour and the celebration of the end of the labour.' He rushed to get it.

'Labour? What labour is he talking about?' asked Father Shackel, sitting down.

'My sister,' said Mavis. 'She had twins the other day. You have a christening job to do, Father.'

'Thank you, Shonny.' Father Shackel took the half-filled glass. 'Well,' he said, having sipped, 'there are some queer things going on, aren't there?'

'When did they let you out?' Shonny asked again.

'Three days ago. Since then I've been in Liverpool. Incredible, but the whole hierarchy's at large – archbishops, bishops, the lot. We can drop the disguise now. We can even wear clerical dress if we wish to.'

'We don't seem to get any news,' said Mavis. 'Just talk, talk, talk these days – exhortation, propaganda –

but we hear rumours, don't we, Shonny?'

'Cannibalism,' said Shonny. 'Human sacrifice. We hear about those things.'

'This is very good wine,' said Father Shackel. 'I suppose one of these days we'll be seeing the ban taken off viticulture.'

'What's viticulture, Dad?' asked Llewelyn. 'Is it the same as human sacrifice?'

'You two,' said Shonny, 'can go back to holding poor old Bessie's trotter. Kiss Father Shackel's hands before you go.'

'Father Shackel's trotters,' giggled Dymphna.

'Enough of that now,' warned Shonny, 'or you'll be receiving a clout on the earhole for yourself.'

'Bessie's a long time dying,' grumbled Llewelyn with youth's heartlessness. 'Come on, Dymph.' They kissed Father Shackel's hands and went chattering out.

'The position isn't at all clear yet,' said Father Shackel. 'All we know is that everybody's getting very scared. You can always tell. The Pope, apparently, is back in Rome. I saw the Archbishop of Liverpool with my own eyes. He's been working, you know, poor man, as a bricklayer. Anyway, we kept the light going through the dark times. That's what's meant by a Church. It's something to be proud of.'

'And now what's going to happen?' asked Mavis.

'We're to return to our priestly duties. We're to celebrate mass again – openly, legally.'

'Glory be to God,' said Shonny.

'Oh, don't think the State's at all concerned with the glory of God,' said Father Shackel. 'The State's scared of forces it doesn't understand, that's all. The leaders of the State are suffering from an accession of super-stitious fear, that's what it is. They've done no good with their police, so now it's the priests they call on. There aren't any churches now, so we have to go up and down our allotted areas, feeding them all God instead of the law. Oh, it's all very clever. I suppose sublimation is the big word: don't eat your neighbour, eat God instead. We're being used, that's what it is. But in another sense, of course, we're using. We're right down to essential function now – the sacramental function. That's one thing we've learnt: the Church can take in any heresy or unorthodoxy – including your harmless belief in the Second Coming – so long as it holds fast to essential function.' He chuckled. 'A surprising number of policemen are being eaten, I gather. God works in a mysterious way. Epicene flesh seems to have the greater succulence.'

'How horrible,' grimaced Mavis.

'Oh yes, it's horrible,' grinned Father Shackel. 'Look, I haven't much time: I've got to get to Accrington to-night and I may have to walk: the buses don't seem to be running. Have you got the communion wafers?'

'Some of them,' said Shonny. 'The kids, God forgive them, found the packet and started eating them, blasphemous little heathens. They'd have wolfed the lot if I hadn't caught them.'

'A little job of baptism before you go,' said Mavis.

'Oh, yes.' Father Shackel was led to the outhouse where Beatrice-Joanna lay with her twins. She looked thin but rosy. The twins slept. Shonny said:

'And after the rites for the new-born, how about the rites for the dying?'

'This,' said Mavis, introducing, 'is Father Shackel.'

'I'm not dying, am I?' said Beatrice-Joanna in alarm. 'I feel fine. Hungry, though.'

'It's poor old Bessie that's dying, poor old lady,' said Shonny. 'I claim the same rights for her as for any Christian soul.'

'A pig doesn't have a soul,' said Mavis.

'Twins, eh?' said Father Shackel. 'Congratulations. Both are boys, are they? And what names have you chosen for them?'

'Tristram for one,' said Beatrice-Joanna promptly. 'And Derek for the other.'

'Can you give me water?' asked Father Shackel of Mavis. 'And also a little salt?'

Llewelyn and Dymphna came panting in. 'Dad,' cried Llewelyn, 'Dad. It's about Bessie.'

'Gone at last, has she?' said Shonny. 'Poor faithful old girl. Uncomforted by the last rites, God have mercy on her.'

'She's not dead,' cried Dymphna. 'She's eating.'

'Eating?' Shonny stared.

'She's standing up and eating,' said Llewelyn. 'We found some eggs in the henhouse and gave her those.'

'Eggs? *Eggs?* Is everybody going mad, including myself?'

'And those biscuits,' said Dymphna. 'Those round white ones in the cupboard. We couldn't find anything else.'

Father Shackel laughed. He sat on the edge of Beatrice-Joanna's bed in order to have his laugh out. He laughed at the mixture of feelings on Shonny's face. 'Never mind,' he said at last, grinning imbecilically. 'I'll find some bread on the road to Accrington. There's bound to be bread somewhere.'

Nine

TRISTRAM'S new cell-mate was a massive Nigerian called Charlie Linklater. He was a friendly talkative man, with a mouth so large that it was a wonder he was able to attain any precision in his enunciation of the English vowel-sounds. Tristram tried frequently to count his teeth, which were his own and flashed often as in pride of the fact, and the total he arrived at seemed always in excess of the statutory thirty-two. This worried him. Charlie Linklater was serving an indefinite sentence for an indefinite crime that, as far as Tristram could make out, involved multiple progeniture along with beating-up of greyboys, flavoured with committing a nuisance in the vestibule of Government Building and eating meat when drunk. 'A nice little rest in here,' he said, 'won't do me no harm.' His voice was rich crimson-purple. Tristram felt thinner and weaker than ever in this polished blue-black meaty presence. 'They talk about meat-eating,' said Charlie Linklater in his lazy way, relaxed on his bunk, 'but they don't know the first thing about it, boy. Why, a good ten years ago I was keeping company with the wife of a man from Kaduna, same as myself. His name was George Daniel, and he was a meter-reader by trade. Well, he comes back un-expected and catches us at it. What could we do but give him the old hatchet? You'd do the same, boy. Well, there we have this body – a good thirteen stone if he was a pound. What could we do but get the old stew-pot going? Took us a week, that did, eating all the time. We buried the bones and nobody one bit the wiser. That was a big meal, brother, and a real good eat.' He sighed, smacked his huge lips, and even belched in appreciative recollection.

'I've got to get out of here,' said Tristram. 'There's food in the outside world, isn't there? Food.' He drooled, shaking the bars but feebly. 'I've got to eat, got to.'

'Well,' said Charlie Linklater, 'for myself there's no hurry right away to get out. One or two people are look-ing for me with the old hatchet and I reckon I'm as well off here as anywhere. For a little while, anyhow. But I'd be happy to oblige in any way I could to get you out of here. Not that I don't like your company, you being a well-behaved and educated man and with good manners. But if it would oblige you to get out, then I'm the boy to assist you, boy.'

When the warder came along to shove the midday nutrition tablets and water between the bars, Tristram was interested to see that he carried a truncheon. 'Any nonsense from you,' said the warder, 'and you'll get a fine big crack with this gentleman'– he brandished it – 'on the soft part of your skull, Mister Bloody-minded. So watch out, that's what I say.'

'That black stick of his will come in very nice,' said Charlie Linklater. 'The way he speaks to you is not very good-mannered,' he added. Then he devised a simple plan for securing Tristram's release. It involved some punitive danger to himself, but he was a man of big heart. Having consumed about nine stone of meter-reader in seven days, he was evidently also a man of steadiness and persistence. Now, in the first simple phase of his simple plan, he built up a show of enmity towards his cell-mate so that there should be no danger of the suspicion of complicity when the time came for the second phase. From now on, whenever the warder looked in through the bars, he would howl out loud at Tristram:

'You stop getting on to me, boy. You keep them dirty words to yourself. I'm not used to being treated like that, nohow.'

'At it again, is he?' nodded the grim warder. 'We'll break his spirit, you just wait and see. We'll have him grovelling before we're through with him.'

Tristram, sunken-jawed because his dentures were broken, opened his mouth in a sort of fish-snarl. The warder snarled back, dentate, and went off. Charlie Linklater winked. Three days of this.

On the fourth day Tristram lay much as the Blessed Ambrose Bayley had lain – out, still, his eyes up to heaven. Charlie Linklater agitated the bars. 'He's dying. Come quick there. This boy here's snuffing it. Come along now.' The warder came grumbling. He saw the prostrate Tristram and ground open the cell-door.

'Right,' said Charlie Linklater, fifteen seconds after. 'You just climb into his clothes, boy. Nice little job, this is,' he said, swinging the truncheon by its leather-substitute loop. 'Just you get into that man's uniform, you two being much of a size.' Between them they stripped the dead-out warder. 'Pimply sort of a back he's got,' commented Charlie Linklater. Tenderly he lifted him on to Tristram's bunk and covered him with Tristram's blanket. Meanwhile, breathing hard with excitement, Tristram buttoned himself into worn warder's blue. 'Don't forget his keys,' said Charlie Linklater, 'and more than that, boy, don't forget his truncheon. That'll really get you places, that will, the little beauty. Now, I reckon he'll be well out for another half an hour, so just take your time and act natural. Pull that cap well down over your eyes, boy. Pity about that beard.'

'I'm grateful,' said Tristram, his heart pumping like mad. 'I really am.'

'Don't think nothing of it,' said Charlie Linklater. 'Now, just give me one little crack on the back of the head with that truncheon, so as it'll look more natural. No need to lock the cell-door, because nobody's going to try and get out, but don't forget to keep them keys jingling, so as to be nice and natural. Go on, now. Hit.' Tristram tapped weakly, as at a breakfast egg, on the oaken skull. 'You can do better than that,' said Charlie Linklater. Tristram, his lips tight, cracked him a beauty. 'Something like, that is,' said Charlie Linklater, showing the whites of his eyes. His bulk crashed to the flags, making the tin mugs rattle on their shelf.

Outside on the corridor Tristram looked both ways with care. At the far end of the gallery two warders leaned gloomily on the well-rails, chatting, gazing down as into the sea. At this end the way was clear: four cells only to the stairhead. Tristram was worried about being a bearded warder. He found a handkerchief in the pocket of the stiff alien trousers and, with a fully stretched hand, he spread this over his muzzle. Toothache or jaw-ache or something. He decided against Charlie Linklater's advice: looking unnatural, he must behave unnaturally. A jangle of keys and clomp of boots, he danced clumsily down the iron stairs. On the landing he met another warder going up. 'What's the matter with you?' this one asked. 'Burk crawk workers-gate,' mumbled Tristram. The other nodded, satisfied, and continued to climb.

Tristram clattered on down. He held his breath. This looked as if it were going to be too easy. Flight after flight of ringing iron, row after endless row of cells, a yellowing card of close print on each landing: *H.M. Prisons. Regulations.* Then at last came the ground floor and the feeling that he was balancing these tiers of cells on his own delirious head. A beef-faced warder, stiff as if artificially braced, collided with him head-on as he turned a random corner. 'Here, here,' he said. 'You all right? New here, aren't you?' 'Humgoil,' chumbled Tristram. 'Gert webbing. Gort foresight.' 'If it's the sick-bay you're after,' said the warder, 'it's straight down there. Can't miss it.' He pointed. 'Inch of bellrope,' chewed Tristram. 'That's all right, mate,' said the warder. Tristram hurried on. Now it was all institutional corridors, the walls buff with nigger-brown dadoes, a strong smell of disinfectant, OFFICERS' SICKBAY said a blue box over a lintel, a light inside it. Tristram walked boldly into a place of cubicles, youths in white coats, the stench of spirit. From the nearest door came the splashing and churning of bath-water, the grunting of a male bather. Tristram found the door open and entered. Blue tiles, steam, the bather lathering his head with eyes tight shut as in direst agony. Forgot to shave,' shouted Tristram. 'Eh?' the bather shouted back. To his minor elation Tristram found an electric shaver clamped to a bracket in the wall. He switched on and started to carve his beard like so much meat. 'Here,' said the bather, his sight restored, 'what's going on? Who let you in?' 'Shaving,' said Tristram, seeing with shock his lantern jaws emerge in the mirror as the swathes fell, with horror the fierce mistrustfulness of his eyes. 'Won't be a minute,' he said. 'Nothing's private these days,' grumbled the bather. 'Not even when you have a bath is it private.' He stirred the water fretfully, saying, 'You might have the decency to take your hat off when you come barging in disturbing a bloke's bath.' 'Shan't be more than two seconds,' said Tristram. He left a moustache to save time. 'You might clear up all that mess on the floor,' said the bather. 'Why should I have to tread in my bare feet on another bloke's whiskers?' And then, 'Here, what's going on? Who are you, anyway? You've got a beard, leastways you had one, and that's not right. Warders don't have beards, not in this prison they don't.' He tried to get out of the bath, a rabbit-bodied man with a black pelt from sternum to pubes. Tristram pushed him back in again, very soapy, and dashed to the door. There was, he was glad to see, a key in it, and this he transferred to the outside. The bather, all suds, tried again to lift himself out. Clean-shaven Tristram mouthed good-bye fishily, went out, then locked the door. 'Here,' the bather could be heard calling, sploshing. In the corridor Tristram calmly said to a white-coated youth, 'I'm new here and seem to have got lost. How do I get out of this place?' The youth led him, smiling, from the sickbay and gave directions. 'Down there, dear,' he said, 'then turn sharp left, then straight on, you can't miss it, dear.' 'Thank you very much,' said Tristram, smiling with his black hole for a mouth. Everybody had been, really and truly, most obliging.

In the wide high gloomy hall there were several warders apparently coming off duty, handing their keys over to a chief officer, his blue new and smart, very thin, his height nearer seven feet than six. 'Right,' he kept saying with little interest, 'Right,' checking the key-numbers with a list, ticking, 'Right,' passing the keys to an assistant who hung them on a wall-board. 'Right,' he said to Tristram. There was a small open port in the massy left-hand metal door of the prison. The warders went out that way. It was as easy as that. Tristram stood on the steps an instant, inhaling freedom, gazing up, astonished at the height of the sky. 'Careful, careful, don't give yourself away,' he counselled his shaking heart. He walked off slowly, trying to whistle. But his mouth was still too dry for that.

Ten

SEED-TIME, eggs trickling in from the battery, Bessie the sow almost frisky, the twins thriving. Beatrice-Joanna and her sister sat together in the living-room, knitting a sort of wool-surrogate into warm baby-coats. In a double cradle hammered together by Shonny, Tristram and Derek Foxe slept in amity. Mavis said:

'Far be it from me to propose that you go out into the night with your double bundle, but I'm only thinking of what's best for you. Obviously, you yourself wouldn't want to stay here for ever, apart from there not really being room. And then there's the danger for all of us. I mean, you've got to make up your mind about the future, haven't you?'

'Oh, yes,' agreed Beatrice-Joanna dispiritedly. 'I see that. You've been very kind. I see all that.'

'So,' asked Mavis, 'what have you in mind?'

'What can I have in mind?' said Beatrice-Joanna. 'I've written three letters to Tristram, care of the Home Office, and all of them have come bouncing back. He may be dead. They may have shot him.' She sniffed two or three times. 'Our flat will have been pounced on by the Housing Department. I've nowhere to go and nobody to go to. It's not a very pleasant situation, is it?' She blew her nose. 'I've no money. All I've got in the world is these twins. You can throw me out if you want to, but I've literally nowhere to go.'

'Nobody's suggesting throwing you out,' said Mavis sharply. 'You're my sister, and these are my nephews, and if you have to stay here, well, I suppose that's all there is to it.'

'Perhaps I could get a job in Preston or somewhere,' said Beatrice-Joanna with very small hope. 'That would help a little, perhaps.'

'There aren't any jobs,' said Mavis. 'And money's the least of anybody's worries. It's the danger I'm thinking about. I'm thinking about Llewelyn and Dymphna and what would happen to them if we were arrested. Because we would be, you know, if they found out, for harbouring a what's-its-name.'

'A multipara is the term. I'm a multipara. You don't see me as your sister, then. You just see me as something dangerous, a multipara.' Mavis, her lips a line, bent to her knitting. 'Shonny,' said Beatrice-Joanna, 'doesn't think that way. It's only you who think I'm a nuisance and a danger.'

Mavis looked up. 'That's a very unkind and unsisterly thing to say. That's completely heartless and selfish. You ought to realize that the time's come now for being sensible. We took chances before the babies were born, a lot of chances. Now you're blaming me for putting my own children before yours. And as for Shonny – he's too good-hearted to live. So good-hearted that he's stupid, going on as he does about God protecting us. I get sick of hearing the name of God sometimes, if you want to know the truth. One of these days Shonny will get us all into trouble. He'll land us all properly in the soup one of these days.'

'Shonny's sane enough and sensible enough.'

'He may be sane, but sanity's a handicap and a liability if you're living in a mad world. He's certainly not sensible. Put out of your head any notion that Shonny is sensible. He's just lucky, that's all. He talks too much and says the wrong things. One of these days, you mark my words, his luck's going to change, and then God help the lot of us.'

'So,' said Beatrice-Joanna after a pause, 'what do you want me to do?'

'You must do whatever you think's best for yourself. Stay here if you have to, stay as long as you think fit. But try and remember sometimes –'

'Remember what?'

'Well, that some people have put themselves out for you and have even run into danger. I'll say it now and I won't say it again. That's an end of it. But I'd just like you to remember sometimes, that's all.'

'I do remember,' said Beatrice-Joanna, her voice tightening, 'and I'm very grateful. I've said that about three times a day every day since I've been here. Except, of course, on the day that I was actually giving birth. I would have done so then, but I had other things to think about. If you like, I'll say it now to make up for it. I'm very grateful, I'm very grateful, I'm very grateful.'

'Now there's no need to be like that,' said Mavis. 'Let's drop the subject, shall we?'

'Yes,' said Beatrice-Joanna, rising. 'Let's drop the subject. Remembering, of course, that it was you who raised it.'

'There's no call to speak in that manner,' said Mavis.

'Oh, to hell,' said Beatrice-Joanna. 'It's time for their feed.' She lifted the twins. There was too much of this, too much of this altogether; she would be glad when Shonny came home from his seed-drills. One woman was enough in a house, she saw that, but what could she do? 'I think I'll keep to my room,' she said to her sister, 'for the rest of the day. If you can call it a room, that is.' Having said this, she could have bitten her tongue out. 'Sorry,' she said. 'I didn't mean that.'

'Do what you like,' said Mavis acidly. 'Go exactly where you want to go. You always have, ever since I can remember.'

'Oh, to hell,' said Beatrice-Joanna, and she bounced out with her pink twins.

'Stupid,' she thought later, lying in the outhouse. 'No way to behave.' She had to reconcile herself to the fact that this was the only place where she could live, the only place until she knew what precisely was going on in the world, where – if above ground, otherwise it didn't matter –Tristram was, how to fit Derek into the scheme. The twins were awake, Derek (the one with the D sewn on his tucker) burbling with a bubble of mother's milk on his mouth, both kicking. Bless their little cotton-substitute socks, the darlings. She had to endure much for their sake, endurance was one of her duties. Sighing, she left the outhouse and went back to the living-room. 'I'm sorry,' she said to Mavis, wondering what precisely she was saying she was sorry for.

'That's all right,' said Mavis. She had laid aside her knitting and was viciously manicuring.

'Would you like me,' said Beatrice-Joanna, 'to do something about getting a meal ready?'

'You can if you want to. I'm not particularly hungry.'

'How about Shonny?'

'Shonny's taken hard-boiled eggs with him. Cook something if you want to.'

'I'm not all that hungry myself.'

'That's all right then.'

Beatrice-Joanna sat down, distractedly rocking the empty cradle. Should she lift the twins from their cot, bring them in? Poor little intruders, let them stay where they were. Brightly she said to Mavis, 'Giving your talons a bit of a sharpening?' She could have bitten her tongue out, etc.

Mavis looked up. 'If,' she snapped, 'you've just come back in here to be insulting –'

'I'm sorry, I'm sorry, I really am. Just a joke, that's all. I just didn't think.'

'No, that's one of your characteristics. You just don't think.'

'Oh, to hell,' said Beatrice-Joanna. Then, 'Sorry, sorry sorry.'

'There's no point at all in your keeping on saying you're sorry if you don't mean it.'

'Look,' said Beatrice-Joanna desperately, 'what do you really want me to do?'

'I've told you already. You must do exactly what you think best for yourself and your *children*.' Her enunciation of this last word made it ring with a dissonant cluster of overtones, suggesting that the only genuine children in that household were Mavis's and that Beatrice-Joanna's were, being illegal, spurious.

'Oh,' said Beatrice-Joanna, snuffing up her tears, 'I'm so unhappy.' She ran back to her gurgling, not at all unhappy twins. Mavis, tight-lipped, went on manicuring her talons.

Eleven

IT was a good deal later in the day that Captain Loosley of the Population Police arrived in his black van. 'Here it is,' he said to young Oxenford, the driver. 'State Farm NW313. It's been a long journey.'

'A disgusting journey,' said Sergeant Image, with the strongly alveolated sibilants of his type. They had seen things in the ploughed fields, horrible things. 'Disgusting,' he repeated. 'We should have filled their buttocks with bullets.'

'Not enough ammo on board, Sarge,' said Oxenford, a literal young man.

'And not our job,' said Captain Loosley. 'Public indecency is the concern of the regular police.'

'Those of them that have not yet been eaten,' said Sergeant Image. 'Go on, Oxenford,' he said with petulance. 'Get out and open that gate.'

'That's not fair, Sarge. I'm driving.'

'Oh, all right, then.' And Sergeant Image extruded his long snaky body to open up. 'Children,' he said. 'Children playing. Pretty children. All right,' he said to Oxenford, 'you drive up to the homestead. I'll walk.' The children ran.

In the house, breathlessly, 'Dad,' Llewelyn cried, 'there are men coming in a black van. Policemen, I think.'

'Black, you say?' Shonny rose to peer out of the window. 'So,' he said. 'We've been expecting them a long time, God forgive them, and they haven't been. And now, when we're lulled asleep, they come lolloping along in their jackboots. Where's your sister?' he asked Mavis sharply. 'Is she away in the outhouse?' Mavis nodded. 'Tell her to lock herself in and keep quiet.' Mavis nodded but hesitated before going. 'Go on, then,' urged Shonny. 'They'll be here in a second.'

'We come first,' said Mavis. 'Remember that. You and me and the children.'

'All right, all right, go on now.' Mavis went to the outhouse. The van drew up and Captain Loosley alighted stretching. Young Oxenford revved up then switched off. Sergeant Image walked up to join his chief. Young Oxenford took off his cap, disclosing a red band on his brow like the mark of Cain, wiped with a spotted handkerchief, then set his cap on again. Shonny opened the door. All was ready.

'Good afternoon,' said Captain Loosley. 'This is State Farm NW313, and you are – I'm afraid I can't pronounce your name, do you see. But that doesn't matter. You have a Mrs Foxe staying with you, haven't you? Are these your children? Delightful, delightful. May we come in?'

'It's not for me to say yes or no,' said Shonny. 'I suppose you must have a warrant.'

'Oh, yes,' said Captain Loosley, 'we have a warrant, do you see.'

'Why does he say that, Dad?' asked Llewelyn. 'Why does he say "Do you see"?'

'It's just his nerves, God have mercy on him,' said Shonny. 'Some people twitch, others say, "Do you see". Come on in then, Mister –'

'Captain,' said Sergeant Image. 'Captain Loosley.' They all came in, keeping their caps on.

'Now,' said Shonny, 'what precisely is it you're looking for?' ?

'This is interesting,' said Sergeant Image, rocking the rough cradle with his foot. 'When the bough breaks the cradle will fall. Down will come baby –'

'Yes,' said Captain Loosley. 'We have reason to believe, do you see, that Mrs Foxe has been living here for the whole period of her illicit pregnancy. "Baby" is the operative word.' Mavis came into the room. 'This,' said Captain Loosley, 'is not Mrs Foxe.' He spoke peevishly, as though they were trying to fob him off. 'She is like Mrs Foxe but she isn't Mrs Foxe.' He bowed to her as in ironic congratulation on a reasonable attempt at deception. 'I want Mrs Foxe.'

'That cradle there,' said Shonny, 'was for pigs. The runt of the litter usually needs special looking after.'

'Shall I,' asked Sergeant Image, 'tell young Oxenford to beat him up a little?'

'Let him try,' said Shonny. Swift red suffused his face as though through the operation of dimmers. 'Nobody beats me up. I've a good mind to ask the lot of you to leave.'

'You can't do that,' said Captain Loosley. 'We're doing our duty, do you see. We want Mrs Foxe and her illegal offspring.'

'Illegal offspring,' parroted Llewelyn. 'Illegal off-spring,' delighted with the phrase.

'Supposing I were to tell you that Mrs Foxe isn't here,' said Shonny. 'She paid us a visit just before Christmas and then moved on. Where to I don't know.'

'What is Christmas?' asked Sergeant Image.

'That's irrelevant,' snapped Captain Loosley. 'If Mrs Foxe isn't here, I take it you'll have no objection to our confirming that for ourselves. I have here,' he fumbled in his tunic side-pocket, 'a sort of all-purposes warrant. It covers search, do you see, and everything else.'

'Including beating-up,' said Mavis.

'Exactly.'

'Get out,' said Shonny, 'the lot of you. I'll not have State hirelings rummaging through my house.'

'You're a State hireling, too,' said Captain Loosley evenly. 'We're all servants of the State. Come now, do please be reasonable, do you see. We don't want any nastiness.' He smiled wanly. 'We've all got to do our duty, when all's said and done.'

'Do you see,' added Dymphna and then giggled.

'Come here, little girl,' said Sergeant Image in-gratiatingly. 'You're a nice little girl, aren't you?' He crouched, rocking on his hunkers, and puss-pussed her, snapping his fingers.

'You stay here,' said Mavis, drawing both children to her.

'Aaargh.' Sergeant Image snarled briefly at Mavis and then, rising, put on a mask of idiotic sweetness. 'There's a little baby in this house, isn't there?' he said wheedlingly to Dymphna. 'A wee sweet little baby, that's right, isn't it?' Dymphna giggled. Llewelyn said stoutly:

'No.'

'And that's the truth, too,' said Shonny. 'The boy spoke no less than the truth. Now will you all get out and stop wasting your time as well as mine? I'm a busy man.'

'It's not my intention,' sighed Captain Loosley, 'to prefer charges against either you or your wife. Produce Mrs Foxe and her offspring and you'll hear no more about it. You have my word for that.'

'Do I have to throw you out?' cried Shonny. 'Because, by the Lord Jesus, I've a mind to set on the lot of you.'

'Bash him a little, Oxenford,' said Sergeant Image. 'It's all a lot of nonsense.'

'We're going to start searching,' said Captain Loosley. 'I'm sorry you're being so unco-operative, do you see.'

'Get upstairs, Mavis,' said Shonny, 'you and the

children. You leave all this to me.' He tried to push his wife out.

'The children stay here,' said Sergeant Image. 'The children will be made to squeal a little. I like to hear children squeal.'

'You unholy Godless bastard,' cried Shonny. He threw himself at Sergeant Image, but young Oxenford was quick to interpose himself. Young Oxenford punched Shonny lightly in the groin. Shonny cried in pain and then began to flail wildly.

'All right,' said a voice from the kitchen doorway. 'I don't want to cause any more trouble.' Shonny dropped his fists.

'*This* is Mrs Foxe,' said Captain Loosley. '*This* is the genuine article.' He showed restrained delight.

Beatrice-Joanna was dressed for outdoors. 'What,' she said, 'will you do to my children?'

'You shouldn't have done it,' wailed Shonny. 'You should have stayed where you were. Everything would have been all right, God forgive you.'

'You have my assurance,' said Captain Loosley, 'that no harm will come either to you or to your children.' He suddenly started. 'Children? Children? Oh, I see. More than one. I hadn't considered that possibility. All the better, of course, do you see, all the better.'

'You can punish me as much as you like,' said Beatrice-Joanna, 'but the children have done no harm.'

'Of course not,' said Captain Loosley. 'No harm at all. We intend harm only to the father. My intention is merely to confront the Metropolitan Commissioner with the fruits of his crime. Nothing more than that, do you see.'

'What is this?' cried Shonny. 'What's going on?'

'It's a long story,' said Beatrice-Joanna. 'It's too late to tell it now. Well,' she said to her sister, 'it looks as though the future's taken care of. It seems that I've found somewhere to go.'

Part Four

Part Four

One

TRISTRAM was ready to begin his anabasis. He yearned, like a compass-needle, towards his wife in the north, the prospect of repentance and reconciliation like the prospect of sore labour's bath. He wanted comfort, her arms, her warm body, their mingled tears, rest. He did not now particularly want revenge.

There was chaos in the metropolis, and that chaos seemed at first like a projection of his own new freedom. Chaos whooped like a big laughing Bacchante and told him, not very far from Pentonville, to club a harmless man with his truncheon and steal his clothes. This was in an alley, after dark, in the hinterland of public cooking-fires and flares spluttering with human fat. Electricity, like other public utilities, seemed to have failed. Here was jungle night, broken glass crackling under one's feet like an undergrowth. Tristram wondered at the maintenance of civilized order in that jail he had left; how much longer could it last? Then, wondering, he saw a man leaning by the mouth of the alley, singing to himself, drunk on something. Tristram raised his club and the man went down at once, obligingly, as if this was what he had been waiting for, and his clothes – a round-necked shirt, a cardigan, a checked suit – came off without effort. Tristram turned swiftly into a free civilian but decided to keep his warder's truncheon. Dressed for dinner, he went off looking for food.

Jungle noises, black skyscraper forest, starred sky dizzily high, the ruddiness of fires. In Claremont Square he came upon people eating. They sat, men and women alike, round a barbecue, about thirty of them. Metal grills of roughly reticulated telegraph wire – these rested on plinths of heaped bricks; beneath were glowing coals. A man with a white cap forked and turned spitting steaks. 'No room, no room,' fluted a thin donnish person as Tristram shyly approached. 'This is a dining club, not a public restaurant.'

'I,' said Tristram, brandishing his truncheon, 'also have a club.' Everybody laughed at this puny threat. 'I've only just got out of prison,' wailed Tristram plaintively. 'I've been starved.'

'Fall to,' said the donnish person. 'Though this may prove, at first, too rich for your stomach. These days,' he epigrammatized, 'your criminal is your only moral man.' He reached over to the nearest grill and picked up, with a pair of tongs, a long hot metal skewer spitted with chunks of meat. 'A kebab,' he said. Then, squinting at Tristram in the firelight, 'You've no teeth. You'll have to get some teeth somewhere. Wait. We have some very nourishing broth over here.' And, most hospitably, he fussed round searching for a bowl, a spoon. 'Try this,' he said, ladling from a metal pot, 'and heartily welcome.' Tristram, like an animal, carried this gift trembling to a corner away from the others. He sucked in a steaming spoonful. Rich, rich, an oily liquid in which were suspended gobbets of smoking pliant rubbery stuff. Meat. He had read about meat. Ancient literature was full of meat-guzzling – Homer, Dickens, Priestley, Rabelais, A. J. Cronin. He swallowed the spoonful, retched, lost it. 'Slowly, slowly,' said the donnish man, coming up to him kindly. 'You will find it delicious fairly soon. Think of it not as what it is but as one of the pulpy fruits of the tree of life. All life is one. Why did they put you in prison?'

'I suppose,' said Tristram, still retching, 'because,' recovering, 'I was against the Government.'

'Which government? At the moment we don't seem to have a government.'

'So,' said Tristram, 'the Gusphase has not yet begun.'

'You seem to be something of a scholar. In prison you must have had leisure to think. Tell me, what do you make of the present times?'

'You can't think without data,' said Tristram. He tried the broth again; it went down much better. 'So this is meat,' he said.

'Man is a carnivore, just as man is a breeder. The two are cognate and the two have been long suppressed. Put the two together and you have no rational cause for suppression. As far as information is concerned, we have no information because we have no information services. However, we can take it that the Starling Government has fallen and that the Praesidium is full of snarling dogs. We shall have a government soon, I don't doubt. Meantime, we band ourselves into little dining clubs for self-protection. Let me warn you, who are just out of prison and hence new to this new world, not to go out alone. I will, if you like, put you up for this club of ours.'

'That's very kind,' said Tristram, 'but I have to find

my wife. She's in Northern Province, just outside Preston.'

'You'll have some difficulty,' said this kind man. 'The trains have stopped running, of course, and there's little road transport. It's a very long walk. Don't go unvictualled. Go armed. Don't sleep in the open. It worries me,' he said, squinting again at Tristram's sunken jaws, 'that you have no teeth.'

Tristram took from his pocket the twice-transferred halves of dental plate. He turned them over and over ruefully. 'A brutal prison warder,' he said unjustly.

'I think,' said the donnish man, 'we may have a dental mechanic among our members.' He went over to the group and Tristram finished his broth. It was heartening, no doubt about that. A memory of an ancient Pelagian poem – or rather one of the author's own notes to it – steamed into his mind. *Queen Mab*. Shelley. 'Comparative anatomy teaches us that man resembles frugivorous animals in everything, and carnivorous in nothing; he has neither claws wherewith to seize his prey, nor distinct and pointed teeth to tear the living fibre.' And again, 'Man resembles no carnivorous animal. There is no exception, unless man be one, to the rule of herbivorous animals having cellulated colons.' That was, perhaps, after all, all bloody nonsense.

'Your teeth can be mended,' said the kindly donnish man, returning, 'and we can fill a scrip for you with cold meat for the journey. I shouldn't, if I were you, think of starting before daylight. You're very welcome to spend the night with me.'

'You're genuinely very kind,' said Tristram genuinely. 'I've never before, I honestly think, met such kindness.'

His eyes began to fill with tears; it had been an exhausting day.

'Think nothing of it. When the State withers, humanity flowers. There are some very nice people about these days. Still, hang on to that weapon of yours.'

Tristram retired that night with his teeth in. Lying on the floor in the donnish man's flat, he champed again and again at the darkness as at so much airy meat. His host, who had given his name as Sinclair, had lighted them both to rest with a wick floating in fat; it had smelled delicious. The homely flame had shown a small untidy room crammed with books. Sinclair, however, had disclaimed any pretensions to being what he called a 'reading man'; he had been, before the electricity failed, an electronic composer, specializing in atmospheric music for television documentaries. Again, before the electricity failed and the elevators were grounded, his flat had been a good thirty storeys higher than this one; today, apparently, the weakest rose and the strongest fell. This new flat of his had belonged to a real reading man, a professor of Chinese, whose flesh had proved, despite his great age, not unsucculent. Sinclair slept innocently on his wall-bed, snoring gently, only occasionally talking in his sleep. Most of his utterances were gnomic, some were plain nonsense. Tristram listened.

'The cat's way is only exceeded by its perpenderosity.'

'I love potatoes. I love pork. I love man.'

'Eucharistic ingestion is our answer.'

That dark term – eucharistic ingestion – became a sort of key to sleep. As though it were indeed an answer, Tristram passed, content and comforted, into oblivion.

Sinking out of time, he rose into it again to see Sinclair, humming and dressing, blinking down at him amiably. It seemed to be a fine spring morning. 'Well,' said Sinclair, 'we must set you on your way, mustn't we? First, however, a good breakfast is essential.' Sinclair washed quickly (the public water supply still seemed in order) and shaved with an antique cut-throat. 'Well-named,' he smiled, naming it, lending it to Tristram. 'It has cut throats enow.' Tristram found no cause to disbelieve him.

The barbecue fires were, it seemed, never allowed to go out. Templar, thought Tristram, Olympic, flashing a modest smile at the members of the dining club, four of whom had guarded and tended the flames through the night. 'Bacon?' said Sinclair, and he heaped a singing tin plate high for Tristram. All ate heartily, with many a merry quip, and drank water by the quart. Then these kind people filled a postman's sack with cold joints and, with several expressions of good will, loaded their guest and sped him on his way.

'Never,' declared Tristram, 'have I met such generosity.'

'Go with God,' said Sinclair, replete and ripe for solemnity. 'May you find her well. May you find her happy.' He frowned and amended that. 'Happy to see you, that is, of course.'

Two

TRISTRAM walked all the way to Finchley. There would

not be, he knew, any sense in taking the road until well past, say, Nuneaton. It was a long long plodding of a town street, between skyscraper dwelling-blocks and factories with smashed windows. He passed jolly or somnolent dining clubs, corpses, bones, but was not himself molested. The endless city had a smell of roasting flesh and stopped-up drains. Once or twice, to his embarrassment, he saw open and unashamed copulation. I love potatoes. I love pork. I love woman. No, that was wrong. Something like that, though. He saw no police; they all seemed absorbed or digested into the generality. At a street-corner near Tufnell Park mass was being said before a small but fairly devout congregation. Tristram knew all about mass from the Blessed Ambrose Bayley and so was surprised to see the priest – a grey-coxcombed boyish man with a roughly painted surplice (the cross, IHS) – doling out what looked like rounds of meat. '*Hoc est enim Corpus. Hic est enim calix sanguinis.*' Some new Council of somewhere or other must be, in this shortage of the orthodox accidents, countenancing that sort of improvisation.

It was a fine spring day.

Just beyond Finchley Tristram sat down to rest in a shop doorway in a safe back-street and drew food from his scrip. He was footsore. He ate carefully and slowly, his stomach – as was evident from a bout of dyspepsia after breakfast –still having much to learn, and, having eaten, sought water. Queen Mab whispered to him about thirst being the necessary concomitant of a flesh diet, great thirst. In the rear living-quarters of the rifled shop Tristram found a tap in working order and, laying his mouth beneath it, drank as if he would drink for ever.

The water tasted faintly foul, faintly corrupt, and he thought: 'Here is where future trouble lies.' He rested a while longer, sitting in the doorway, clutching his truncheon, watching the passers-by. They all kept to the middle of the road, an interesting characteristic of the later part of the Interphase. He sat idly reviewing the thoughts and feelings it seemed to him he ought to have. It surprised him that he now felt so little desire to smash in the face of his brother. Perhaps it had all been a malicious lie of that ambitious and aggrieved captain; one needed proof, one needed definite and incontrovertible evidence. The meat growled in his stomach; he belched an utterance that sounded like 'paternity lust'.

Would the child, if there was to be a child, be born yet? He had lost track of time somehow. He felt that Beatrice-Joanna would, in all this chaos, be safer than before. She must still be up north (if that man had told the truth); she had nowhere else, anyway, to go. He himself, he was sure, was doing the only possible thing. He too had nowhere else to go. How he detested his brother-in-law, however: the bluff bluster, pious shouts apt for tug-of-war teams always on his lips. This time he would bluster back and out-God him; he was not going to be bullied by anyone any more.

Keeping to the pavement, he made Barnet by mid-afternoon. Hesitating between the roads to, respectively, Hatfield and St Albans, he was surprised to see a motor-van come coughing slowly up, north-bound like himself. It was painted a sort of earth-colour and the ghost of its provenance – *Ministry of Infertility* – showed faintly under the single coat. Tristram, hesitating between roads, hesitated before gesturing for a lift. A nerve in his sore left foot decided for him and, by-passing his brain, shot up its reflex message to his thumb.

'I'm only going as far as Aylesbury,' said the driver. 'You might pick up something else there. If we get to Aylesbury, that is.' The car shuddered agreement. 'You're making a long trip,' he said, glancing curiously at Tristram. 'There's not much travelling done these days.' Tristram explained. The driver was a lean man in a strange uniform: greyboy's tunic and civilian trousers dyed the earth-colour of the van itself, an earth-coloured cheese-cutter on his knees, white bands looped through his shoulder-straps. When Tristram spoke of his escape from prison he laughed in a brief snort. 'If you'd waited till this morning,' he said, 'you would have been bowed off the premises. They opened up their gates, apparently, because of the failure of the food supply. At least, that's what they told me at Ealing.'

Tristram also barked a short laugh. All Charlie Linklater's work for nothing. He said, 'You can understand that I'm very much out of touch. I just don't know what's going on.'

'Oh,' said the man. 'Well, there's not a lot I can tell you. There doesn't seem to be a central government at the moment, but we're trying to improvise some kind of regional law and order. A sort of martial law you could call it. You behold in me one of the resuscitated military. I'm a soldier.' He snorted another laugh.

'Armies,' said Tristram. 'Regiments. Battalions. Platoons.' He had read of such things.

'We can't have all this,' said the man. 'Indiscriminate cannibalism and the drains out of order. We've got our wives and children to think of. We've got something started in Aylesbury, anyway. We've even got people doing a bit of work again.'

'What do you eat?' asked Tristram.

The soldier laughed very loud. 'It's officially called tinned pork,' he said. 'We've got to eat something. Waste not want not. We've had to do a fair amount of shooting, you see, in the name of law and order,' he said seriously. 'Meat and water. It's a bit too much of a tiger's diet, perhaps, but the canning makes it seem civilized. And we have hopes, you know, we have hopes that things will start growing again. And, believe it or not, I actually did some fishing last week-end.'

'Much of a catch?'

'Chub,' said the soldier. He laughed again. 'Measly little chub.'

'And,' said Tristram, 'if I may ask, what's been the purpose of your journey?'

'This journey? Oh, we'd had a report of a police ammunition dump along the road from Ealing to Finchley. Some swine had got there first, though. One of these gangs. They knocked off my corporal. He wasn't a very good corporal, but they shouldn't have knocked him off. Probably eating him now, blasted cannibals.' He spoke quite calmly.

'It would seem,' said Tristram, 'that we're all cannibals.'

'Yes, but, damn it all, we in Aylesbury are at least civilized cannibals. It makes all the difference if you get it out of a tin.'

Three

WEST of Hinckley Tristram saw his first ploughed fields. He had done well on the whole: a night in barracks in civilized Aylesbury; a walk in weather continuing fair along the Bicester road with a lift in an army truck five miles out of Aylesbury as far as Blackthorn; lunch in armed but kindly Bicester and even a shave and haircut there; a walk up the railway line to Ardley and there a surprise – an ancient steam train run on wood as far as Banbury. Tristram had only the few septs and tanners and tosheroons he had found in the pockets of the man he had truncheoned, but the amateurs who manned the three-coach train were archaeologists vague about fares. Tristram spent the night in a cobwebbed cellar on the Warwick Road and reached Warwick, with the aid of a lift on a truck musical with small arms, well before lunch-time the next day. At Warwick, which was sullen under martial law, he was told to beware of Kenilworth, this town apparently being ruled by a sort of Fifth Monarchy fanatics who preached a doctrine of rigid exophagy; Coventry, he was assured, was safe enough to the stranger. So Tristram plodded the secondary road through Leamington, the journey eased by a pillion lift on a cheerful dispatch-rider's motor-cycle. Coventry seemed almost a normal city except for its flavour of the garrison: communal messes, roll-calls outside factories, a curfew at nightfall. Tristram was asked eagerly for news at the city-frontier, but of course he had none to give. Still, he was made welcome and given the freedom of the Engineers' Sergeants' Mess. A couple of tins of meat were crammed into his pockets when he left at dawn and, for the first time in many years, he actually felt like singing as he marched, in this miraculous weather, towards Nuneaton. He was near the northern limit of Greater London now; he fancied he could snuff country air. At Bedworth he was picked up in a staff car (a Falstaffian colonel and his adjutant, red-faced on alc) and was taken through Nuneaton on to the Shrewsbury road. Here at last was country indeed: the flatness of ploughed fields, hardly a building in sight, the sky no longer challenged by proud monoliths. He lay down behind a gate and took a nap in the smell of earth. Thanked be Almighty God.

When he awoke he thought he was dreaming. He thought he heard a flute playing breathily and voices singing more breathily still. The words of the song seemed to resolve themselves into a statement so direct and final that it was as though he was hearing 'Eucharistic Ingestion' all over again. The words were something like 'Apples be ripe and nuts be brown, petticoats up and trousers down', and the simple tune went round and round, an endless *da capo*. And he saw, he saw, he saw men and women in the furrows – a pair here and a pair there – making, with ritual seriousness, beast after beast after beast with two backs. Petticoats up and trousers down in the spring sun, in the sown furrows, ripe apples and brown nuts, country copulatives. Six men, five men, four men, three men, two men, one man and his, and their – Why did the song say 'dog'? Sowing, not mowing, a meadow. But they would mow in due time, they would quite certainly mow. All life was one. That blight had been man's refusal to breed.

Four

'COME on, now,' called the leader crossly. He had the look of a morris-dance organizer, stringy and sniffly, red-nosed and blue-cheeked. 'Listen, please, everybody,' he said plaintively. 'The following partners have been drawn.' He read from the list in his hand. 'Mr Lipset with Miss Kemeny. Mr Minrath with Mrs Graham. Mr Evans with Mrs Evans. Mr Hilliard with Miss Ethel Duffus.' He read on. Tristram, blinking in the warm sun, sat outside the inn at Atherstone, watching benevolently as the men and women paired. 'Mr Finlay with Miss Rachel Duffus. Mr Mayo with Miss Lowrie.' As for country dancing, those called did a stand-and-face-your-lover line-up, giggling, blushing, bold-faced, bashful, game, ready. 'Very well,' said the leader, tiredly. 'Into the fields.' And off, hand in hand, they went. The leader saw Tristram and, shaking his head resignedly, came over and sat next to him on the bench. 'These are strange times we're living in,' he said. 'Are you just passing through?'

'On my way to Preston,' said Tristram. 'Why, if I may ask, do you have all this organizing?'

'Oh, the usual thing,' said the leader. 'Greed, selfishness. Some people getting all the plums. That man Hilliard, for instance. And poor Belinda Lowrie left out in the cold all the time. I wonder if it really does any good,' he wondered gloomily. 'I wonder if it's really anything more than sheer self-indulgence.'

'It's an affirmation,' said Tristram. 'It's a way of showing that reason is only one instrument for running our lives. A return to magic, that's what it is. It seems very healthy to me.'

'I foresee danger,' said the leader. 'Jealousy, fights, possessiveness, the breaking-up of marriages.' He was determined to look on the black side.

'Things will sort themselves out,' soothed Tristram. 'You'll see. A recapitulation of whole aeons of free love, and then the Christian values will be reasserted. Nothing to worry about at all.'

The leader gloomed at the sun, at the clouds gently and seriously propelled across the blue acres. 'I suppose you're normal,' he said at length. 'I suppose you're one of those like that man Hilliard. A real told-you-so, born and bred, that man. He was always saying that things couldn't go on as they were for ever. They laughed at me when I did what I did. Hilliard laughed louder than anybody. I could kill Hilliard,' he said, clenching his fists with the thumbs inside.

'Kill?' said Tristram. 'Kill in these days of,' he said, 'love?'

'It was when I was working at the Lichfield Housing Office,' bubbled the leader, 'that this thing happened. There was the question of a vacancy and me getting up-graded. I was senior, you see.' If not days of love, these were certainly days of open and frank confiding. 'Mr Consett, who was in charge, told me it was a toss-up between me and a man called Maugham, very much my junior Maugham was, but Maugham was homo.

Well, I thought about that a good deal. I was never that way inclined myself but, of course, there was something I could do. I thought about it a good deal before taking action, because it was, after all, a pretty momentous step to take. Anyway, after a good deal of thought and lying in bed, tossing and turning, worrying about it, I made up my mind and went to see Dr Manchip. Dr Manchip said it was quite an easy job, no danger at all, and he did it. He said a general anaesthetic wasn't necessary. I watched him do it.'

'I see,' said Tristram. 'I wondered about your voice –'

'That's right. And look at me now.' He extended his arms. 'What's done can't be undone. How do I fit into this new world? I should have been warned, somebody should have told me. How was I to know that that sort of world wasn't going to go on for ever?' He lowered his voice. 'You know what that man Hilliard's been calling me lately? He's been calling me a *capon*. And he smacks his lips, joking of course, but it's not in very good taste.'

'I see,' said Tristram.

'I don't like it at all. I don't like it one little bit.'

'Sit tight and wait,' counselled Tristram. 'History is a wheel. This sort of world can't go on for ever, either. One of these days we're bound to go back to liberalism and Pelagianism and sexual inversion and, and – well, your sort of thing. We're obviously bound to, because of all this.' He waved his hand in the direction of the ploughed fields, whence came muffled noises of intense concentration. 'Because,' he clarified, 'of the biological purpose of all this.'

'But in the meantime,' said the leader sadly, 'I've

people like Hilliard to contend with.' He shuddered. 'Calling me a capon, indeed.'

Five

Tristram, being still young and not ill-looking, was kindly received by the ladies of Shenstone. He excused himself courteously, pleading that he must reach Lichfield by nightfall. He was sped on his way with kisses.

Lichfield burst on him like a bomb. Here some kind of carnival was in progress (though it was no farewell to flesh, far from it) and Tristram's eyes were confused by a torch-procession and by banners and streamers dancing aloft: *Lichfield Fecundity Guild* and *South Staffs Love Group*. Tristram mingled with the crowd on the pavement to watch the parade go by. First marched a band of pre-electronic instruments booming and shrilling what sounded like that thin flute-tune of the fields outside Hinckley, but the tune was now, in all its brass, beefy, blood-red, confident. The crowd cheered. Next came two clowns buffeting and falling at the head of a comic squad in boots, long tunics, but no trousers. A woman behind Tristram screamed, 'Eeeee, there's our Arthur, Ethel.' The tunics and caps of this leering, waving, shouting, staggering bare-legged phalanx had evidently been stolen from the Poppol (where were they now, where were they?) and a card on a stick was held high, lettered neatly COPULATION POLICE. They belaboured each other with truncheons of stuffed sack-ing or thrust at the air with them in ithyphallic rhythms. 'What's that word mean, Ethel?' cried the woman behind Tristram. 'Real jaw-breaker, that is.' A small man with a hat on told her in one brief Lawrentian term. 'Eeeeeee,' she screamed.

Next toddled little boys and girls in green, sweet and pretty, soaring multicoloured sausage balloons moored to their fingers. 'Awwww,' went a droop-mouthed lank-haired girl next to Tristram. 'Em's nice, ennem?' The balloons jostled high in the torchlit air, an airy languid pillow-fight. After the children leaped and staggered more buffoons, men in antique billowing female skirts, enormously and unevenly breasted, others in skintight motley with Panurgian codpieces. Dancing clumsily, they engaged in brief spasmodic parodies of the claw-buttock act. 'Eeeeeee,' yelled the woman behind Tristram, 'I shall fair pass out of laughing, that I shall.' Then, to a hush of admiration followed by sincere cheers, there trundled up a white-decked float of paper flowers with, high on a throne, a buxom lass in blue, paper-flower-crowned, a staff in her grip, clustered about by all her starry fays, smiling and waving nubility, Lichfield's, so it would appear, festal queen. 'Real lovely she is,' said another woman. 'Joe Treadwell's daughter.' The float was pulled – crackling flower-twined ropes – by young men in white shirts and red leggings, handsome and muscular. After this float there walked sedate members of the clergy, bearing, in embroidered silk-surrogate, the motto *God Is Love*. The local army marched behind, terrible with banners: *General Hapgood's Boys* and *We Saved Lichfield*. The crowd cheered full-throatedly. And then, at the end, young girls trod daintily (not one of them more than fifteen), each with a streamer and each streamer attached to the top of a high thick pole, the Priapic emblem which evoked redoubled cheers, borne in the arms of a long-robed comely matron, a blown rose in this garden of callow cowslips. The procession moved on to the town's outskirts and the crowd jostled, thumped, pushed on to the road to follow it. From the unseen head of the parade the jaunty six-eight tune – mulberry bush, nuts and may, apples be ripe – blasted and thumped brassily on, clearing the way through the spring night. Tristram was caught in the crowd, borne irresistibly, apples be ripe, through the town, home of a swan, and nuts be brown, and a lexicographer, petticoats up, *Lich* meaning a corpse in Middle English, and trousers down, how inappropriately named – Lichfield – tonight. Men and women, youths and girls, thrust, elbowed, laughed, in the procession's wake, the high white wooden phallus gleaming ahead, swaying, the focus of pretty ribbons, old men bent but game, middle-aged women solidly eager, young lusty boys, girls shy but ready, faces like moons, hatchets, flat-irons, flowers, eggs, mulberries, all the noses of the world (haughty Italian, crushed Oriental, snub, splayed, spurred, bulbous, crested, tilted, flared), corn-hair, rust-hair, Eskimo-straight, crinkled, undulant, receding, gone, tonsures and bald spots, cheeks warmed to ripe-apple and nut-brown in the flares and fires and enthusiasm, the swish of petticoats, on to the sown furrows of the fields, and trousers.

Down, somewhere, had gone Tristram's near-empty food-sack; his truncheon had disappeared. His arms were free for dancing and embracing. On the green at the town's end the band had settled, squat on benches, blasting, cracking, clashing, skirling away. The Priapic pole was being plunged into a hole already dug in the centre of the green, the streamers flapping and entwining the men who pushed it down and tamped the soil at its base. The local army was smartly fallen out and started to pile arms. There were flares and a bonfire, there were glowing and spitting barbecues. *Lichfield Sausages*, said a notice. Tristram joined hungry wolfers of these, doled out free on skewers, and chewed the salty meat, ho', 'ery ho', his mouth smoking.

Dancing began round the Priapic pole, youths and putative maidens. On the periphery of the green (a euphemistic term for the brown near-bald half-acre) their elders twirled and clodhopped lustily. A warm dark woman in her thirties came up to Tristram and said, 'How about you and me, duck?' 'Gladly,' said Tristram. 'You look proper sad,' she said, 'as if you was pining away after somebody. Am I right?' 'Another couple of days, with a bit of luck,' said Tristram, 'and I'll be with her. In the meantime —' They rolled into the dance. The band played their rollicking six-eight tune over and over. Soon Tristram and his partner rolled into the furrows. Many were rolling into the furrows. It was a warm night for the time of year.

At midnight, the revellers breathing hard, unbuttoned about the fires, the contest for the male festal crown was fanfared. The queen sat aloof on her float, her dishevelled and rosy retinue settling their skirts, with many a giggle, at her feet. Below the float, at a rough table, passing from hand to wrinkled hand a flask of alc, sat the judges, elders of the town. There was a short list of five competitors in a trial of physical strength and agility. Desmond Seward bent a poker – teeth gritted, thews bursting – and walked forty yards on his hands. Jollyboy Adams turned innumerable somersaults and then leapt over a fire. Gerald Toynbee held his breath for five minutes and performed a frog-dance. Jimmy Quair walked on all fours, supinated, a little boy (his brother, as it turned out) striking an Eros-pose upon his, Jimmy Quair's, stomach. This, for its novelty and aesthetic appeal, drew much applause. But the crown went to Melvin Johnson (illustrious surname) who, balanced on his head, feet high in the air, recited loudly a triolet of his own composition. It was strange to see the upside-down mouth, hear the right-way-up words:

> This lovely queen, if I should win her,
> Shall have my heart for a medallion.
> She'll never lack a hearty dinner,
> This lovely queen, if I should win her.
> My fire shall rouse the fire that's in her,
> She'll ride my sea, a golden galleon,
> This lovely queen. If I should win her,
> She'll have my heart for a medallion.

In vain for the captious to grumble that the rules of the contest said nothing about facility in versifying and how, anyway, had this competitor shown strength and agility? He would show it soon enough, laughed some. There were roars of approval at the judges' unanimous decision. Melvin Johnson was crowned with castellar tinfoil and borne, amid cheers, on strong shoulders to meet his queen. Then the royal pair, hand in hand, youths and maidens singing behind them an old nuptial song whose words Tristram could not catch, proceeded majestically to the field for the consummation of their love. At a decent distance the common sort followed after.

There they all were under the moon, seed busy above seed busy below: Charlie Aaron with Gladys Woodward, Dan Abel with Monica Wilson, Howard Wilson with Clara Hoskyns-Abrahall, Freddie Adler with Diana-Gertrude Williams, Bill Agar with Mary Westcott, Harold Auld with Louisa Wertheimer, Jim Weeks with Pam Asimov, Ford Wolverton Avery with Lucy Vivian, Denis Brodrick with Dorothy Hodge, John Halberstram with Jessie Greenidge, Tristram Foxe with Ann Onymous, Ron Heinlein with Agnes Gelber, Sherman Feyler with Margaret Evans, George Fisher with Lily Ross, Alf Meldrum with Joanie Crump, Elvis Fenwick with Brenda Fenwick, John-James De Ropp with Asmara Jones, Tommy Eliot with Kitty Elphick – and scores more. With the sinking of the moon and the rising of the wind they sought the fires, sleeping till dawn in a red crackling haze of fulfilment.

Tristram woke at dawn to hear bird-twitterings; he rubbed his eyes at the cool distant bass flute of a cuckoo. A priest appeared with his field-altar and a yawning cross boy-servitor. '*Introibo ad altare Dei.*' 'To God Who giveth joy to my youth.' The consecration of the roasted meat (bread and wine would doubtless be back soon), the donation of a eucharistic breakfast. Washed but un-shaven, Tristram kissed his new friends good-bye and took the north-west road to Rugeley. The fine morning weather might well hold all day.

Six

THERE were Dionysian revels at Sandon, Meaford and the cross-roads near Whitmore, but at Nantwich there was the sophistication of a fair. Tristram was interested to see a brisk flow of small money at the stalls (rifle-range, aunt sally, try-your-strength, roll-a-coin-on-to-a-lucky-square): people must be working and earning again. Food (he noticed small spitted birds among the kebabs and sausages) was being sold, not given away. Barkers urged lubricious males to pay a tosheroon to see Lola and Carmenita in their sensational seven-veils speciality. It seemed that, in one town at least, the novelty of free flesh had begun to pall.

But, in its lowliest form, an art had been revived. How long was it since anybody in England had seen a live play? For generations people had lain on their backs in the darkness of their bedrooms, their eyes on the blue watery square on the ceiling: mechanical stories about good people not having children and bad people having them, homos in love with each other, Origen-like heroes castrating themselves for the sake of global stability. Here in Nantwich customers queued outside a big tent to see *The Unfortunate Father: A Comedy*. Tristram shrugged over his small handful of coin and counted out the price of admission: one and a half septs. His feet were weary; it would be somewhere to rest.

This, he thought, crammed on a bench, was what the first Greek comedy must have been like. On a creaking platform, lighted by two uncertain floods, a narrator wearing a large false phallus introduced, and commented coarsely on, a simple story of bawdry. A bald impotent husband (impotence symbolized by a flaccid codpiece) had a flighty wife, regularly impregnated by lusty lovers, and, in consequence, a house full of children. The poor man, reviled and ridiculed and taunted, eventually in a blazing temper tackled a pair of these cuckolders in the street and was cracked soundly on the pate for his pains. But, lo, a miracle. The bash on the head did strange things to his nervous system: the codpiece swelled and rose: he was no longer impotent. Cunningly feigning, however, to be as he had been, he found his way easily into the homes of those of his wife's lovers who had womenfolk, swiving them while the man of the house was at work. Uproarious. Finally, he sent his own wife packing and turned his house into a seraglio, the comedy ending with a phallic song and dance. Well, thought Tristram, leaving the tent at twilight, soon men would be dressing up as goats and presenting the first neo-tragedy. Perhaps in a year or two there would be mystery plays.

By one of the smoking food-stalls a little man was selling single sheets of paper, quarto, and doing a brisk trade. '*Nantwich Echo*,' he called. 'One tanner only.' Many were standing, reading, open-mouthed. Tristram, trembling a little, spent one of his last coins and took off his paper to a corner, as furtive as when, a few days before, he had carried off his first meat-meal. This – a newspaper – was almost as archaic as a comedy. There were two sides of blurred print, under the name NNTWTSH EKO the legend 'Put out by Min of Inf microwave transmitter picked up 1.25 p.m. G. Hawtrey Publisher.' Private enterprise: beginning of the Gusphase. Tristram gobbled the news without chewing. Mr Ockham invited by His Majesty to form a government, names of cabinet members to be announced tomorrow. Emergency national martial law, immediate establishment of central control of regional (irregular) armed forces, regional commanders to report forthwith for instructions to provincial headquarters as listed below. Regular communications and information services expected to be resumed within forty-eight hours. Return to work in twenty-four hours ordered, dire penalties (unspecified) for refusal.

Return to work, eh? Tristram thought about that, looking up from his paper. The men and women that stood around, reading with their lips or skimming, open-mouthed, puzzled and wondered. There was no throwing of hats in the air or huzzaing to celebrate this news of the reimposition of stability. Return to work. Officially he must still be workless, a committal to jail automatically depriving a government servant of his post. He would push on to State Farm NW313. Surely one's wife and children came first? (Children? One of them was dead.) Officially, anyway, he had received no information.

He would try to reach Chester tonight. He bought himself the viaticum of a large sausage for a tanner and sought the Chester road munching. His marching feet teased out from deep memory the rhythm of a gnomic quatrain written by some forgotten poet:

> The northern winds send icy peace,
> The southern gales blow balmy.
> Pelagius is fond of police;
> Augustine loves an army.

Seven

CAPTAIN LOOSLEY devoured crackling morsels of the news received on the dashboard microwave radio. 'There,' he said with nasty satisfaction, 'that'll teach them, do you see. There'll be a bit more respect for law and order.' As Tristram Foxe had so rudely told him that day in jail, he had no knowledge of historiography, no sense of the cycle. Young Oxenford, driving, nodded without much conviction. He was fed up; it had been a rotten journey. The police rations had been meagre and his stomach growled. The nuclear motor of the Poppol van had misbehaved several times, and Oxenford was no nuclear mechanic. Coming out of Chester he had mistaken the road and gone blithely west (this being at night and he no astro-navigator either), only at Dolgelley discovering his error (signposts had been uprooted for fuel). At Mallwyd, on the Welshpool road, men and women with lilting speech and magicians' faces had halted them. These people had been charmed by Beatrice-Joanna's twins ('There's pretty') but antagonized by the haughty demeanour and trembling gun of Sergeant Image. 'Queer the poor bugger is,' they said, taking his weapon with gentle fingers. 'Boil up lovely he will,' they had nodded, fingering his soft joints as they undressed him. They had also taken the uniforms of Captain Loosley and young Oxenford, saying, 'Come in nice these will for the army. Proper, these are.' Seeing the two shivering in their underclothes they had said, 'There's pity now. Who knows for some brown paper to cwtch their chests?' Nobody did. 'Treating you kind we are, see,' they said finally, 'because of her in the back. Fair play.' And they had sped them on to Welshpool with waves, Sergeant Image protesting loudly at treachery, writhing in the grip of strong butchers.

Taking their uniforms, the people of Mallwyd had perhaps saved their lives, but Captain Loosley was too stupid to see it. As for Beatrice-Joanna, her sole anxiety was for her babies. She feared these towns and villages with their fires and hearty meat-eating faces, faces that looked in on her sleeping pair and grinned amiably. The smiles and words of admiration seemed to her to be equivocal: cooing might soon turn to lip-smacking. Whatever official fate waited in the capital, it would, surely, not stoop to teknophagy? Anxious for her babies, Beatrice-Joanna forgot to feel hungry, but malnutrition spoke loud in the quality and quantity of her milk. Involuntarily she occasionally yearned towards the smell of roasting or simmering as they sped through a town; whenever the van was stopped by held-up meaty hands and curious eyes examined the pair in their underwear, herself with the twins at her breasts, she would feel sick at the thought of what was being roasted and boiled.

But why? Sense was primal, and sense was not revolted; it was always the great traitor *thought* that threw its shoe into the works.

'Things look almost back to normal, do you see,' said Captain Loosley as, at last, they took the Brighton road. 'Too many smashed windows, though, and look at that twisted metal in the road, do you see. Overturned vehicles. Barbarous, barbarous. Martial law. Poor Sergeant Image. We should have taken the names, do you see, of those responsible. Then they could be summarily punished.'

'Don't talk so bloody wet,' said young Oxenford. 'The way you go on makes me proper bloody sick sometimes.'

'Oxenford,' cried Captain Loosley, shocked. 'I don't think you quite know what you're saying. Just because we haven't our uniforms on, do you see, is no excuse for forgetting the deference due to, due to –'

'Aw, shut it. It's all over. Haven't you got the bloody sense to see it's all over? How the hell you got where you have got bloody well beats me.' They were now coming into Haywards Heath. 'First thing I do when I get back and get some clothes on is to join the bloody army. I'm finished with this lot because this lot is finished anyway.' They were coming out of Haywards Heath.

'This lot is *not* finished, do you see,' said Captain Loosley. 'There must always be an organization for keeping the population down, whether by force, do you see, or by propaganda. I forgive you, Oxenford,' he added generously. 'The fate of Sergeant Image must have unnerved you as, I confess, it's unnerved me, do you see, a little. But don't let it happen again. Remember, please, the difference in our ranks.'

'Aw, shut it,' said Oxenford again. 'I'm bloody freezing cold and I'm bloody hungry and I've a bloody good mind to stop the van and leave you to get on with it while I go and join that lot there.' He gestured roughly with his head towards a gipsy-like company at the roadside who were placidly eating round a fire.

'The army will get them,' said Captain Loosley calmly. 'They'll be picked up, never fear.'

'Aaaaarch,' suddenly sneezed Oxenford. And again, 'Aaaaah Chag. Blast it and damn it, I've got a cold, a real beauty. Blast your eyes, Loosley. Aaaaaaah Shok.'

'The Metropolitan Commissioner will have something to say about this, do you see,' warned Captain Loosley. 'Sheer unmitigated insubordination.'

'I thought,' said Oxenford sarcastically, 'that the purpose of the exercise was to get the Metropolitan Commissioner given the sack. I thought that was the idea.'

'That's where you're stupid, Oxenford. There will be another Metropolitan Commissioner,' said Captain Loosley loftily. 'He'll know how to deal with insubordination.'

'Aaaarch,' went young Oxenford, and then, 'Chow,' nearly running into a lamp-standard. 'It won't be you, anyway,' he said rudely. 'It won't be you who'll get the bloody job, and that's a fact. And, anyhow, I'll be in the army tomorrow or the next day. A man's life that'll be. Howrashyouare. Dog damn and blast it. Not running after poor defenceless women and kids, same as we've been doing.'

'I've heard quite enough, do you see,' said Captain Loosley. 'That will do very well, Oxenford.'

'Raaaaaarch. Blast it.'

Soon they were running into Brighton. Sunlight was merry on the sea, on the coloured dresses of the women and children, on the drab suits of the men. There seemed to be fewer people about; you couldn't have your cake and eat it too. Now they came to the lofty Government offices. 'Here we are,' said Captain Loosley. 'Drive straight in there, Oxenford, where it says *In*. Strange, I can't remember that *In* being there, do you see, when we left.'

Oxenford laughed raucously. 'You poor silly bloody clot,' he said. 'Can't you see where that *In* has come from? Can't you, you daft fool?'

Captain Loosley stared at the façade. 'Oh,' he said. 'Oh, dear.' For the great sprawling sign – *Ministry of Infertility* – had changed; its last word had lost its negative prefix.

'Ha ha,' went young Oxenford. 'Ha ha ha.' And then, 'Raaaaaaarch! Damn and blast it.'

Eight

'AND as far as possible,' said the television face of the Right Honourable George Ockham, Prime Minister, 'to pursue the good life with a minimum of State interference.' It was the face of a business tycoon – fat-jowled with firm but self-indulgent lips, hard-bargain-driving eyes behind hexagonal glasses. It could be seen only intermittently because of a transmission fault: it alternated with rapid ripples or itself dissolved into geometrical tropes and fancies; it wobbled, wambled; it split itself into autonomous grimaces; it flew pentecostally up out of the screen and, in frame after rising frame, chased its own flight. But the firm calm steady business voice remained undistorted. It spoke long, though – in the true Augustinian manner – it had little to say. Difficult times might well still lie before them, but, thanks to the spirit of hard-headed British compromise that had weathered so many crises in the past, the nation would undoubtedly win through to happier days. Confidence was the thing; Mr Ockham asked for confidence. He had confidence in the British people; let them have confidence in him. His image nodded itself to extinction and television darkness.

Tristram himself nodded, picking his teeth in the eleemosynary eating-centre which had been set up by the Chester Ladies' Fecundity Association on the north bank of the Dee. He had just consumed, listening to Mr Ockham, a fair meat-meal served by rosy bantering Cheshire girls in pleasant though austere surroundings, daffodils in jars spouting to the ceiling. Many men in his position were, and had been, eating there, though mostly, it seemed, provincial men: men let, bewildered, out of prison, now on the road to find families evacuated from the towns during diet-riots and the first dining-club atrocities; jobless men tramping to newly re-opened factories; men (but there ought to be *women,* too; where were the women?) evicted from their low-storey flats by the strong and ruthless – all tannerless.

Tannerless. Money was a problem. Tristram had found a bank open that afternoon, a branch of the State 3 in which his few guineas were deposited, doing brisk business again after the long moratorium. He had been told politely by a teller that he must draw at his own branch though, and Tristram had a grim smile at this, he was very welcome to pay in money if he wished. Banks. Perhaps those who mistrusted them were not so foolish. A man at Tarporley, so he had heard, had sewn three thousand guinea-notes into his mattress and been able to open up a general store while the banks were still closed. The small capitalists were crawling out of their holes, rats of the Pelphase but Augustine's lions.

'– Cordially invited,' a woman's voice was calling over a loudspeaker, 'to attend. Eight o'clock. A light barbecue supper will be served. Partners,' and this sounded sinister, 'for everyone.' The voice clicked out. More of an order than an invitation. A bonfire dance by the river, not in the fields. Did they hope that Dee salmon would soon start leaping again? Two things idly struck Tristram this fine, but chill, spring evening: the toughness of women; the fact that everything, however small, had to be paid for. Sighing, he rose from the table; he would take a stroll through Chester's streets. At the door an eager woman said, 'You won't forget, will you? Eight o'clock sharp. I'll be watching out for you, you greedy boy.' She giggled, a plump woman, more easily thought of as an aunt than a mistress. Greedy? In what way had he shown himself greedy? Was the term facetiously proleptic, in no wise a food-referent? Tristram combined a smirk and a grunt and went out.

Had Chester smelled like this in the days of Roman occupation – smelled of soldiery? *Army of the West – GHQ*, cried the sign-board; noble, thrilling the sound of that, Arthurian almost. As, in the days of Caesar's legionaries, the town must have smoked with the breath of slithering horses, so now the exhausts of motor-cycles gushed and plumed caerulean – dispatch-riders arriving with top-secret messages in nests of envelopes, leaving – gloved and helmeted – with such letters, kicking their machines afire to burn up one of the tentacle-roads that roared out of the city-camp, camp-city. Cryptic sign-posts pointed to *Director of Ordnance Supplies, Director of Medical Supplies, Office of Quartermaster-General.* There were lorries clattering out their freights of lumpish soldiers in their improvised uniforms; a work-ing squad – with brooms for rifles – was dismissed in a side-street; a couple of chaplains were learning shyly to salute. Cans were being unloaded into the guarded food-store.

By what hypocritical gesture of the head were the supplies being maintained? Civilian contracts with no questions asked; the troops called the anonymous tinned meat 'bully', and there was no such animal as that; the keeping of law and order was not incompatible with tolerance of the quiet work of the slaughter-house. Martial law was the only way, Tristram supposed. An army being primarily an organization set up for mass murder, morality could never be its concern. Clear the road-arteries for traffic, the country's blood; watch the water-supply; keep the main streets well-lighted, the alleys and back-lanes can look after themselves. Theirs not to reason why. I'm a simple soldier-man, sir, damn your eyes, not one of your flaming politicians: leave the dirty work to them.

The *Daily Newsdisc* was functioning once more. Tristram heard the metal voice booming from the

Garrison Officers' Mess (dim lights, a white-coated orderly, cutlery ringing silverily) and stopped to listen. The cult of Quetzlcoatl revived in Mexico: love-feasts and human sacrifice reported from Chihuahua, Moctezuma, Chilpanzingo. Meat-eating and the salting-down of meat all along Chile's long thin strip. Vigorous canning in Uruguay. Free love in Utah. Riots in the Panama Canal Zone, a loose-loving loose-feeding people unsubmissive to the newly-raised militia. In Suiyuan Province, Northern China, a local magnate with a pronounced limp had been mactated with due ceremony. 'Rice babies' had been moulded in the East Indies and drowned in the paddies. Good news of grain crops in Queensland.

Tristram walked on, seeing troops off duty laughing, their arms round local girls. He heard a band tuning up for a dance, fairy lights delicate on the buds of the riverside trees. He began to formicate all over with the languor of one digesting meat. This was the world, acquiesce in it: the mutter of love-making and the mass, the grinding of meat and the wheels of the military. Life. No, damn it, no. He pulled himself together. He was on the last stage of his journey now. With luck and lifts he might even reach Preston by morning. He had been long enough on the road; he must look forward to one known and loved pair of arms, a languor consecrated by love and private darkness, away from the fires and the gay feasts. He tramped briskly to the mouth of the road leading north and stood, jerking his raised thumb, under a signpost pointing to Warrington. He was not perhaps showing due gratitude to the duennas of the Chester Ladies' Fecundity Association, but never mind.

Fecundity ought to be a fruit of the Holy Ghost reserved to the married, anyway. Too much fornication going on.

After six or seven unheeded thumb-jerks, just as he was about to start walking, an army lorry squeal-ground to a halt by him. 'Wigan,' said the soldier-driver, 'with this here lot behind.' He gave his head a savage jolt towards the rear in indication. Tristram's heart bounded. Twenty miles north of Wigan lay Preston. Three miles west of Preston, on the Blackpool road, lay State Farm NW313. He climbed aboard, full of thanks. 'Well,' said the driver, his hands gripping the big wheel at a diameter's span, 'I reckon it won't be all that long now then, mister.'

'No,' agreed Tristram fervently.

'Tell me, then, mister,' said the driver. 'Who do you think it's going to be?' He sucked loudly at a natural pre-molar, a youngish fattish fair man with a greasy cap.

'Eh?' said Tristram. 'I'm afraid I didn't – I was thinking of something else, I'm afraid.'

'*Afraid,*' repeated the driver in satisfaction. 'That's just about it, isn't it? That's the word. There's a lot going to be afraid before long, mister, you among them, I dare say. But it stands to reason you've got to have a war. Not because anybody wants it, of course, but because there's an army. An army here and an army there and armies all over the shop. Armies is for wars and wars is for armies. That's only plain common sense.'

'War's finished,' said Tristram. 'War's outlawed. There hasn't been any war for years and years and years.'

'All the more reason why there's got to be a war,' said the driver, 'if we've been such a long time without one.'

'But,' said Tristram, agitated, 'you've no conception what war was like. I've read books about the old wars. They were terrible, terrible. There were poison gases that turned your blood to water and bacteria that killed the seed of whole nations and bombs that smashed cities in a split second. All that's over. It's got to be over. We can't have all that again. I've seen photographs,' he shivered. 'Films, too. Those old wars were ghastly. Rape, looting, torture, arson, syphilis. Unthinkable. No, no, never again. Don't say things like that.'

The driver, tilting his wheel gently, his shoulders jigging like a bad dancer's, sucked hard. 'I didn't mean that sort, mister. I meant, you know, fighting. Armies. One lot having a bash at another lot, if you see what I mean. One army facing another army, like it might be two teams. And then one lot shoots at another lot, and they go on shooting till somebody blows the whistle and they say, "This lot's won and this lot's lost." Then they dish out leave and medals and the tarts are all lined up waiting at the station. That's the sort of war I mean, mister.'

'But who,' asked Tristram, 'would go to war with whom?'

'Well,' said the driver, 'that would have to be sorted out, wouldn't it? Arrangements would sort of have to be made, wouldn't they? But, you mark my words, it's got to come.' The cargo behind him danced tinnily, jauntily, as they went over a hump bridge. 'A hero's death,' said the soldier suddenly with a sort of complacency. The battalion of tinned meat jingled applause, like some giant chestful of medals.

Nine

TRISTRAM got a lift in a Military Police van from Wigan to Standish, then the road was suddenly empty of traffic. He walked slowly and with some difficulty through the plenilunar night, his left foot giving him trouble – a thick seg and the shoe-sole worn to a neat hole. Still, he shogged along bravely, with quiet excitement trotting in front of him, its tongue out, and the night shogged with him towards morning. His feet suggested a rest at Leyland, but his heart would have none of that. On to dawn in Preston: a breather there, perhaps an eleemosynary breakfast, then on to his goal, three miles west. Morning and the town approached stealthily.

What was that ringing noise? Frowning, Tristram poked his little fingers into his ears, agitating the wax with a deafening rumble. He automatically sniffed at the waxy finger-tip (the only pleasant odour of all that the body secreted), listening. That bell-noise came from the world, not his head: it clanged out of the town itself. Bells to welcome the pilgrim in? Nonsense. It was not bells, either: it was an electronic fabrication of bells – slow-pulsing from shaking loudspeakers, throwing up a metallic spray of harmonics, demented silver. Wondering, Tristram approached. He entered Preston in full morning and was swallowed by crowds and the jubilant clanging, crying to the strangers who surrounded him, 'What is all this? What's going on?' They laughed in answer, deaf, dumb, mouthing in the mad swirl of auricular metal. A shuddering bronze lid, which miraculously seemed to let in more light, had come down in silver over the township. People were moving towards the source of the mad angelic din; Tristram followed. It was like entering the very heart of noise, noise as ultimate reality.

A grey freestone anonymous building – provincial architecture, no more than ten storeys – and loud-speakers flaring down from its roof. Tristram entered, jostled, out of the lemon sunlight, and inside the build-ing opened his mouth at the vast cubic hollowness. Never in his life had he seen an interior so large. It could not be called a room – a hall, meeting-place, place of assembly; there must be a special word and he searched for it. It was an improvisation: the cells of the old block (flats or offices) had been shelled out; room-walls had been knocked down, as jagged brick buttresses showed; the floor-ceilings of several storeys cleared, stripped, so that the eyes were shocked at the height. Tristram recognized an altar on a rostrum at the far end; rows of rough benches, people sitting waiting, kneeling praying. The appropriate terms began to creak back from his reading, as *platoon*, *battalion* had come back before in a context that, for some reason, seemed similar. *Church. Congregation.* 'You're oldin oop traffic, lad,' said a genial voice behind. Tristram took a, took a – what was the word? Took a *pew*.

Priests, a plurality of them, marched burlily in with big fat candles, a platoon (no, a section) of boy-servitors. '*Introibo ad altare Dei –*' Mixed voices, a whole storey up, in a gallery at the rear of the building, replied in song: '*Ad Deum Qui laetificat juventutem meam.*' This was some very special occasion. This was like playing chess with carved ivory horses and elephants, not with bits of shaped prison soap. *"Alleluia"* kept crashing into the liturgy. Tristram waited patiently for the Consecration, the eucharistic breakfast, but the grace before meat was very long.

A heavy-lipped bull of a priest turned from the altar to the congregation, standing at the rostrum's edge, blessing the air. 'Brethren,' he said. A speech, an oration, an address, a *sermon*. 'This is Easter Day. This morning we celebrate the resurrection or rising-from-the-dead of Our Lord Jesus Christ. Crucified for preaching the kingdom of God and brotherhood of man, His dead weight dragged down from the cross and stamped in the earth – as weed is stamped or fire-ash – He yet rose on the third day in raiment glorious as the sun and moon and all the fires of the firmament. He rose to bear witness to the world that there is no death, that death is but appearance and not reality, that the seeming forces of death are but shadows and their prevalence but a prevalence of shadows.' The priest belched gently on a fasting stomach. 'He rose to extol life everlasting, not a white-lipped ghost-life in some tenebrose noosphere –' ('Ee,' said a woman behind Tristram) '– but a totality or unity of life in which the planets dance with the amœbæ, the great unknown macrobes with the microbes that swirl in our bodies and the bodies of the beasts our fellows, all flesh is one and flesh is also corn, grass, barley. He is the sign, the eternal symbol, the perpetual recurrence made flesh; He is man, beast, corn, God. His blood also becomes our blood through its act of refreshing our sluggish warm red, coiling along its palpitating channels. His blood is not only the blood of man, beast, bird,

fish; it is also the rain, the river, the sea. It is the ecstatically pumped seed of men and it is the flowing richness
of the milk of the mothers of men. In Him we become
one with all things, and He is one with all things and
with us.

'Today in England, today throughout the English-
Speaking Union, we joyfully celebrate, with sackbut and
psaltery and loud alleluias, the resurrection of the Prince
of Life. Today, too, in far lands which in the barren
past rejected the flesh and the blood of the Eternal Life-
giver, this His rising from the tomb is hailed with a joy
like to our own, though under figures and names of out-
landish meaning and heathenish sound.' The man to
Tristram's right frowned at that sentence. 'For, though
we call Him Jesus and the veritable Christ, yet is He
beyond all names and above them, so that Christ re-arisen
will hear Himself addressed in joy and worship as
Thammuz or Adonis or Attis or Balder or Hiawatha,
and to Him all is one as all names are one, as all words
are one, as all life is one.' The preacher was silent for a
space; spring coughs hacked out from the congregation.
Then, with the irrelevance proper to a religious dis-
course, he cried with a main voice, 'Therefore, fear not.
In the midst of death we are in life.'

'Aaaargh, bloody nonsense!' called a voice from the
rear. 'You can't bring the dead back, blast you, for all
your fine talk!' Heads swivelled gratefully; there was
a scuffle; arms flailed; Tristram could not see very well.

'I think,' said the preacher, unperturbed, 'it would be
better if my interrupter left. If he will not leave volun-
tarily perhaps he could be assisted to leave.'

'Bloody nonsense! Whoring after false gods, God forgive your black heart!' And now Tristram could see who it was. He knew that moon-face, red with generous anger. 'My own children,' it yelled, 'sacrificed on the altar of Baal that you worship as the true God, God forgive you!' The big body, in its sack farmer's garments, was being pulled out fighting by struggling panting men, leaving the presence correctly backwards, its arms pinned painfully behind it. 'God forgive the lot of you, for I never shall!'

'Excuse me,' murmured Tristram, pushing out of his pew. Somebody had placed a gagging hand over his brother-in-law's retreating mouth. 'Bob,' came the muffled protest. 'Bob blasp be bop ob boo.' Shonny and his rough hard-breathing escort were already through the doorway. Tristram walked fast up the aisle. 'To resume,' the preacher resumed.

Ten

'So,' said Tristram hopelessly, 'they just took her away.'

'And then,' said Shonny dully, 'we waited and waited, but they didn't come home. And then the next day we knew what had happened. Oh, God, God.' He made a big red plate of his hands and plopped the pudding of his head on to it, sobbing.

'Yes, yes, terrible,' said Tristram. 'Did they say where they were taking her to? Did they say they were going back to London?'

'I blame myself,' said Shonny's hidden head. 'I trusted

God. It was the wrong God I was trusting, all these long years. No God who was good could let that happen, God forgive Him.'

'All for nothing,' sighed Tristram. 'All that journey wasted.' His hand trembled round his glass. They were seated in a small shop that sold water barely touched by alc.

'Mavis has been wonderful,' said Shonny, looking up, dripping with tears. 'Mavis took it like a saint or an angel. But I'll never be the same again, never. I tried telling myself that God knew why it had happened, that there was a divine reason for everything. I even came to mass this morning, ready to be like Job and to praise the Lord in the transport of my miseries. And then I saw. I saw it in that priest's fat face; I heard it in his fat voice. A false God has taken possession of them all.' He breathed in hard with a curious rattling noise like sea-dragged shingle. The few other drinkers (men in old clothes, not celebrating Easter) looked up.

'You can have other children,' said Tristram. 'You still have your wife, your home, your work, your health. But what am I to do? Where can I go, who can I turn to?'

Shonny glared at him evilly. There was scum round his lips and his chin was ill-shaven. 'Don't talk to me,' he said. 'You with your children that I've protected all these months at the risk of the lives of my whole family. You and your sly twins.'

'Twins?' Tristram stared. 'Twins, did you say?'

'With these hands,' said Shonny, and he presented them to the world, huge and hooked, 'I brought your twins to birth. And now I say: Better if I hadn't. Better if I'd let them shift for themselves, like little wild animals. Better if I'd strangled them and given them to your false greedy God with His lips dripping with blood, picking His teeth after His favourite accursed meal of little children. Then, perhaps, He would have left mine alone. Then, perhaps, He would have permitted them to come home from school unmolested, as on any other day, and let them live. Live,' he shouted. 'Live, live, live.'

'I'm sorry,' said Tristram. 'You know I'm sorry.' He paused. 'Twins,' he said in wonder. And then, vigorously, 'Where did they say they were going? Did they say they were going back to my brother in London?'

'Yes, yes, yes, I suppose so. I suppose they said something like that. It doesn't matter, anyway. Nothing matters any more.' He sucked at his glass without relish. 'My whole world's shattered,' he said. 'I have to build it up again, searching for a God I can believe in.'

'Oh,' cried Tristram in sudden irritation, 'don't be so sorry for yourself. It's people like you who've made the kind of world you say you no longer believe in. We were all safe enough in that old liberal society.' He was talking of less than a year back. 'Hungry, but safe. Once you kill the liberal society you create a vacuum for God to rush into, and then you unleash murder and fornication and cannibalism. And,' said Tristram, his heart suddenly sinking, 'you believe it's right for man to go on sinning for ever, because that way you justify your. belief in Jesus Christ,' for he saw that whatever government was in power he would always be against it.

'That's not right,' said Shonny, with surprising reasonableness. 'Not it at all. There are two Gods, you see.

They get mixed up, and it's hard for us to find the right one. Like,' he said, 'those twins, Derek and Tristram she called them. She got them mixed up when they were naked. But it's better to have it that way than to have no God at all.'

'Then what the hell are you complaining about?' snarled Tristram. The best of both worlds, as always; women always got the best of both worlds.

'I'm not complaining,' said Shonny, with frightening meekness. 'I'm going to put my trust in the real God. He'll avenge my poor dead children.' Then he clamped the two half-masks of his hands, dirty hands, over his fresh sobbing. 'You can keep your other God, your other filthy God.'

'I don't believe in either,' Tristram found himself saying. 'I'm a liberal.' Shocked, he said, 'I don't really mean that, of course. What I mean is –'

'Leave me to my misery,' cried Shonny. 'Get out and leave me alone.'

Embarrassed, Tristram mumbled, 'I'm going. I'd better start my return journey. They say there are trains running now. They say the State airlines are functioning again. So,' he said, 'she called them Tristram and Derek, did she? That was very clever.'

'You have two children,' said Shonny, removing his hands from his blear eyes. 'I have none. Go on, get to them.'

'The fact is,' said Tristram, 'the fact is that I've no money. Not a solitary tanner. If you could lend me, say, five guineas or twenty crowns or something like that –'

'You'll get no money from me.'

'A loan, that's all. I'll repay it as soon as I get a job.

It won't be long, I promise.'

'Nothing,' said Shonny, making an ugly mouth like a child. 'I've done enough for you, haven't I? Haven't I done enough?'

'Well,' said Tristram, puzzled, 'I don't know. I suppose you must have, if you say so. I'm grateful, anyway, very grateful. But you can see, surely, that I've got to get back to London and it's too much to ask me, surely, to return as I came, walking and cadging lifts. Look at this left shoe. I want to get there quickly.' He feebly banged the table with both fists. 'I want to be with my wife. Can't you see that?'

'All my life,' said Shonny sombrely, 'I've been giving, giving, giving. People have put upon me. People have taken and then laughed behind my back. I've given too much in my time. Time and work and money and love. And what have I ever got in return? Oh, God, God.' He choked.

'Be reasonable. Just a loan. Two or three crowns, say. I am, after all, your brother-in-law.'

'You're nothing to me. You're just the husband of my wife's sister, that's all. And a damned bad lot you've turned out to be, God forgive you.'

'Look here, I don't like that. You've no call to say that sort of thing.'

Shonny folded his arms, as if ordered to by a teacher, and shut his lips tight. Then, 'Nothing from me,' he said. 'Go somewhere else for your money. I've never cared for you or for your type of person. You and your Godless liberalism. And cheating, too. Having children on the sly. She should never have married you. I always said that, and Mavis said the same. Go on, get out of my sight.'

'You're a mean bastard,' said Tristram.

'I am what I am,' said Shonny, 'as God is what He is. You'll get no help from me.'

'You're a damned hypocrite,' said Tristram with something like glee, 'with your false "Lord have mercy on us" and "Glory be to God in the highest". High-sounding blasted religious phrases and not a scrap of real religion in you.'

'Get out,' said Shonny. 'Go quietly.' The bald waiter by the bar was biting his nails anxiously. 'I don't want to throw you out.'

'Anybody would think you owned the damned place,' said Tristram. 'I hope you remember this some day. I hope you remember that you refused help when it was desperately needed.'

'Go on, go. Go and find your twins.'

'I'm going,' said Tristram. He got up and plastered his rage with a grin. 'You'll have to pay for the alc, anyway,' he said. 'That's one thing you'll have to pay for.' He made a vulgar schoolboy's noise and went out in tearing anger. He stood on the pavement for a moment, hesitant, then, deciding to turn right, he caught, trudging on his way, through the smeared window of the cheap shop, a last glimpse of poor Shonny with his pudding head shaking in his hands.

Eleven

TRISTRAM walked hungry and wondering what to do,

rage still quaking inside, through the sunny Easter Preston streets. Should he stand in the gutter and beg, sing with his hand out? He was dirty and ragged enough for a beggar, he knew, gaunt, bearded, his hair a crinkly tangle. Someone out of ancient history or myth had been that not too unhappy teacher of Social Studies of less than a year ago, groomed, neat, eloquent, home to eat synthelac pudding prepared by a personable wife, the shiny black news spinning sedately on its wall-spindle. Things had not been too bad, really: just enough food, stability, a sufficiency of money, stereoscopic television on the bedroom ceiling. He choked back a dry sob.

Not far from a bus-terminal – red single-deckers filling up with passengers for Bamber Bridge and Chorley – Tristram's nostrils dilated at a briskly wind-borne smell of stew. It was a coarse charity kind of aroma – greasy metal and meat-fat mitigated by herbs – but he slavered lavishly, sucking the saliva back in as he followed his nose. In a side-street the smell blew out richly at him, heartening as low comedy, and he saw both men and women queueing outside a double-fronted shop whose windows had been rendered opaque with whitewash whorls like amateur reproductions of Brancusi's portrait of James Joyce. A metal plaque above the door said, white on scarlet, *WD North-West District Communal Feeding Centre*. God bless the army. Tristram joined the line of vagrants like himself – dusty-haired, clothes creased with sleep, fish-eyed with disappointment. One jockey of a wretched man kept doubling up as though punched in the guts, complaining monotonously of the belly-warch. A very thin woman with filthy grey hair stood upright in pathetic dignity, above these people, above begging except absent-mindedly. A quite young man sucked with desperate force at his mouth without teeth. Tristram was suddenly nudged by a jocular male bag of rags, smelling powerfully of old dog. 'What fettle?' he asked of Tristram. And then he said, nodding towards the greasy stew-aroma, 'Oo's getten chip-pan on.' Nobody else smiled. A young shapeless woman with hair like teased wool said to a bowed and sunken Oriental, 'Ad to ditch kid on't way, like. Couldn't carry im no more.' Wretched wanderers.

A ginger man in uniform, capless, arms akimbo but bent painfully forward the better to show his three chevrons of rank, now stood in the doorway and said, surveying the queue compassionately, 'The scum of the earth, the dregs of humanity,' and then, 'Right. In you come. No pushing and shoving. Plenty for everybody if you can call it a body. In, then.' The queue pushed and shoved. Inside, on the left, three men in dirty cooks' white stood with ladles over steaming drums of stew. On the right a private soldier, his tunic far too large, clattered out dull-gleaming pannikins and spoons. The hungrier members of the queue barked at each other, drooling as their doles were ladled out, clapping dirty paws over their portions, protective lids, as they staggered with them over to the rows of tables. Tristram had eaten the day before, but the morning's anger had made him ravenous. The room, whitewashed, coarsely functional, was full of the noise of sucking, the splash and tremulous clatter of spoons. Tristram, maddened by the odorous steam, supped up his stew in seconds. Hunger was now greater than before. The man next to him was licking his empty bowl. Somebody, eating too

greedily, had been sick on the floor. 'Waste,' said somebody else, 'sheer bloody waste.' There seemed to be no
second helpings. Nor was it possible to sneak out and
re-join the queue: the akimbo sergeant was watchful at
the door. It did not, as a matter of fact, seem possible to
get out at all.

A door diagonally opposite to the entrance now
opened and a uniformed man in early middle age
marched in. He was capped, polished, brushed, pressed,
holstered, and carried the three stars of a captain. His
steel-rimmed army-issue spectacles gleamed benevolently. Behind him stood a stocky two-striped man,
clipboard under his arm. Tristram, with wonder and
hope, saw that the captain carried, in addition to his
stars, a grey bag that chinked discreetly as he walked.
Money? God bless the army. God very much bless the
army. The captain stalked around the tables, surveying,
weighing, and the corporal toddled after. At Tristram's
table, 'You,' said the captain – his accent was cultured –
to an old champing man with wild hair, 'could use, perhaps, a tosheroon or so.' He dug into the bag and, half-
contemptuously, tossed a bright coin on to the table.
The old man made the ancient gesture of touching his
forelock. 'You,' said the captain to a young hungry man
who was, ironically, very fat, 'could probably make use
of a loan. Government money, no interest charged,
repayable within six months. Shall we say two guineas?'
The corporal presented his clipboard, saying, 'Sign here.'
The young man, with shame, confessed that he could
not write. 'A cross, then,' comforted the corporal, 'then
out through that door.' He nudged towards it, the door
he and the officer had entered by. 'Ah,' said the captain

to Tristram, 'tell me all about yourself.' His face was remarkably unlined, as though the army possessed some secret face-iron; he smelled curiously spicy. Tristram told him. 'A schoolmaster, eh? Well, you shouldn't have anything to worry about. How much shall we say? Four guineas? Perhaps you can be persuaded to settle for three.' He rustled the notes out of the bag. The corporal pushed his clipboard forward and seemed ready to stick an inkpencil in Tristram's eye. 'Sign here,' he said. Tristram signed, shaky, the notes clutched in the same hand. 'Now out through that door,' nudged the corporal.

The doorway seemed not to be a way out. It led into a long wide kind of hallway, whitewashed and smelling of size, and a number of ragged people were being indignant with a young and unhappy-looking sergeant. 'It's no good going on at me about it,' he said in a Northern voice pitched tight and high. 'Day after day we get them in here going on at me as if it was my fault, and I have to tell them it's nowt to do with me. Nothing,' he translated, looking at Tristram. 'Nobody made you,' he told everybody reasonably, 'do what you've just done now, did they? Some – that is to say, the old ones – got a little present. You got a loan. That'll be taken out of your pay, so much per week. Now, you needn't have taken the King's money if you didn't want to, and you needn't have signed. It was all quite voluntary.' He pronounced this last word to rhyme with 'hairy'. Tristram's heart lunged down deep then up again into his throat, as if it were on elastic.

'What is all this?' he said. 'What's going on?' To his surprise he saw the dirty-grey lady there, ramrod with *grande dame* hauteur. 'This creature,' she said, 'has the impertinence to say that we've joined the army. I never heard such nonsense. *Me* in the army. A woman of my age and position.'

'I daresay you'll do all right,' said the sergeant. 'They like them a bit younger as a rule, but you'll as like as not get a nice job looking after the auxiliaries. Women soldiers,' he explained courteously to Tristram, as though Tristram were the most ignorant one there, 'are called auxiliaries, you see.'

'Is this true?' asked Tristram, fighting for calm. The sergeant, who seemed a decent young man, nodded gloomily. He said:

'I always tell people never to sign anything till they've read it. That thing that Corporal Newlands has out there says at the top that you've volunteered to serve with the colours for twelve months. It's in pretty small printing, but you could have read it if you'd wanted.'

'He had his thumb over it,' said Tristram.

'I can't read,' said the young fat man.

'Well, then, that's your funeral, isn't it?' said the sergeant. 'They'll teach you to read, never fear.'

'This,' said the grey lady, 'is preposterous. This is an utter scandal and a disgrace. I shall go back there at once and give them back their filthy money and tell them precisely what I think of them.'

'That's the way,' said the sergeant admiringly. 'I can just see you in the orderly room, giving them what for. You'll do pretty well, you will. You'll be what they call a real old battle-axe.'

'Disgraceful.' And she made, a real old battle-axe, for the door.

'What's done can't be undone,' said the sergeant philo-

212

sophically. 'What's been signed can't be unsigned. Fair means or foul, they've got you. But twelve months isn't much, now, is it? They talked me into signing on for seven years. A right twit, I was. A mug,' he translated for Tristram. 'Between you and me, though,' he confided to all, 'there's a lot more chance of promotion if you're a volunteer. Eee, she's at it,' he said, cocking an ear. From the dining-hall the raised voice of the grey woman could be clearly heard. 'Do well, she will.' Then, 'They'll be having what they call Con Scrip Shun before long, so Captain Taylor says. A volunteer will be in a different position altogether from one of those. That stands to reason.'

Tristram began to laugh. There was a chair just inside the doorway and he sat on it the better to laugh. 'Private Foxe,' he said and laughed, crying.

'That's the way,' said the sergeant approvingly. 'That's the real army spirit. Keep smiling is what I say, it's better to laugh than do the other thing. Well,' he said, standing at ease, nodding as other pressed vagrants came in, 'you're in the army now. You might as well make the best of it.' Tristram continued to laugh. 'Just like he's doing.'

Part Five

One

'Itsy bitsy booful,' went Derek Foxe, first to one dribbling chuckling twin, then to the other. 'Boo boo boo boop a doop,' he booed to his little namesake and then, scrupulously fair, that identical phatic utterance to tiny Tristram. He was never anything but scrupulously fair, as his subordinates at the Ministry of Fertility could testify; even Loosley, demoted to rather junior executive rank could – though he was now trying to prove Derek a homosexual – hardly prate of injustice. 'Worple worple worple,' chortled Derek in serial duplicate, typing the twins with two fingers. These meanwhile, bubbling like fish, secure in their play-pen, podgily clutched the rails and performed a treadmill action. Tiny Tristram alone said, like Upanishadian thunder, 'Da da da.' 'Ah,' said Derek seriously, 'we ought to have more, lots, lots more.'

'So they can be put in the army and shot at?' said Beatrice-Joanna. 'Not likely.'

'Oh, that –' Derek, hands clasped behind, did a brief quarterdeck-pacing act round the drawing-room. He then drank off his coffee. It was a spacious drawing-room; all the rooms of the seaward-looking flat were spacious. There was space nowadays for men of Derek's rank, for their wives or pseudo-wives, their children. 'Everybody's got to take his chance,' he said. 'Her chance, too. That's why we ought to have lots more.'

'Nonsense,' said Beatrice-Joanna. She was stretched on a deep-piled chunky couch that was eight feet long and claret-coloured. She was leafing through the latest issue of *Sheek*, a fashion magazine which was all pictures. Bustles, her eye noted, were decreed by Paris for day-wear; daring décolletages were *de rigueur* for evening; Hongkong cheongsams were lascivious with fourfold slits. Sex. War and sex. Babies and bullets. 'In the old days,' she mused, 'I'd have been told that I've already exceeded my ration. And now your Ministry tells me that I've not fulfilled my quota. Mad.'

'When we're married,' said Derek, 'properly married, that is, you may feel differently about it.' He padded round to the rear of the couch and kissed her nape, its broth of goldish flue delicate in the weak sun. One of the twins, perhaps tiny Tristram, made, as on a satirical sound-track, a synchronic farting lip-noise. 'Then,' said Derek jocularly, 'I can *really* start talking about wifely duties.'

'How long now?'

'About six months. That will make it a full two years since you last saw him.' He kissed her delicious nape once more. 'The statutory period for desertion.'

'I keep thinking about him,' said Beatrice-Joanna. 'I can't help it. I had a dream a couple of nights ago. I saw Tristram quite clearly, wandering through the streets, crying out for me.'

'Dreams don't mean anything.'

'And I've been thinking about that business of Shonny saying he'd seen him. In Preston.'

'Just before they put the poor man away.'

'Poor, poor Shonny.' Beatrice-Joanna gave the twins a glance of desperate fondness. Shonny's brain turned by the loss of his children, the defection of his God, he now recited long liturgies of his own composition – in a cell in Winwick Hospital, near Warrington, Lancs. – trying to munch consecrated bedclothes. 'I can't help feeling that. That he's been wandering everywhere, all over the country, looking for me.'

'There were ways and means,' said Derek. 'Were you honestly expected to live off air, you and the two children? I've said often, and I say again now, that the most charitable thing is to think of Tristram long dead and long eaten. Tristram is ended, over. Now it's you and me. The future.' He looked, bending over her, masterfully smiling, groomed and smooth, very much like the future. 'Heavens,' he said, without anxiety. 'The time.' A clock on the far wall meekly showed it him – a stylized golden sun of a clock, fiery rays like hair-locks set all round it. 'I must fly,' he said, without hurry. And then, with even less hurry, into her ear, 'You wouldn't really like things to be any different, would you? You're happy with me, aren't you? Say you're happy.'

'Oh, I'm happy.' But her smile was wan. 'It's just that I – that I like things to be right, that's all.'

'Things are right. Very much right.' He kissed her fully on the mouth with a relish that smacked nothing of valediction. But he said, 'Now I really must fly. I've a busy afternoon ahead of me. I'll be home about six.' He did not forget the twins, kissing each on its flossy pate and blowing final phatic vocables at them. Waving, smiling, brief-case under arm, he left: the Ministry car would be waiting below.

After about three minutes Beatrice-Joanna glanced round the room somewhat furtively, then tiptoed over to the switch which operated the *Daily Newsdisc*, shiny-black as a liquorice pancake on its wall-spindle. She could not altogether explain to herself this sensation of small guilt at wanting to hear the day's news again: after all, the *Daily Newsdisc* – now one of a number of free-enterprise organs, auditory, audio-visual, even (the *Weekly Feel*) tactile – was there for anybody's re-listening. What itched in Beatrice-Joanna's brain-stem was a hint that there was something disingenuous about the news these days, something crafty and implausible which Derek and people like him knew all about (laughing up their sleeves at it) but didn't want people like her to know all about. She wanted to see if she could find a crack in the too-smooth plaster which now –

'– Secession of China from Ruspun and the declaration of China's intention – made by Premier Poh Soo Jin in Peking – to establish an independent association of states to be known in Kuo-Yü as Ta Chung-kuo, anglicized as Chinspun. Indications are already reported of aggressive intentions towards both Ruspun and Enspun, as witness raids on Kultuk and Boryza and massing of infantry in Southern Canton. There is every sign, says our Midway Island observer, of an intended annexation of Japan. With the laying bare of the western flank of Enspun –' Beatrice-Joanna clicked off the manic synthetic voice. Sheer damned nonsense. If the world were really considering starting a real war, surely there should be talk of soaring planes and plunging warships as well as trudging armies with simple portable weapons; there should, surely, be threats of the resurrection of one of those ancient but efficacious province-blasting nuclear devices. But there wasn't. That British Army improvised last year and now superseded – for the maintenance of civil order – by reasonable blue-clad bobbies, was pure infantry with minimal support of specialist corps; in the magazines and on the news-reels one saw the soldiers climbing the ramps of troopers – off for training, it was said, on the Annexe Islands or for police work in dissident corridors – up-thumbing at the cameras with a partially dentate leer, the best of British luck and pluck.

Beatrice-Joanna had almost convinced herself that she had been convinced, one evening before the stereo-telly in this very flat, that she had seen in penumbral background to the close-up of an up-thumbing cheerful Tommy a face she knew. 'Nonsense,' of course, from Derek, stretched in his purple dressing-gown. 'If Tris-tram were in the army Army Records would have his name. You sometimes forget I'm his brother and I have a certain duty. I consulted Army Records and they know nothing. I've said before, and I say again now, the most charitable thing is to think of Tristram long dead and long eaten.' Still –

She pressed an electric buzzer on a wall-panel of switches and buzzers; almost at once a cheerful (cheer-ful as a Tommy) brown girl glided in, bowing in spasms, dressed in servant's black silk-substitute. She was a pretty little orchestra of races and her name was Jane. 'Jane,' said Beatrice-Joanna, 'please get the twins ready for their afternoon outing.' 'Yes, yes, madam,' said Jane, and she wheeled the castered play-pen across the sea-green fitted carpet, clucking and creasing her face at the two treadmilling infants.

Beatrice-Joanna went to her bedroom to make herself ready for the afternoon's walk. Her dressing-table carried, in neat order, a whole pharmacy of creams and unguents; her wall-fitted wardrobes were full of gowns and costumes. She had servants, children, a handsome and successful pseudo-husband (co-ordinating sub-minister at the Ministry of Fertility, soon, it was said, to be Minister), all that love could give and money could buy. But she did not think she was really happy. A dim film in some basement projection-room of her mind occasionally flickered a sequence of things as they had been. Often called a flower by Derek (and, previously, by Tristram), had she really been a flower she would have belonged to the class Diandria. She needed two men in her life, her day to be salted by infidelity.

She now unlocked a carved camphorwood box and took from it a letter she had written the day before; it smelled deliciously of mingled camphor and sandalwood. She read through it for the seventh or eighth time before definitely making up her mind to send it. It said:

'Dearest dearest Tristram, there have been such changes in this mad world, so many strange things have been happening since we parted so unhappily, that there is nothing I can say here that will make much sense to either of us except that I miss you and love you and long for you. I'm living with Derek now, but don't think badly of me for that: I have to keep a home going for your two sons (yes, I do honestly believe they are really yours). Perhaps you have already tried to write to me, perhaps – and I firmly believe this – you have tried to get in touch with me, but I know how difficult life has been. Your brother has been most kind to me and I think he genuinely loves me, but I don't think any letter you write c/o him would ever reach me. He has his precious career to think of, a man with children standing a better chance of promotion to Minister of Fertility than a man with none, or so he says. You will remember how every day when we were together I used to take my walk by the sea, not far from Government Building. Every afternoon I still do that, wheeling my two sons in their pram, from three to four. Looking out to sea I now pray daily that the sea will send you back to me. This is my hope. I love you and if I ever hurt you I am sorry. Come back to your always loving Beattie.'

She refolded this and placed it in a fine-quality subtle-smelling envelope. Then she took her dainty ink-pencil and addressed the envelope in her bold mannish hand to Tristram Foxe, Esq., B.A., British Army. There was just a chance; it was the only way, anyway. As for Army Records – Derek must either be most influential or a great liar; she herself, one furtive afternoon after seeing that television newsreel, had telephoned the War Office (the house telephone was an extension of the Ministry switchboard) and, after endless shuttling from department to department, had finally contacted a little Scots voice which admitted to being Army Records but said coldly that private individuals could not be informed of troop locations. Something to do with security. But she was not, said Beatrice-Joanna, concerned primarily with anything so sophisticated as location; her enquiry was more fundamental, more ontological. The voice had clicked itself sternly off.

Derek had come home smiling at six and wanted to know, smiling, why she had been telephoning Army Records. Didn't she believe him, her pseudo-husband, didn't she trust him? That was the whole point: she didn't. One could forgive mendacity and untrustworthiness in a lover but hardly in a husband, even pseudo. She didn't tell him this, however. Still, his love seemed to be an unscrupulous sort of love, and that was flattering, but she preferred that sort of love in a lover.

So she went out with the twins in a pram in the winter marine sunshine, the little black-clad nurse clucking and moon-smiling at the two bubbling little men in their warm woollies, and she posted the letter in a pillar-box whose top had been whitened by seagull-droppings. It was like launching a letter in a bottle on the sea, that great unpunctual deliverer.

Two

'Sah,' snarled R.S.M. Backhouse, with a terrifying jaw-twist. '7388026 Sergeant Foxe T. Sah.' Tristram marched in in a sort of lope and saluted without grace. Lieutenant-Colonel Williams looked up sadly from his desk; his swarthy adjutant, standing behind, gave a grin of pain.

'Sergeant Foxe, eh?' said Lieutenant-Colonel Williams.

He was a handsome tired greying man wearing, at the moment, clumsy reading-spectacles. The aura of long service which beat from him was, of course, illusory: all the soldiers of all the new armies were rookies. But Lieutenant-Colonel Williams, like all the senior officers, came out of that old liberal police force almost entirely superseded by the greyboys; he had been a scholarly superintendent of the Special Branch. 'Foxe with an "e", I see,' he said now, 'like the *Book of Martyrs* man.'

'Sir,' said Tristram.

'Well,' said Lieutenant-Colonel Williams, 'there's this question of your terms of reference as a sergeant-instructor.'

'Sir.'

'Your duties are, I think, straightforward enough. You have, according to Q.M.S.I. Bartlett, fulfilled them adequately. You have done good work in the class for illiterates, for example. You have, in addition, taught elementary arithmetic, report-writing, use of the telephone, military geography and current affairs.'

'Sir.'

'And it's these current affairs that have been causing the trouble. That right, Willoughby?' He peered up at his adjutant who, picking his nose, stopped picking his nose and nodded eagerly. 'Now, let me see. You seem to have been holding certain discussions with the men. Something about Who Is The Enemy? and What's All The Fighting About? You admit that, I take it.'

'Yes, sir. In my opinion, the men have a perfect right to discuss why they're in the army and what –'

'A soldier,' said Lieutenant-Colonel Williams wearily, 'has no right to opinions. That is laid down, rightly or wrongly. Rightly, I suppose, as it's laid down.'

'But, sir,' said Tristram, 'surely we have to know what we're involved in. We're told that there's a war on. Some of the men, sir, refuse to believe it. I'm inclined to agree with them, sir.'

'Indeed?' said Lieutenant-Colonel Williams coldly. 'Well, be enlightened, Foxe. There is fighting, so there must be war. There is not perhaps a war in the ancient sense, but war and fighting are, I should have supposed, in the organized sense, in the sense of armies being involved, as good as synonymous.'

'But, sir –'

'I hadn't finished, Foxe, had I? As far as these two questions of who and why are concerned, those are – and you must take it from me apodictically – no business of soldiers. The enemy is the enemy. The enemy is the people we're fighting. We must leave it to our rulers to decide which particular body of people that shall be. It's nothing to do with you or with me or with Private Snooks or Lancejack Dogsbody. Is that quite clear?'

'But, sir –'

'Why are we fighting? We're fighting because we're soldiers. That's simple enough, isn't it? For what cause are we fighting? Simple again. We're fighting to protect our country and, in a wider sense, the whole of the English-Speaking Union. From whom? No concern of ours. Where? Wherever we're sent. Now, Foxe, I trust all this is perfectly clear.'

'Well, sir, what I –'

'It's very wrong of you, Foxe, to disturb the men by starting them thinking and making them ask questions.'

He examined the sheet in front of him, droning. 'Very interested, Foxe, I take it you are, in the enemy and fighting and so forth?'

'Well, sir, in my view –'

'We're going to give you an opportunity for closer contact. Good idea, Willoughby? You approve, Sergeant-major? I'm taking you, Foxe, off instructional duties w.e.f. today, 1200 hours. You'll be posted from HQ Company to one of the rifle companies. It's B Company, I believe, Willoughby, that's short of a platoon sergeant. Right, Foxe. It will do you a lot of good, lad.'

'But, sir –'

'Salute!' cried R.S.M. Backhouse, formerly a sergeant of police. 'About turn! Quick march!' Tristram left-right-left-right-lefted out, furious and apprehensive. 'Better report now,' said the R.S.M., in the more brotherly tones of the mess.

'What did he mean,' asked Tristram, 'when he talked about closer contact? What was he getting at?'

'I reckon he meant what he said,' said the R.S.M. 'I reckon some will be on the move before long. Won't be no time for teaching them their ABC and their once times table then, there won't. Right, Sarnt, off you go.'

Tristram, no very soldierly figure, tramped to B Company Office, his boots ringing and sparking on the metal deck. This – Annexe Island B6 – was an artifact of limited area anchored in the East Atlantic, intended originally to accommodate population overflow, now compactly holding a brigade. All that could be seen of the natural world was a bitter winter sky and, railed off all round, the grey acid sea. This endless dual ambient made one glad to turn inward, to the empty discipline, the childish training, the warm fug of barrack-room and company office. Tristram entered B Company lines, reported to the C.S.M. – a slack-mouthed stupid Nordic giant – and then was admitted to the presence of Captain Behrens, O.C. B Company. 'Good,' said Captain Behrens, a fat white man with very black hair and moustache. 'That makes the company about up to strength. You'd better cut along and report to Mr Dollimore – he's your platoon commander.' Tristram saluted, nearly fell over executing his about-turn, and cut along. He found Lieutenant Dollimore, an amiable young man with idiot spectacles and mild acne rosacea, giving his platoon a lesson in the naming of parts of the rifle. Rifles – there had been, Tristram knew, rifles in those ancient pre-atomic wars; the organization, nomenclature, procedure, armament of this new British Army all seemed to have come out of old books, old films. Rifles, indeed. 'Cocking piece,' pointed Mr Dollimore. 'No, sorry, that's the firing pin. Bolt, striker – What's this one called, Corporal?'

'Sear spring, sir.' A squat middle-aged two-striper looked on, standing to attention, prompting, helping, as now.

'Sergeant Foxe reporting, sir.'

Mr Dollimore gazed with mild interest at Tristram's idiosyncratic salute and snapped it with a bizarre allomorph of his own – a briefly fluttering coxcomb of fingers at his brow. 'Good,' he said, 'good, good.' A wash of vapid relief animated his face. 'Naming of parts,' he said. 'You can take over.'

Tristram looked at the platoon in bewilderment. Thirty men were squatting in the lee of a sleeping-hut, grinning or gawping up. He knew most of them; most of them had had to come to him for rudimentary educational instruction; most of them were still analphabetic. The other ranks of this entire brigade (East Atlantic) were pressed thugs, corner-boys, sexual perverts, gibberers, morons. Still, as far as the naming of the rifle's parts was concerned, he and they were much on a level of ability. 'Very good, sir,' said Tristram and, cunning, 'Corporal.'

'Sarnt?'

'You can take over.' Tristram shuffled into step with Mr Dollimore, who was walking in the direction of his mess. 'What do you actually do with them, sir?'

'Do with them? Well, there's not very much one *can* do, is there?' Mr Dollimore opened his mouth suspiciously at Tristram. 'I mean, all that's laid down is that they learn how to fire that gun of theirs, isn't that it? Oh, and to keep themselves clean, of course, as far as they can.'

'What's going on, sir?' said Tristram somewhat sharply.

'What do you mean – what's going on? That's all that's going on, that that I told you.' They marched metallically, sparkily, across the open winter Atlantic deck of the barren man-made island.

'What I meant was,' said Tristram, with more patience, 'have you heard anything about our going into action?'

'Action? Action against whom?' Mr Dollimore paused in his march the better to stare at Tristram.

'Against the enemy.'

'Oh, I see.' Mr Dollimore used a tone implying that there were hosts other than the enemy that one could go into action against. Tristram crawled all over with a ghastly intimation that Mr Dollimore must be regarded as expendable; if he was expendable, then so was his platoon sergeant. And then, it being just noon, a scratchy record hissed from the loudspeakers, a synthetic bugle blared its angelus, and Mr Dollimore said, 'I just hadn't thought of that. I thought *this* was meant to be a sort of action, really. I thought we were sort of doing a sort of protection job.'

'We'd better go and look at Battalion Orders,' said Tristram. An orderly-room orderly was pinning them up – flapping desolate surrender flags in the Atlantic wind – as they approached the prefabricated huts (ringing with typewriter-bells) of Battalion Headquarters. Tristram nodded, grim, reading faster than his officer. 'That's it, then,' he said. Mr Dollimore, mouth open at it, said, 'Oh, oh, I see. What's that word? Oh, oh, I see.' It was all there, crisp and cold as a lettuce though less digestible. A movement order from Brigade: a draft of six hundred officers and men – two hundred from each battalion – to parade for embarkation at 0630 hours the following day. 'Yes, yes,' said Mr Dollimore eagerly, 'we're in it, you see.' He pointed with joy as though he had his name in the papers. 'There – 2nd Battalion: B Company.' And then, surprisingly, he stood to awkward attention and said, 'Now God be thanked Who has matched us with His hour.'

'I beg your pardon?' said Tristram.

'If I should die, think only this of me,' said Mr Dollimore. It was as if part of his school reading had been an index of first lines. ' "Ye have robbed, said he," ' said he, ' "ye have slaughtered and made an end." '

'That's more like it,' said Tristram, though his head reeled. 'That's a good deal more like it.'

Three

THEY could hear sea transport hooting in at midnight. The men had been sent to bed at ten, stuffed with cocoa and bully, having suffered an inspection of rifles and feet, had deficiencies of clothing and equipment made up, and been issued with many rounds of live ammunition. After three other ranks had been shot accidentally dead and the C.S.M. of HQ Company sustained a flesh wound in the buttock, this issue was withdrawn as premature: the troops would be given their bullets – strictly for the enemy – at the base camp at the port of disembarkation.

'But who is this damned enemy?' asked Sergeant Lightbody for the thousandth time. He lay in the bunk above Tristram, on his back, head resting on folded hands, a handsome sardonic young man with a Dracula jaw. Tristram was writing a letter to his wife, sitting up with blankets round his knees. He was sure she would not receive it, as he was sure she had not received the thirty-odd others he had written, but writing to her was like launching a prayer, a prayer for better times, normality, the decent ordinary comforts of home and love. '– Moving off into action tomorrow. Where, God knows. Be assured that you will be in my thoughts as always. We shall be together again soon, perhaps sooner than we think. Your loving Tristram.' He wrote her name on a cheap canteen envelope and sealed the letter in; he then scribbled his invariable covering note: 'Swine who call yourself my brother, give this to my wife, you unloving hypocritical bastard. All everlasting hate from T.F.' He addressed his outer envelope to D. Foxe, Government Building, Brighton, Greater London, being quite sure that Derek was of that type who would have power, in his trimmer's Vicar-of-Bray way, whatever party reigned. Derek was quite probably behind this war, if there was a war. The C.O.'s definition of 'enemy' was wrong. 'You know what I think?' said Sergeant Lightbody, when Tristram had answered that first question to himself and his own satisfaction but not aloud at all. 'I think there is no enemy. I think that as soon as we get aboard that trooper they'll just sink it. I think they'll drop a few bombs on it and smash us all to smithereens. That's what I think.'

'There aren't any bombing planes,' said Tristram. 'Bombing planes don't exist any more. They went out a long time ago.'

'I've seen them on the films,' said Sergeant Lightbody.

'Very ancient films. Films of the twentieth-century wars. Those ancient wars were very complex and elaborate.'

'They'll split us with torpedoes.'

'Another obsolete technique,' said Tristram. 'No warships, remember.'

'All right,' said Sergeant Lightbody. 'Poison gas, then. They'll get us somehow. We won't have a chance to fire a single shot.'

'Possible,' conceded Tristram. 'They wouldn't want to damage our uniforms or equipment or the ship itself.'

He shook himself, asking, 'Who the hell do we mean when we talk about "they"?'

'Obvious, I should have thought,' said Sergeant Lightbody. 'By "they" we mean the people who get fat through making ships and uniforms and rifles. Make them and destroy them and make them again. Go on doing it for ever and ever. They're the people who make the wars. Patriotism, honour, glory, defence of freedom – a load of balls, that's what it is. The end of war is the means of war. And *we* are the enemy.'

'Whose enemy?'

'Our own. You mark my words. We shan't be alive to see it, but we're in now for an era of endless war – endless because the civilian population won't be involved, because the war will be conveniently far away from civilization. Civilians love war.'

'Only,' said Tristram, 'presumably, so long as they can go on being civilians.'

'Some of them will be able to – those who govern and those who make the money. And their women, of course. Not like the poor bitches we'll be fighting side by side with – if they kindly allow us to live, that is, till we get to the other shore.'

'I've not,' said Tristram, 'clapped eyes on one single auxiliary since I joined.'

'Auxiliaries? That's a load of balls, too. Battalions of women, that's what they've got, whole damned regiments of them. I ought to know – my sister got conscripted into one. She writes now and again.'

'I didn't know that,' said Tristram.

'According to her, they seem to do pretty well what we do. Damn all, in other words, except practising how

233

to shoot. Marking time till they drop a bomb on the poor bitches.'

'Do you,' asked Tristram, 'very much mind the prospect of being killed?'

'Not all that much. It's best to be caught by surprise. I shouldn't like to lie in bed, waiting for it. When you come to think of it,' said Sergeant Lightbody, settling himself snug as in his coffin, 'that business about "Let me like a soldier fall" has a lot in its favour. Life's only choosing when to die. Life's a big postponement because the choice is so difficult. It's a tremendous relief not to have to choose.' In the distance the sea transport bellowed, as in derision of these trite aphorisms.

'I intend to live,' said Tristram. 'I have so much to live for.' The sea transport bellowed again. It did not waken the four other sergeants in the billet; they were rough men, inclined to jeer at Tristram because of his accent and pretensions to polite learning, now snoring after a heavy mess-night on alc. Sergeant Lightbody said nothing more and was soon lightly asleep himself, neatly asleep, as if he had carved himself a dainty helping of oblivion. But Tristram was in a strange bed in a strange barrack-room, the bed of Sergeant Day (discharged dead of a botulism) whom he was now replacing. All night long the sea transport roared as if hungry for its freight of expendables, unwilling to wait till breakfast-time, and Tristram, tossing in dirty blankets, listened to it. Endless war. He wondered. He did not think that possible, not if the law of the historical cycle was a valid law. Perhaps, all these years, the historiographers had been unwilling to recognize history as a spiral, perhaps because a spiral was so difficult to

234

describe. Easier to photograph the spiral from the top, easier to flatten the spring into a coil. Was war, then, the big solution after all? Were those crude early theorists right? War the great aphrodisiac, the great source of world adrenalin, the solvent of ennui, *Angst*, melancholia, accidia, spleen? War itself a massive sexual act, culminating in a detumescence which was not mere metaphorical dying? War, finally, the controller, the trimmer and excisor, the justifier of fertility?

'War,' bawled the trooper in the metal bay. And, turning over in his heavy sleep, 'War,' imploded snoring Sergeant Bellamy. All over the world, at this very moment, infants by the million were fighting into the outer air bellowing 'War'. Tristram yawned, and his yawn was 'War'. He was desperately weary but could not sleep, despite the lullaby ('War' on so many instruments) around him. The night, however, was not very long; it became arbitrary morning at 0400 hours, and Tristram was thankful not to have to undergo the agony of his fellow-sergeants, groaning back to the world, cursing to be dead again as the synthetic bugle bounced reveille all over the camp.

Four

SPARKS on the morning-night road outside its barrack-room as No. 1 Platoon fell in, coughs, hawks, curses five feet above the sparks. Corporal Haskell syringed light from a thin torch on to the nominal roll held by his sergeant. Tristram, in steel helmet and a raglan great-coat of ancient design, called the names into the wind:

'Christie.'

'Sarnt.'

'Crump.'

'Boogger off.'

'Gashen. Howell. Mackay. Muir. Talbot.' Several men answered, some obscenely. 'Better count them,' said Tristram. Corporal Haskell took his thin-rayed torch to each trio of faces, disclosing serially decollated masks, horrible apparitions in the Atlantic blackness. 'Twenty-nine, Sarnt,' said Corporal Haskell. 'O'Shaughnessy got hisself shot last night.'

'Platoon shun,' suggested Tristram. 'Move to the right in threes. By the left quick march.' This total order was roughly obeyed. The platoon sparked off, left-wheel-ing, right-wheeling, halting on the wrong foot at the company lines. The other platoons came shambling up severally, fire at their heels, barked at, and the platoon commanders came out to take posts. Captain Behrens eventually appeared, a milk-white ghost in an officer's raincoat, to march the company off to the battalion parade-ground. Here, arc-lamped like a tattoo, mass was said by the Battalion chaplain, yawning and shivering as he made his obeisances at the canopied altar. There was bread to be transubstantiated (a bumper harvest last year) but still no wine: blackcurrant-flavoured alc went into the chalice. The chaplain, a long unhappy-looking man, blessed the troops and their cause; some of the troops ironically blessed him back.

Breakfast and, above the champing and sucking, the C.O. gave his valedictory speech over the loudspeakers.

'You will be fighting an evil and unscrupulous enemy in the defence of a noble cause. I know you will cover yourselves in glo in glo in glo in glo craaaaaark come back alive and therefore I say godspeed and all the luck in the world go with you.' A pity, thought Tristram, drinking tea-substitute in the sergeants' mess, a pity that a cracked record should make that perhaps sincere man sound so cynical. A sergeant from Swansea, Western Province, got up from the table singing in a fine tenor, 'Cover yourselves in glow, in glow, in glo-o-ow.'

At 0600 hours the battalion's share of the draft, having drawn the unexpired portion of the day's rations, marched – packed, strapped, water-bottled, helmeted, rifled, all cartridge-pouches (except for those of the officers and N.C.O.s) safely empty – down to the quay. Their transport waited, sparsely lighted but its name covered in glow: T3 (ATL) *W. G. Robinson London*. The smell of sea, oil, unclean galleys, merchant seamen in turtle jerseys spitting from the top deck; the sudden appearance of a bawling scullion emptying swill over the side; the plaintive pointless hoot of the siren. Tristram took in the scene as they were fallen out to wait – the drama of hard shadow, bales, gantries, the scurrying RTO men, the troops already unwrapping their rations (bully between doorsteps) as they stood or squatted. Mr Dollimore, withdrawn from his fellow-subalterns, gaped ever and anon up at the black sky as at a source of eventual glory. The tripartite draft completed itself – more troops marching on to lip-farts, cheers and up-your-pipe V-signs. The brigade major appeared, dressed as for a riding-lesson, saluted and saluting. Breath rose from speaking mouths like cartoon-dialogue. Oil was steadily pumped in by pipe, the nozzle asp-like at the ship's breast. A C.S.M. from another battalion took off his helmet to scratch a head obscenely bald. Two privates punched each other in yelping gleeful play-fight. A tall captain irritably rubbed his crotch. The ship's siren booed. A lance-corporal's nose bled. Like a Christmas tree the covered gangway suddenly lit up with pretty lights. Some troops groaned. 'Attedtiod,' called a loudspeaker voice, muffled and denasalized. 'Attedtiod. The ebbarkatiod will dow cobbedce. Ebbark id order of codstituedt battaliods, duberically.' Officers called and pleaded, taking post with the rocking ship for background. Tristram beckoned Corporal Haskell. Between them they ranged their platoon, blaspheming and chortling, at right angles to the ship's side. Mr Dollimore, recalled from dreams of England far and honour a name, counted with mouth and fingers. The six platoons from 1st Battalion went aboard first; one man's rifle fell over the side to everyone's joy; a clumsy near-imbecile tripped, nearly collapsing the men ahead like a card-pack. But, on the whole, it was a smooth embarkation. 2nd Battalion, No. 1 Platoon leading it up. Tristram saw his men into a troop-deck with hammock-hooks (hammocks to be drawn later, and fixed mess-tables; cold air hummed in, but the bulkheads sweated. 'Not sleepin in one of them buggers,' said Talbot, told about hammocks. 'Doss down on the floor like, that's about it.' Tristram went off to find his own quarters.

'There's one thing I'll bet,' said Sergeant Lightbody, easing his pack off, 'and that's that they'll batten down the hatches or whatever the nautical term is. You'll see. They won't let us up on deck. Rats in a trap, by God or

Dog.' He lay down, as though highly satisfied, on the shallow tray of a lower bunk. From the thigh-pocket of his antique battle-dress he drew out a scarred volume. 'Rabelais,' he said. 'Do you know of this old writer? *"Je m'en vais chercher un grand peut-être."* That's what he said on his death-bed. "I go to seek a great perhaps." Me too. All of us. "Ring down the curtain, the farce is finished." That's something else he said.'

'That's French, isn't it?'

'French. One of the dead languages.'

Sighing, Tristram heaved himself on to the upper bunk. Other sergeants – tougher, stupider perhaps – were already starting card-games; one group was even quarrelling over an alleged mis-deal. *'Vogue la galère!'* called Sergeant Lightbody's voice. The ship did not obey at once but, after about half an hour, they heard the clank of casting-off and, soon after that, the steady engine throbbing like a sixty-four-foot organ-stop. As Sergeant Lightbody had prophesied, no one was allowed on deck.

Five

'When's grub up, Sarge?'

'There'll be no grub up, today,' said Tristram patiently. 'You drew rations, remember. But you're supposed to send someone to the galley for cocoa.'

'I ate it,' said Howell. 'I ate me dinner when we was waiting to get on board. Bloody imposition I call it. Bloody half-starved and bloody f – ed about and being bloody sent to be bloody shot at.'

'We're being sent to fight the enemy,' said Tristram. 'We'll have our chance to shoot, never fear.' He had spent much of the battened-down morning cleaning his pistol, a rather beautifully made weapon which, thinking to serve out his time as a pacific instructor, he had never expected to have to use. He imagined the surprised expression of somebody toppling, shot dead by it; he imagined a face exploding in a riot of plum-jam, the mashing of the lineaments of surprise or any other emotion; he imagined himself, dentures and contact-lenses and all, suddenly become a man, performing the man's act of killing a man. He closed his eyes and felt the finger on the trigger of the pistol in his mind gently squeeze; the surprised face before him was the face of Derek; Derek, in the single smart crack, became jam pudding perched on a stylish jacket. Tristram, opening his eyes, was at once aware of how he must look to his troops – fierce, with slit eyes and a killer's grin, an example to them all.

But the men were restless, peevish, bored, inclined to reverie, in no mood for dreaming of blood. They sat about, chins in palms, elbows on knees, their eyes glassy with visions. They passed round snapshots while somebody played – most melancholy of instruments – a mouth-organ. They sang:

> We'll be coming home,
> Coming, coming home.
> Some day soon,
> January or June,
> Evening, morning or afternoon –

Tristram, back on his bunk, brooding, felt a shiver break over him as he listened to the sad little song. It seemed to him that he had been suddenly transported to a time and place he had never visited before, a world out of books and films, ineffably ancient. Kitchener, napoo, Bottomley, heavies, archies, zeppelins, Bing Boys – the words, fragrant and agonisingly evocative, sang over the song like a descant.

> – So just you stand and wait
> By the garden gate
> Till my ship comes bouncing o'er the foam.
> We'll be together
> For ever and ever,
> Never more to roam –

He lay transfixed, breathing hard. This was no operation of what the old SF writers called a 'time-warp': this was really a film, really a story, and they had all been caught in it. The whole thing was fictitious, they were all characters in somebody's dream.

> – He'll be coming,
> We'll be coming,
> I'll be coming home.

He vaulted from his bunk. He shook Sergeant Lightbody. 'We've got to get out of here,' he panted. 'There's something wrong, something evil.'

'Just what I've been trying to tell you all along,' said Sergeant Lightbody calmly. 'But we can't do anything about it.'

'Oh, pipe down for Christ's sake,' called a sergeant trying – for all sea-time was one – to sleep.

'You don't understand,' said Tristram urgently, still shaking. 'It's evil because it's unnecessary. If they want to kill us why don't they just get on with it, here and now? Why didn't they kill us over on B6? But they don't want that. They want us to go through an illusion –'

'An illusion of choice,' said Sergeant Lightbody. 'I'm inclined to agree with you now. I think it's going to be a rather prolonged illusion. Not too prolonged, I hope.'

'But why, why?'

'Perhaps because we've a government that believes in everybody having the illusion of free will.'

'Do you think this ship's really moving?' Tristram listened. The ship's engines organ-stopped on, comforting to the belly as a warm poultice, but it was impossible to tell whether –

'I don't know. I don't care.'

The ship's Orderly Sergeant came in, a boily young man with horse-teeth and a neck like twisted cables. He wore a cap and an arm-band – SOS. 'What's going on up there?' asked Tristram.

'How should I know? Bleeding fed up I am, copping this lot.' He dove into his thigh-pocket. 'Ought to be a post corporal,' he said. He shuffled letters. Letters? 'Got enough to flipping do. The O.C. Troops is a right bastard. Here,' he said, throwing the bundle in the middle of a card-game 'Roll on, Death, and let's have a go at the angels.'

'Where did you get those?' frowned Sergeant Lightbody, puzzled.

'From the Ship's Orderly Room. They reckon they got them dropped by helicopter.' There was a scramble. One of the card-players whined, 'Just as I got a decent effin hand, too.'

One for him, one for Tristram. His first, his very first, his literally the absolutely bloody first since joining. Was this ominous, part of the film? He knew the writing; it made his heart dance. He lay on his bunk, very weak and trembling, to slice it open with a delirious finger, sweating. Yes, yes, yes, yes. It was her, she, his loving – sandalwood and camphorwood. Dearest dearest Tristram, changes in mad world, strange happening parted so unhappily, nothing can say here except miss you, love you, long for – He read it four times, then seemed to faint. Coming to, he found he was still clutching it. – Pray daily sea will send you back to me. Love you and if ever hurt you sorry. Come back to your – Yes, yes, yes, yes. He would live. He would. They wouldn't get him. He trembled down from his bunk to the deck, squeezing the letter like his week's pay. Then he unashamedly knelt down, closed eyes, joined hands. Sergeant Lightbody gaped at that. One of the card-players said, 'Bugger there having a word with the C.O.' and dealt swiftly and with skill.

Six

THREE more days in the ship's womb, perpetual electric light, beating of the engines, sweating of the bulkheads, hum of the ventilators. Hard-boiled eggs for breakfast, slabs of bread and bully for lunch, cake for tea, cocoa and cheese for supper, constipation (a new day-long preoccupation) at the troops' heads. And then, one sleepy afterlunch, hooting from above and counter-hooting, very distant, later a heavy grating unwinding of a mile of anchor-chain, the voice of the Ship's R.S.M. over the Tannoy: 'Disembarkation at 1700 hours, tea-meal at 1600 hours, parade on troop-decks in F.S.M.O. at 1630 hours.'

'Can you hear that noise?' asked Sergeant Lightbody, frowning hard in the direction of his cocked left ear.

'Guns?'

'That's what it sounds like.'

'Yes.' Bits of old song spiralled through Tristram's brain, fuming up from some forgotten source: '– We were up at Loos When you were on the booze, The booze that no one here knows.' (Where was Loos and what were they doing there?) 'Take me back to dear old Blighty, Put me on the train to –' (Blighty was a wound that got you repatriated, wasn't it? The wound glowed desirably, so did England; England and the wound became one. How tragic man's lot.) Drearily, members of his platoon were droning in sentimental reprise:

> We'll be together
> For ever and ever,
> Never more to roam –

Tristram chewed and chewed at the dry seedcake they were given for tea; he almost had to push the bolus down with his finger. After tea he put on the greatcoat which, with its row of metal buttons straight down the front, gave him the look of a child's drawing of a man, and the shallow steel helmet like an inverted bird-bath. He heaved on his back-pack and hung his side-pack; he clipped on his ammunition-pouches and dryly clicked his pistol. Soon, an upright soldier, he was ready for his platoon and Mr Dollimore. When he entered their mess-deck he found Mr Dollimore already there, saying, 'This old country we love so well. We'll do our best for her, won't we, chaps?' His eyes shone through their glasses, his forehead was as moist as the bulkheads. The platoon averted their eyes, embarrassed. Tristram suddenly felt a great love for them.

Sea-air blew in icily: the hatches were open. Over the Tannoy the Ship's R.S.M. began, indifferently, to call out the order of disembarkation. Tristram had time to clomp out on deck. Darkness, rare lamps, ropes, hawsers, spitting jerseyed seamen, razor cold, thumps and crashes from the land, explosive flashes. 'Where are we?' Tristram asked a sailor with a flat face. The sailor shook his head and said that he didn't speak English: '*Ying kuo hua, wo pu tung.*' Chinese. The sea hissed and whooshed, the language of a foreign sea. Foreign? He wondered.

Platoon after platoon minced down the steep ramp in their great boots. A dark quay reeked of oil. Lamps were few, as if some modified black-out regulation prevailed. RTO men loped round with clipboards. MPs strolled in pairs. A red-tabbed major with a false patrician accent haw-hawed, slapping his flank with a leather-bound baton. Mr Dollimore was summoned, with other subalterns, to a brief conference near some sheds. Inland the

245

crumps of heavies and squeals of shells, sheet lightning, all part of the war film. An unknown captain with corniculate moustaches spoke to open-mouthed Mr Dollimore and his fellows, gesticulating much. Where were the brigade's own captains? Tristram, uneasy, could see no officer of the brigade higher than lieutenant. So. Captain Behrens had merely escorted his company to the ship. Only lieutenants and below, then, considered expendable. Mr Dollimore came back, rather breathily saying that they had to march to the base camp, a mile inland.

They marched off, led by the strange captain, platoon after platoon. The troops sang softly, nocturnally:

> We'll be coming home,
> Coming, coming home.
> Some day soon,
> January or June,
> Evening, morning or afternoon –

Moonless the early evening. The flashes showed pruned trees like stage cut-outs on either side of the metalled road. Hedgeless, farmless country. But Corporal Haskell said, 'I know this place. I swear I do. There's something in the air. Soft. Kerry or Clare or Galway. I travelled this whole west coast in peacetime,' he said almost apologetically. 'Buying and selling, you know. I know this part of Ireland like the back of my hand. A rainy softness,' he said, 'if you catch my meaning. So it's the Micks we're going to fight. Well. Devils for a scrap they are. No hard feelings after, though. Cut your head and plaster it.'

Approaching the base camp they marched to attention. Barbed-wire perimeter, concrete gate-posts, an unsteady gate skirred open by the sentry. Huts with lights. Little activity. A man walking singing, balancing cakes on top of mugs of tea. The doleful hollow clatter of table-laying in a hovel lettered SERGEANTS' MESS, the smell of frying in fat not hot enough. The draft was halted; the men were told off, platoon after platoon, to follow to their allotted barrack-rooms conducting C3 lance-corporals in plimsolls (smug with the smugness of depot staff); the sergeants were led to quarters without comfort – one bare transit-camp red bulb in the ceiling, dusty kapok-oozing biscuits to lie on, no bedsteads, no extra blankets, a dirty stove unlighted. A gaunt C.Q.M.S. was their conductor. 'Where are we?' asked Tristram. 'Base Camp 222.' 'Yes, we know that, but where?' He sucked his teeth in answer and went off.

'Listen,' said Sergeant Lightbody, standing, their kit dumped, by the door with Tristram. 'Do you notice anything queer about that crumping noise?'

'There are so many noises.'

'I know, but just listen. It's coming from over there. Dada *rump*, dada *rump*, dada *rump*. Can you pick it out?'

'I think so.'

'Dada *rump*. Dada *rump*. What does it remind you of?'

'It's a very regular sort of rhythm, isn't it? I see what you mean: *too* regular.'

'*Exactly*. Doesn't it remind you a bit of the C.O.'s farewell speech?'

'Good God,' said Tristram, freshly shocked. 'A

cracked gramophone record. Would that be possible?'

'Very much possible. Loud amplifiers. Magnesium flashes. Electronic war, gramophony war. And the enemy, poor devils, are seeing and hearing it too.'

'We've got to get out of here,' trembled Tristram.

'Nonsense. You're as trapped here as you were on that ship. An electrified perimeter, a sentry told to shoot without asking questions. We've got to see it through.'

But they walked together to the twelve-feet-high wire fence. It was a sturdy piece of knitting. Tristram sprayed the damp ground with the platoon torch. 'There,' he said. In the tiny spotlight lay a sparrow's corpse, charred as from a grill. Then a rabbity lance-corporal approached them, capless, tunic collar undone, swinging an empty tea-mug. 'Keep away from there, mate,' he said, with depot staff insolence. 'Electric, that is. A lot of volts. Burn you to buggery.'

'Where exactly are we?' asked Sergeant Lightbody.

'Base Camp 222.'

'Oh, for God's sake,' cried Tristram. '*Where?*'

'That doesn't apply,' said the lance-corporal with a sagacity worthy of his stripe. '*Where* doesn't mean anything. It's just a bit of land, that's all.' They could hear motor noises in crescendo on the road outside the camp. A three-ton lorry bounced by with full lights, travelling to the coast, then another, another, a convoy of ten. The lance-corporal stood to attention till the last tail-light had passed. 'The dead,' he said, with quiet satisfaction. 'Lorry-loads of corpses. And just to think, only two nights ago some of that lot were in here, taking a stroll before supper as you are, talking to me as it might be yourselves.' He shook his head in factitious grief. The distant gramophone record went Dada *rump*, dada *rump*.

Seven

NEXT morning, shortly after mass, they were told that they would be going up to the front that very evening, a 'show' of some sort being imminent. Mr Dollimore shone with joy at the prospect. 'Blow out, you bugles, over the rich dead!' he quoted, tactless, to his platoon.

'You seem to have the death-urge pretty strongly,' said Tristram, cleaning his pistol.

'Eh? Eh?' Mr Dollimore recalled himself from his index of first lines. 'We shall survive,' he said. 'The Boche will get what's coming to him.'

'The Boche?'

'The enemy. Another name for the enemy. During my officers' training course,' said Mr Dollimore, 'we had films every evening. It was always the Boche. No, I'm telling a lie. Sometimes it was Fritz. And Jerry, sometimes.'

'I see. And you also had war poetry?'

'On Saturday mornings. After break. For our morale, Captain Auden-Isherwood said. That was one of my favourite lessons.'

'I see.'

A cold dry day with a dusty wind. Barbed wire of high voltage, WD signboards, blasted-looking country beyond the perimeter, dispiriting as that bilious Atlantic had been, all round B6. There were still distant crashes and bumps – a twenty-four-hour performance, probably with three shifts of lance-corporal disc-jockeys – but no fire in the sky. At noon an ancient aircraft – strings, struts, an open cockpit and waving goggled aeronaut – lurched over the camp and away again. 'One of ours,' Mr Dollimore told his platoon. 'The gallant R.F.C.' Luncheon of bully and dehydrated greens reconstituted; a couple of hours on the charpoy; a tea-meal of fish-paste and Arbuckle's Individual Fruit Pies. Then, with the sun's wreck seaward – a celestial panful of broken eggs – came the drawing of ammunition from the quartermaster's stores, also a tin of bully per man and a grey hunk of cornbread. The bully-tin had a Chinese label whose key-words were:

Tristram grinned at that; any fool could read the bifurcated second word (the essence of man, then, to the Chinese, was bifurcation?) if he had a sister who worked in China. What, incidentally, had happened to her? What to his brother in America? He had received one letter in eleven months, one only, from one person dear to him, but that person most dear. He patted his breast-pocket where it lay safe. *Shou Jên*, eh? The Romanized transliteration was clear at the bottom of the label. Ripe, soft, properly cooked man.

Twilight, and they paraded in marching order, water-bottles filled, bayonets fixed, steel helmets covered with steel-helmet covers. Mr Salter of one of the other battalions appeared to take the parade, newly promoted to

Captain Salter and self-conscious about it. He seemed to have directions written out for him on a bit of paper; there was no guide. He told them, squeaking a little, to move to the right in threes, and Tristram, moving, wondered for the first time at that anachronism. Surely, in that prototypical war, they had formed fours? But the essence of modern war seemed to be eclectic simplicity: let us not be too pedantic. They marched to attention out of camp. Nobody waved them good-bye except the sentry who should, by rights, have saluted with his rifle. They left-wheeled and, after a quarter-mile, marched at ease. Nobody sang, though. The fixed bayonets looked like a Birnam Wood of spikes. Between crumps, bumps, thumps – more widely spaced than before and, surely, that cracked record had been discarded – one could hear the glug of bouncing water in water-bottles. There were flashes of sky-fire; on either side of the road the black cut-out tree-corpses stood out bleakly in the sudden light.

They marched through a hamlet, a contrived Gothic mess of ruins, and a few hundred yards outside it were given the order to halt. 'You will now micturate,' ordered Captain Salter. 'Fall out.' They fell out; the duller men found out quickly what that long word meant: the road was cosy with the comfortable warm noise of hissing. They were fallen in again. 'We are very near the front line now,' said Captain Salter, 'and subject to enemy shelling.' ('Nonsense,' thought Tristram.) 'We will march in file, hugging the left of the road.' From *tre corde* to *una corda*, like a piano damped. The draft was attenuated into a single long string, and the march was resumed. After another mile they came, on the left, to what seemed to be a ruined country house.

Captain Salter consulted his scrap of paper in a sky-flash, as if to see whether this was the right number. Seemingly satisfied, he marched boldly in by the front door. The long stream followed. Tristram was interested to find that they had entered a trench. 'Queer sort of 'ouse this is,' grumbled a man, as if he had genuinely thought they had been invited to supper there. It was a mere shell, like something from a film-set. Tristram flashed the platoon torch down at the earth – holes, a tangle of wires, the sudden scurry of a small beast with a long tail – and immediately heard 'Put that bloody light out.' He obeyed; the voice sounded authoritative. Warnings were passed down the endless line – 'Hole – 'ole – 'owl; wire – wayer – wah' – like specimens of English sound changes. Tristram stumbled on at the head of No. 1 Section of his platoon, seeing the whole montage clearly as the sky flashed with fireworks (that's what they were, that's what they *must* be). Surely there should be a reserve line, a support line, sentries on fire-steps, smoke and stink from dug-outs? The whole labyrinth seemed quite deserted, nobody to welcome them in. Suddenly they turned right. Ahead men were stumbling, cursing softly, being crammed into dug-outs.

'The enemy,' whispered Mr Dollimore with awe, 'is only about a hundred yards away. Over there.' He pointed, lit up finely by a great flash, in the direction of no-man's-land or whatever it was called. 'We must post sentries. One every forty or fifty yards.'

'Look,' said Tristram, 'who's in charge. What are we? Who do we belong to?'

'Dear me, what a lot of questions.' He gazed mildly, in a new firework flash, on Tristram.

'What I mean,' said Tristram, 'is – are we reinforce-ments for some troops or other already in the line, or are we –? *What* are we? Where are our orders coming from? What orders have we got?'

'Now, Sergeant,' said Mr Dollimore paternally, 'don't worry about all these big issues. Those will be taken care of, never fear. Just make sure the men get settled in properly. Then arrange about sentries, will you?' Mean-while, the harmless racket continued: the record-players banged away at their simulacra of passionate war: the loudspeakers must be very close. Lights of exquisite intensity spewed, like fancy oil, out of the ground. 'Woonderful,' said a man from Northern Province, peep-ing out of his dug-out.

'What,' said Tristram, persistent, 'is the point of post-ing sentries? There's no enemy over there. The whole thing's a fake. Very shortly this trench will blow up and the blowing-up will be done by remote control, by some bloody big spider sitting at base. Don't you see? This is the new way, the modern way, of dealing with excess population. The noises are fakes. The flashes are fakes. Where's our artillery? Did you see any artillery behind the lines? Of course you didn't. Have you seen any shells or shrapnel? Stick your head over that parapet and what do you think will happen?' Tristram clam-bered up some bags filled with earth, a neat pattern, obviously bricklayers' work, and looked out. He saw, momentarily lighted by a firework, a flat stretch of country with a distant vista of trees, hills beyond. 'There,' he said, stepping down.

'I've a good mind,' said Mr Dollimore, shaking, 'to put you under arrest. I've a good mind to strip you right down. I've a good mind –'

'You can't.' Tristram shook his head. 'You're only a lieutenant. Your Temporary Acting Captain Salter can't do it, either. And that's another thing you can tell me – where are the senior officers? There's not one officer of field rank anywhere to be found. Where's Battalion HQ, for instance? I come back to my former question – who's giving the orders?'

'This is insubordination,' shook Mr Dollimore. 'This is also treason.'

'Oh, come, nonsense. Look,' said Tristram, 'it's your duty to tell these men what's going on. It's your duty to march them back to the Base Camp to stop them getting officially slaughtered. It's your duty to start asking a few questions.'

'Don't tell me my duty.' Mr Dollimore, surprisingly, unholstered his pistol. 'I've a good mind to shoot you,' he said. 'I'm entitled to. Spreading alarm and despondency.' It was as though he had acute dengue: the pistol rocked violently.

'You've got the safety-catch on,' said Tristram. 'Such bloody nonsense. You wouldn't have the guts. I'm getting out of here.' He about-turned.

'Oh, no, you're not.' And to Tristram's extreme astonishment, Mr Dollimore, safety-catch evidently off, fired. Crack, and the bullet whined well off target, bedding itself safe in an earth-bag. Some of the troops peeped out, chewing or, chewing suspended, gaping at the noise of a real weapon.

'All right,' sighed Tristram. 'But just wait, that's all. You'll see that I'm right, you idiot.'

Eight

BUT Tristram was not entirely right. His own common sense ought to have told him that there was a flaw in his violent supposition. Mr Dollimore shook off to whatever pathetic headquarters A/T/Captain Salter had contrived. Tristram looked in on his platoon. Corporal Haskell said, 'Know what I found, Sarge? A bit of shamrock. That proves where we are pretty well, doesn't it?'

'Can you think why we should be here?' asked Tristram.

Corporal Haskell made a frog-face and said, 'Fighting the Micks, as I said. Though why we should be fighting them, God alone knows. Still, we don't know half of what goes on, do we? From what I heard on the news a couple of weeks ago, I should have thought it would have been the Chinese. Perhaps the Irish and the Chinese are all tied up together.'

Tristram wondered whether he ought to enlighten Corporal Haskell, a good decent family man by the look of him. *They'd never believe me.* A callow officer-voice was singing that some yards up the trench. A session of ancient war-songs, then, on these officers' training courses? Tristram wondered whether he could risk now making his quiet get-away. But, seeing the whole thing as a trap, a contrivance, he knew that there was no way back, behind the lines. If there was any way at all, it lay ahead, over the top and the best of luck. He said to Corporal Haskell, 'Are you quite certain this is the west coast of Ireland?'

'As certain as I'm certain of anything.'

'But you couldn't say exactly where?'

'No,' said Corporal Haskell, 'but I'd say we definitely weren't as far north as Connaught. That means it must be Galway or Clare or Kerry.'

'I see. And how would one set about getting to the other coast?'

'You'd have to pick up the railway, wouldn't you? All old steam trains they have here in Ireland, or used to have when I was doing my travelling. Let me see. If this is Kerry, then you could get from Killarney to Dungarvan. Or further north it might be from Listowel across Limerick and Tipperary and Kilkenny to Wexford. Or, supposing we're in County Clare –'

'Thank you, Corporal.'

'Couldn't be done, of course, not if we're at war with the Micks. They'd cut your throat as soon as they heard the way you speak.'

'I see. Thanks, anyway.'

'You weren't thinking of doing a bunk, were you, Sarge?'

'No, no, of course not.' Tristram left the close stinking dug-out, full of lolling men, and went to have a word with the nearest sentry. The sentry, a spotty lad called Burden, said:

'They've been moving in over there, Sarge.'

'Where? Who?'

'Over there.' He bowed his steel helmet towards the opposed trenches. Tristram listened. Chinese? There was a murmuring of rather high-pitched voices. The recorded noises of battle had slackened a great deal. So.

His heart sank. He had been wrong, quite wrong. There *was* an enemy. He listened more closely. 'Been moving in real quick, they have, quiet too. Seem to be a very well behaved lot.'

'It won't be long now, then,' said Tristram.

As if to confirm that statement, Mr Dollimore came stumbling along the trench. He saw Tristram and said, 'You, is it? Captain Salter says you ought to be put under close arrest. But he also says it's too late now. We attack at 2200 hours. Synchronize watches.'

'Attack? How attack?'

'There you are again, asking your foolish questions. We go over the top at 2200 hours sharp. It is now –' he checked '– exactly 2134. Fixed bayonets. Our orders are to take that enemy trench.' He was bright and feverish.

'Who gave the orders?'

'Never you mind who gave the orders. Alert the platoon. All rifles loaded, not forgetting one up the spout.' Mr Dollimore stood upright, looking important. 'England,' he suddenly said, and his nose filled with tears. Tristram, having nothing further to say in the circumstances, saluted.

At 2140 hours there was sudden silence like a smack in the face. 'Cor,' said the men, missing the cosy noise. Lights ceased to flash. In this unfamiliar hushed dark the enemy could more clearly be heard, coughing, whispering, in the light tones of small-boned Orientals. At 2145 men stood, breathing hard through their mouths, all along the trench. Mr Dollimore, pistol trembling, eyes never leaving his wrist-watch, was ready to lead his thirty over (some corner of a foreign field) in brave assault, owing God a death (that is for ever England). 2150 and all hearts were all but audible. Tristram knew his own part in this impending suicide: if Mr Dollimore's office was to pull the men over, his own was to push them: 'Get up and out there, you scabs, or I shoot every cowardly one of you.' 2155. 'O God of battles,' Mr Dollimore was whispering, 'steel my soldier's heart.' 2156. 'I want my mum,' mock-sobbed a Cockney humorist. 2157. 'Or,' said Corporal Haskell, 'if we were far south enough you could get from Bantry to Cork.' 2158. The bayonets trembled. Somebody started hiccoughs and kept saying, 'Pardon.' 2159. 'Ah,' said Mr Dollimore, and he watched his second-hand as if it were an act in a flea circus. 'We're coming up now to, we're coming up now to –'

2200. Whistles skirled shrilled deadly silver all along the line, and the phonographic bombardment clamoured out at once dementedly. In mean spasmodic flashes Mr Dollimore could be seen, clambering over, waving his pistol, his mouth stretched in some inaudible OCTU battle-cry. 'Go on, you lot,' shouted Tristram, prodding with his own gun, pushing, threatening, kicking. The troops mounted, some with fair agility. 'No, no,' panicked one small gnarled man, 'for Christ's sake don't make me.' 'Over you go, blast you,' snarled Tristram's dentures. Corporal Haskell yelled, from above, 'Jesus, they're coming for us!' Rifles bitterly cracked and spattered, filling the sharp air with the. sharper smoked-bacon tang of a thousand struck matches. Bullets dismally whinged. There were deep bloody curses, there were screams. Tristram, his head above the parapet, saw etched black cut-out bodies facing each other in hand-to-hand, clumsy, falling, firing, jabbing, in some old film about soldiers. He distinctly observed Mr Dollimore falling back (always this element of the absurd: as if he were in a dance and were trying to keep to his feet to go on dancing) and then crashing with his mouth open. Corporal Haskell was caught savagely in the leg; firing as he fell he opened his mouth (as for the host) for a bullet and his face disintegrated. Tristram, one knee on the topmost earth-bag, emptied his pistol wildly at the staggering advance. It was slaughter, it was mutual massacre, it was impossible to miss. Tristram reloaded, now belatedly infected with poor dead Dollimore's ague, scrambling backwards into the trench, his booted toes digging into the interstices of the earth-bags, his helmeted head, eyes and shooting hand above the parapet. And he saw the enemy. A strange race, small, bulky at chest and hips, high-screaming like women. They were all going down, the air full of tasty smoke, still zinging with bullets. And, seeing, a cold reserved chamber of his brain fitting everything into place, all this foreshadowed by that Sacred Game of Pelagian times, he retched and then vomited a whole sour gutful of chewed meat. One of his own men turned back to the trench, clawing air, having dropped his rifle, choking, 'Oh, bloody Christ.' And then a groan from behind his sternum as bullets entered his back. He toppled like a tumbler over, taking Tristram with him, all arms and legs, essence of man, bifurcation. Tristram, smashed hard against the rocking duckboards, struggled with the dead-weight incubus that snored out the last of its life, then heard from the flanks, as from stage-wings, the dry rain of machine-

gun fire, manifestly a live noise against the sham caco-
phony of bombardment. 'Finishing them off,' he
thought, 'finishing them off.'

Then all the big noise ceased, nor were there any
specifically human sounds, only animal gasps of those
late in dying. One last flash showed him his watch:
2203. Three minutes from start to finish. With great
difficulty he heaved the corpse off his stomach on to the
trench-floor; it groaned, collapsing. Fearful, he crawled
away sorely to whimper alone, the smell of the
monstrous smoked-bacon breakfast still swirling above.
His sobs started up irrepressibly; soon he was howling
with despair and horror, seeing, as if the darkness were
a mirror, his own wretched screwed face, tongue licking
the tears, the lower lip thrust out quivering with anger
and hopelessness.

When this ghastly transport had spent itself, he
fancied he heard the renewal of battle above him. But
it was only single cracks of pistol-shot, irregularly
spaced. Looking up in terror he saw torch-beams searching, as if for something lost in the shambles of bodies.
He stiffened in great fear. 'The old coop de gracy,' said a
coarse voice. 'Poor little bitch.' Then a couple of cracked
peremptory shots. A torch searched, searched, over the
trench-lip, searching for him. He lay, his face bunched
anew, like one who had met violent death. 'Poor old
bugger,' said the coarse voice and a resonant bullet
seemed to meet bone. 'Sergeant here,' said another voice.
'He's had it all right.' 'Better make sure,' said the first.
'Oh, hell,' said the other, 'I'm sick of this job. Real sick.
It's dirty, it's filthy.' Tristram felt the torch-beam travel
over his shut eyes, then pass on. 'All right,' said the

first. 'Pack it in. If they'll let you. You,' to someone more distant. 'Leave all pockets alone. No looting. Have some respect for the dead, blast you.' The boots crunched on over the field; more odd shots. Tristram lay on in dead stiffness, not budging even when some small animal ran over him busily, sniffing and twitching whiskers on his face. Human silence returned, but he lay on for an age longer, frozen.

Nine

At last, in that dead but safe stillness, Tristram torch-lighted his way into the dug-out where Corporal Haskell had taught him the geography of Ireland, where the first section of his platoon had awaited, singing, lolling, fidgeting, action. It was still, sealed by its blanket-door, foul-smelling, odorous of life. Packs and water-bottles lay about, perhaps including his own, for he had dumped these impedimenta with one of the sections on moving into the trench. The battery-fed dug-out lantern had been doused before the attack and he did not re-light it. His torch showed a pile of money on the table – guineas, septs, tosheroons, crowns, tanners, quids, florins; this, he knew, was the pooled cash of the platoon, useless to the dead but a prize for the survivors – an ancient tradition. Tristram, sole survivor, bowed his head as he fed the money into his pockets. He then filled a random pack with tinned meat, strapped a full water-bottle on to his belt, and loaded his pistol. He sighed, facing another anabasis.

He stumbled out of the trench, tripping over the corpses in the tiny no-man's-land, not daring to use his torch yet in the open. He felt his way into and out of the opposed trench, a very shallow one, and then marched, wincing at the pain of that fall from parapet to duckboards so long ago, fearful of possible lurking gunmen. Bare ground stretched under faint starlight. After what he judged to be a mile's walking he saw lights ahead on the horizon, dim, widely spaced. Cautious, his pistol out, he trudged on. The lights glowed bigger, more like fruit than seeds. Soon he saw, fear beating hard in him, a high wire fence stretching on either hand indefinitely, a pattern of illuminated and penumbral close steel weaving. Probably electrified, like the Base Camp perimeter. There was nothing for it but to walk parallel to it (there was no cover of trees or bushes) and seek, ready with bluff, threats, force, some legitimate way through, if any.

At length he saw, and carefully approached, a sort of gateway let into the endless fence, the gate itself a firm metal frame garnished with barbed wire. Beyond was a wooden shack with a single dim-lighted window and, outside the door of this shack, stood a greatcoated, helmeted sentry nearly asleep on his feet. Hut, gate, wire, dark, sentry – nothing else. The sentry came alive with a startled jerk, seeing Tristram, and pointed his rifle. 'Open up,' ordered Tristram.

'Where've you come from?' His rather dim-witted face was uneasy.

'I've got a rank, haven't I?' blustered Tristram. 'Let me through. Take me to the N.C.O. in charge.'

'Sorry, Sergeant. It was a bit of a shock, like. First

time I've seen anybody coming through from that side.' This was going to be easy. The sentry opened the gate, which whirred along the ground on casters, and said, 'This way.' There was evidently no other way. 'Sergeant.' He led Tristram to the shack of a guard-room, opened the door, showed him in. A bulb of low wattage glowed like an orange from the ceiling; on the wall were framed standing orders and a map. Corporal Haskell's nose had been astonishingly accurate: it was a`map of Ireland. At a table, cleaning his nails, his feet on a chair, sat a corporal not unlike Charles Baudelaire in hair and expression. Tristram rapped, 'Stand up, Corporal.' The corporal knocked the chair over in his haste, responding to Tristram's officer-accent more than his stripes. 'All right,' said Tristram, 'sit down again. Are you in charge here?'

'Sergeant Forester's asleep, Sarnt. I'd better wake him up.'

'Don't trouble.' He decided to swell his bluff to skin-bursting. 'What I'm after is transport. Where can I get transport?'

The corporal stared as Charles Baudelaire stares from his daguerreotype. 'Nearest M.T. park's at Dingle. Depends where you want to get to.'

'I've got to report about this last show,' said Tristram. 'May I see that map?' He walked over to the fubsy multi-coloured beast that was Ireland. Dingle was, of course, on Dingle Bay; Dingle Bay and Tralee Bay had carved a peninsula out of County Kerry. He saw everything now: various islands and teats on the west coast were marked with WD flags, leased presumably for ostensible training purposes by the Government of All

Ireland to the British War Department. 'I see, I see,' said Tristram.

'Where would it be,' said the corporal, 'that you'd be wanting to get to?'

'You should know better than to ask that question,' reproved Tristram. 'There *is* such a thing as security, you know.'

'Sorry, Sarnt. Sarnt,' asked the corporal shyly, 'what *really* goes on in there, Sarnt?' He pointed in the direction of the huge enclosed battleground.

'You mean to say you don't know?'

'Nobody's allowed in, Sarnt. Nobody's ever let in there. We just hear the noises, that's all. A very real kind of training it is, from the sound of it. But nobody's ever allowed through to see it, Sarnt. That's in the standing orders.'

'And how about letting people out?'

'Well, there's nothing about that, you see. Nobody ever comes out this way, that's why, I suppose. You're the first I've ever seen, and I've been on this job nine months. Hardly worth while having a gate here, is it?'

'Oh, I don't know,' said Tristram. 'It's served its purpose tonight, hasn't it?'

'That's true,' said the corporal, in a kind of awe as at the provisions of all-providing providence. 'That's very true.' And then, helpfully, 'Of course, you could always get a train to wherever it is you've got to go to, couldn't you, Sarnt?'

'The station?'

'Oh, only a mile or two down that road. Branch-line to Tralee. There's a train takes shift-workers to Killarney about two in the morning. You'd easily get that if that's any good to you.'

To think, just to think: it was still the same night and yet it seemed a whole slab of time somehow outside time since the blasting of those whistles. Sergeant Lightbody, he suddenly remembered, had talked about going to find a great perhaps: queer to think that he had already long found it. No longer a perhaps, of course. Tristram shivered.

'You don't look all that good, Sarnt. Are you sure you can make it?'

'I can make it,' said Tristram. 'I've got to make it.'

Epilogue

Epilogue

One

TRALEE to Killarney, Killarney to Mallow. Tristram had bad dreams most of the way, slumped, greatcoat-collar up, in a corner seat. A high-pitched voice seemed to be keeping the score over the steam-train's noise: 'Say twelve hundred seen off tonight, say ten stone average, women being lighter than men, say twelve thousand stone deadweight. Multiply by one thousand, making twelve million stone – on the bone, on the hoof – for one night's (convert to tons at leisure) good global work.' His platoon paraded, pointing sadly at him because he was still alive. Coming into Mallow he awoke fighting. An Irish labourer held him down, calming him, saying, 'Dere y'are, fella.' He travelled by day from Mallow to Rosslare. He spent the night in a hotel in Rosslare and in the morning, having seen Military Police prowling around, bought a ready-made suit, raincoat, shirt, pair of shoes. He stuffed his army clothes into his pack – first having given away his tins of meat to a poor whining crone who said, 'May Jesus, Mary and Joseph bless ya, acushla.' His pistol in his pocket, he boarded the packet for Fishguard as a civilian.

It was a rough February crossing, St George's Channel rearing and snorting like a dragon. He felt ill at Fishguard and spent the night there. The next day, in chilled sunshine like hock, he travelled south-east to Brighton. At least, the ticket he bought was for Brighton. After Salisbury he yielded to a compulsive desire to count and re-count his money, the platoon's money: it came consistently to thirty-nine guineas, three septs, one tanner. He shivered perpetually, so that the other occupants of his compartment gave him curious stares. As they drew in to Southampton he decided he was really ill but probably had enough strength to alight at Southampton and find accommodation there to have the illness out. There were plenty of good reasons for not arriving, staggering and collapsing, in obvious need of help, everything beyond his control, at Brighton.

Near Southampton Central Station he found an Army hostel – the five bottom storeys of a skyscraper. He went in, showed his paybook, and paid for five nights' accommodation. He was taken by an old man in a faded blue servant's jacket to a small cold room, monastic, but with plenty of blankets on the bed. 'You all right?' said the old man. 'All right,' said Tristram. When the old man had left, he locked the door, undressed quickly and crept into bed. There he relaxed his hold and let the fever, like some devil or lover, take complete possession of him.

The endless shivering and sweating ate up time, place, sensation. He calculated, by the natural alternation of dark and light, that he lay in his bed for thirty-six hours, the sickness worrying and gnawing his body like a dog with a bone, the sweating so intense that his bladder was given a holiday, feeling himself grow palpably thinner and lighter, ridden at the crisis by a conviction that his body had become transparent, that each several inner organ shone phosphorescent in the dark, so that it seemed a scandalous waste no sister-tutor could bring her anatomy students to view him. Then he fell into a trench of sleep so deep that no dream or hallucination could reach him. He woke to morning, feeling he must have slept, like a bear or tortoise, a whole season away, for the sun in the room was like a spring sun. He yanked time painfully out of its hiding-place and computed that it must still be February, still winter.

Intense thirst drew him out of bed. He staggered to the wash-basin, took his chilled dentures out of their glass, then filled this again and again with the hard southern chalky water, glugging it down till finally he had to lie on his bed gasping. He had stopped shaking, but he still felt paper-thin. He rolled himself in his blankets and slept again. His brimming bladder woke him next time and, a little secret, he voided it in the wash-basin. Now he felt able to walk though very cold. That was because he had not eaten. The sun was setting, a chill evening closing in. He dressed without washing or shaving and went downstairs to the canteen. Soldiers sat about, drinking tea, moaning and bragging, their numbers not yet dry. Tristram asked for boiled hen-eggs and natural milk. Meat he did not dare even think of. He ate very slowly and felt a sort of promise of strength returning. He was intrigued to see that an ancient custom (its introduction to England attributed to a mythical seaman named John Player) had been re-vived: a few soldiers were choking over rolled paper tubes, the ends aglow. Cover yourselves in glow, in glow, dada *rump*. Tears burst audibly. He had better get back to bed.

He slept solid for another uncomputed slab of dark and light. When he woke, and this was suddenly, he found himself transferred to a region of great mental clarity. 'What do you propose?' asked the foot of the bed. 'Not to get caught,' answered Tristram aloud. He had been pressed into the army on 27 March, Easter Day of the previous year, and was due for demobilization exactly one year later. Till that date – over a month off – he could do nothing safely. He had failed to die: the War Department would probably chase him till he had made good that dereliction of duty. Would they, though, really care? He thought they would: they would be unhappy brooding over a nominal roll with a query instead of a tick against one name, a paybook missing. Perhaps even here, in this Army Hostel, he would not be safe. He felt, he thought, well enough to leave.

He washed and shaved thoroughly and then dressed with care as a civilian. He almost floated down the stairs, light as a shorn sheep: that illness had done him some good, purged him of gross humours. There were no military policemen in the vestibule. He had expected to walk out into morning but found, fully launched into the maritime city, that afternoon was well advanced. He ate fried fish in a back-street restaurant, then found, not too far from it, a dirty-looking lodging-block which would suit him well. No questions, no curiosity. He paid a week's rent in advance. His money would just about,. he thought, last.

Two

TRISTRAM spent the following four weeks fairly profitably. He recollected his function – that of a teacher of history and related subjects – and so, financed by his poor dead platoon, he treated himself to a brief course of rehabilitation. He sat all day in the Central Library, reading the great historians and historiographers of his age – Stott's *Twentieth-Century Ideological Struggles*; Zuckmayer and Feldwebel's *Principien der Rassensgeschichte*; Stebbing-Brown's *History of Nuclear Warfare*; Ang Siong-Joo's *Kung-Ch'an Chu I*; Sparrow's *Religious Substitutes in the Prototechnic Age*; Radzinowicz on *The Doctrine of the Cycle*. They were all thin books in logogrammatic form, that clipped orthography designed to save space. But now there seemed to be enough space. For evening relaxation he read the new poets and novelists. The writers of the Pelphase seemed discredited, he noticed: one could not perhaps, after all, and it was a pity, make art out of that gentle old liberalism. The new books were full of sex and death, perhaps the only materials for a writer.

On 27 March, a Monday, in fine spring weather, Tristram travelled by rail to London. The War Office was situated in Fulham. He found it to be a block of offices in a skyscraper of moderate height (thirty storeys) called Juniper Building. A commissionaire said, 'You can't come in here, sir.'

'Why not?'

'Not without an appointment.'

273

Tristram snarled, 'Out of my way. You don't seem to know who I am,' and he pushed the commissionaire aside and strode into the first office he came to. Here a number of fattish blonde women in uniform were clacking at electric speech-machines. 'I want to see someone in charge,' said Tristram.

'You can't see anyone without an appointment,' said one of the young women. Tristram strode through this office and opened a door with a glazed upper half. A lieutenant sat, busily thinking, between two empty correspondence-trays. He said:

'Who let you in?' He had spectacles with big black frames, a sweet-eater's complexion, close-bitten nails, a patch of nap on his neck where he had shaved ill. Tristram said:

'That's a pointless sort of question, isn't it? My name's Sergeant Foxe, T. I'm reporting as the sole survivor of one of those pleasantly contrived miniature massacres on the West Coast of Ireland. I should prefer to talk to someone more important than you.'

'Survivor?' The lieutenant looked startled. 'You'd better come and report to Major Berkeley.' He rose from his desk, disclosing a desk-worker's paunch, then went out by a door opposite to the one by which Tristram had entered. A knock at this latter was answered by Tristram himself. It was the commissionaire. 'Sorry I let him get past me, sir,' he began to say. And then, 'Oh,' for Tristram had his pistol out: if they wanted to play at soldiers, let them. 'Barmy,' said the commissionaire and slammed the door quickly; his fast-retreating shadow could be seen through the glaze. The lieutenant returned. 'This way,' he said. Tristram followed him down

274

a corridor illuminated only by the light from other glazed doors; he pocketed his pistol.

'Sergeant Foxe, sir,' said the lieutenant, opening up on an officer pretending to be desperately engaged in the composition of an urgent despatch. He was a red-tabbed major with very fine auburn hair; he presented, writing, to Tristram a bald spot of the size and roundness of a communion host. On the walls were group photographs of dull-looking people mostly in shorts. 'Just one moment,' said the major severely, writing hard.

'Oh, come off it,' said Tristram.

'I beg your pardon?' The major glared up; his eyes were weak and oyster-coloured. 'Why aren't you in uniform?'

'Because, according to the terms of contract listed in my paybook, my engagement terminated today at 1200 hours precisely.'

'I see. You'd better leave us, Ralph,' said the major to the lieutenant. The lieutenant bowed like a waiter and left. 'Now,' said the major to Tristram, 'what's all this about your being the only survivor?' He did not seem to expect an immediate answer, for he followed up with, 'Let me see your paybook.' Tristram handed it over. He had not been asked to sit down, so he sat down. 'Hm,' said the major, opening, reading. He clicked a switch and spoke into a microphone: '7388026 Sergeant Foxe, T. File immediately, please.' And then, to Tristram, 'What have you come to see us about?'

'To register protest,' said Tristram. 'To warn you that I'm going to blow the bloody gaff.'

The major looked puzzled. He had a long nose which he now rubbed, puzzled. A buff file shot from a wall-slit

275

into a wire basket; the major opened this file and read attentively. 'Ah,' he said, 'I see. Everybody's been looking for you, it seems. By rights you should be dead, shouldn't you? Dead, with the rest of your comrades. You must have made a very quick getaway. I could still have you arrested as a deserter, you know. Retrospectively.'

'Oh, nonsense,' said Tristram. 'As the sole survivor I was the head of that unfortunate murdered lot. It was up to me to make the decisions. I decided to send myself on a month's leave. I was also ill, and no wonder.'

'That's irregular, you know.'

'Let's not hear anything from you or your bloody murdering organization about irregularity,' said Tristram. 'A lot of murdering swine, that's what you are.'

'I see,' said the major. 'And you dissociate yourself from us, do you? I should imagine,' smoothly, 'you've done more killing than, say, I have. You've actually taken part in an E.S.'

'What's an E.S.?'

'Extermination Session. That's what the new battles are called, you know. I should imagine you did your share of – well, shall we call it self-defence? Otherwise, I can't see how you managed to survive.'

'We were given certain orders.'

'Of course you were. Orders to shoot. That's only reasonable, isn't it, when you're being shot at?'

'It was still murder,' said Tristram violently. 'Those poor, wretched, defenceless –'

'Oh, come, they weren't exactly defenceless, were they? Beware of clichés, Foxe. One cliché leads on to another, you know, and the final term of the series is

276

always absurd. They were well trained and well armed and they died gloriously, believing they were dying in a great cause. And, you know, they really were. And you survived, of course, for the most inglorious reason. You survived because you didn't believe in what we're fighting for, what we'll always be fighting for. Of course, you got dragged in at the beginning when the system was most imperfect. Our conscription system's very selective now. We don't call up suspicious people like you any more.'

'You just take advantage of the poor devils who don't know any better – is that it?'

'Of course. We're better off without the morons and the enthusiasts. Which means also the corner-boys and the criminals. And, as far as the women are concerned, the cretinous over-producers. That's genetically very sound, you know.'

'Oh God, God,' moaned Tristram, 'it's all sheer bloody madness.'

'Hardly. Look, you acted under orders. We all act under orders. The orders of the War Department come ultimately from the G.P.L.A.'

'Murderers, whoever they are.'

'Oh, no. The Global Population Limitation Authority. They don't, of course, actually give orders in the military sense. They merely report on population in relation to food supply – always with an eye to the future, of course. And their idea of a food supply is not the old primitive minimal notion – they're concerned with a high standard involving margins. I'm not an economist, incidentally, so don't ask me what margins are.'

'I know all about that,' said Tristram. 'I'm a historian.'

277

'Yes? Well, as I say, you should either have been kept on instructional duties – and somebody's going to get a rocket sooner or later over transferring you to combatant duties – or, what was I saying? Yes, you shouldn't have been called up at all.'

'I can see why you say that,' said Tristram. 'I know too much now, don't I? And I propose to write and talk and teach about your cynical murderous organization. This is no longer a police state. There are no spies, there's no censorship. I'll tell the bloody truth. I'll get the Government to act.'

The major was unperturbed. He stroked his nose in slow rhythm. 'Despite its name,' he said, 'the War Department is not really a branch of government at all. It's a corporation. The term "War Department" is merely a link with the past. A corporation with a charter. The charter comes up for renewal every three years, I think it is. I don't think there's any likelihood of its not being renewed. You see, what other way is there of keeping the population down? The birth-rate rose phenomenally last year and it's still rising. Not, of course, that there's anything wrong in that. Contraception is cruel and unnatural: everybody has a right to be born. But, similarly, everybody's got to die sooner or later. Our age-groups for call-up will get progressively older – as far, of course, as the healthy and mentally normal sections of the population are concerned; the trash can go shortly after puberty. Everybody must die, and history seems to show (you're a historian, so you'll agree with me here), history seems to show that the soldier's death is the best death. Facing fearful odds, as the poet says. Ashes of his fathers, temples of his gods, and so on. I don't think you'd find anybody against the present system. The War Department is a bit like prostitution: it cleanses the community. If we didn't exist, a great deal of nastiness would bubble up in the State. We're the mother-of-pearl, you see. The ruffians, the perverts, the death-wishers: you don't want those in the civil community. So long as there's an army there'll never be a police state, no more greyboys or rubber truncheons or thumbscrews or rifle squads at inconveniently early hours. The final problems of the body politic have been solved. Now we have a free state – order without organization, which means order without violence. A safe and spacious community. A clean house full of happy people. But every house, of course, has to have a drainage system. We're that.'

'It's all wrong,' said Tristram. 'All, all wrong.'

'Yes? Well, when you can think out something better come and tell us all about it.'

With a tiny itch of hope, Tristram said, 'Do you think people are fundamentally good?'

'Well,' said the major, 'they now have a chance to be good.'

'Exactly,' said Tristram. 'Which means that it won't be long before the return of liberalism. I don't think a Pelagian State would renew your charter.'

'No?' The major was not very interested.

'You're signing your own death warrant just by existing.'

'That's a bit too epigrammatical for me,' said the major. 'Look, I've enjoyed this talk, but I really am rather busy. You should by rights, you know, go through the proper channels as far as your demobilization is concerned. But I'll sign your discharge, if you like, and give you a chitty for the cashier's department.' He began to write. 'A gratuity of twenty guineas for each month of service. A month's *official* demobilization leave on full pay. Right. They'll work out the details for you. They'll pay you cash, seeing that you're such a suspicious sort of man.' He smiled. 'And,' he added, 'don't forget to hand that pistol in.' Tristram found, shocked, that he had been pointing it at the major. 'You'd better give it to me. We don't like violence all that much, you know. Shooting is for the army, and you're out of the army now, *Mister* Foxe.' Tristram meekly placed the pistol on the major's desk. He saw now that it would, after all, be wrong to shoot Derek. 'Any more questions?' said the major.

'Just one. What happens to the dead?'

'The dead? Oh, I see what you mean. When a soldier is discharged dead the soldier's paybook is collected and a letter of condolence sent to his – or her, of course – next-of-kin. After that the War Department has no further responsibility. Civilian contractors take over. We've learned something, you know, from the past: waste not, want not. What the civilian contractors do is their own affair. But the money comes in handy. The money keeps this corporation going. We're completely independent, you see, of the Treasury. I think that's something to be proud of. Any more questions?'

Tristram was silent.

'Good. Well, the best of luck, old man. Now I suppose you'll have to start looking for a job. You shouldn't have much difficulty with your qualifications.'

'And experience,' added Tristram.

'As you say.' Smiling cordially, he stood up to shake hands.

Three

TRISTRAM took the next tube-train to Brighton, saying to himself in time with the train's beat: 'Patience, patience, patience, patience.' The word summed up so much: patience of different lengths and weights, different lengths of waiting. When Brighton towered all around him his brain shuddered with memories, with expectations. Patience. Keep away from the sea, just for a little while. Do things properly.

He found the Education Department where it had always been: in Adkins Street, just off Rostron Place. Frank Gosport was in the Appointments Section, as he'd been before. He even recognized Tristram. 'You're looking well,' he said, 'really well. Just like somebody who's taken a long holiday. What can we do for you?' He was a pleasant round man, beaming, with fluffy hair like duck-down.

'A job,' said Tristram. 'A good job.'

'Hm. History, wasn't it? Civics and so on?'

'You've got a good memory,' said Tristram.

'Not all that good,' said Gosport. 'I can't recall your first name. Derek, isn't it? No, stupid of me, it can't be Derek. Derek Foxe is the Co-ordinating Secretary of the Ministry of Fertility. Of course, of course, he's your brother. It's all coming back to me. Your name begins with a T.' He pressed buttons on the wall; on the wall opposite, in letters of mild flame, details of vacancies appeared, frame after frame of mildly flaming letters. 'See anything you fancy?'

'South London (Channel) Unitary School (Boys) Division Four,' said Tristram. 'Who's Principal there now?'

'Same as before. Joscelyne. He got married, you know, to a real old battle-axe. Clever man, that. He swung with the tide, you know.'

'Like my brother Derek.'

'I suppose so. Fancy anything there?'

'Not really. Too many bad memories. I like the look of that lectureship at the Technical College. History of War. I think I could do that.'

'It's something new. Hardly any applicants. Shall I put you down for it?'

'I think so.'

'You could start at the beginning of the summer term. Do you know anything about war? My son's just had his calling-up papers.'

'Is he glad about it?'

'He's a young lout. The army ought to knock some sense into him. Good. You'd better go and look at the College sometime. It's a very nice building, I believe. The Principal's all right. Name of Mather. I think you'll get on all right.'

'Fine. Thanks.'

In Rostron Place Tristram found a house-and-flat agent's office. He was offered a very respectable apartment in Winthrop Mansions – two bedrooms, living-dining-room, fair-sized kitchen, fitted with refrigerator, stereotelly, and wall-spindle for the *Daily Newsdisc* or any of its auditory rivals. Having seen it, he took it, signing the usual form of agreement and paying a month's rent in advance. Then he did some shopping: kitchen utensils, provisions (a very fair variety in the new free-enterprise shops) and some underclothes, pyjamas and a dressing-gown.

And now. And now. And now. His heart pounding and fluttering like a bird in a paper-bag, he walked, trying to walk slowly, down to the sea-front. Crowds of people in the spring sun, encircled by fresh marine air, gulls cackling like heckelphones, the stony majesty of the offices of the Government. The Ministry of Fertility – bas-relief of an egg cracking open to display new-born wings – with a plaque saying: *Incorporating Departments of Food, Agriculture, Fecundity Research, Religion, Ritual and Popular Culture. Motto:* ALL LIFE IS ONE. And, looking, smiling nervously, Tristram decided that he didn't finally want to go in there after all, that there was nothing he could profitably say or do to his brother. He swung down in his swing for the last time, braking with his feet dug in the ground. For the victory was his, Tristram's, as this afternoon would show. What was most dearly his, Tristram's, he, Tristram, would, before ninety minutes or less were up, have regained. Finally. Utterly. That was the only kind of victory he needed.

High above Government Building the bronze robed figure with the baroque beard, baroque robe-folds, glared at the sun in this windless day, hair and clothes stirred by the baroque wind of the sculptor's fancy. Who was it? Augustine? Pelagius? Christ? Satan? Tristram fancied he caught the shine of tiny horns in the stirred mass of stone hair. He would have to wait, they would all have to wait. But he was very nearly confident that the cycle would start again, that figure preach to the sun and sea-clouds about man's ability to organize the good life, his lack of need for grace, the godhead implicit in him. Pelagius, Morgan, Old Man of the Sea.

He waited.

Four

'SEA,' whispered Beatrice-Joanna, 'teach us all sense.' She stood by the promenade rails, the gurgling woolly rosy twins belabouring each other softly in their perambulator. There it stretched all before her, endowed with delirium, panther-skin, mantle pierced with thousands upon thousands of the sun's idols, hydra absolute, drunk with its own blue flesh, biting its scintillating tail in a tumult like silence. 'Sea, sea, sea.'

Beyond the sea Robert Starling, late Prime Minister of Great Britain and Chairman of the Council of Prime Ministers of the English-Speaking Union, in a Mediterranean villa, surrounded by his sweet boys, eating delicately, sipping fruit-juice, reading the classics with his feet up, delicately calculated the end of his exile. On other shores of the sea the thalassographers prepared their attempts on the unplumbed green riches with new engines, cunning meters. Untouched life lurked, miles down, leagues down.

'Sea, sea.' And she prayed for someone, and the prayer was at once answered, but the answer did not come from the sea. It came from the warmer land behind her. A gentle hand on her arm. She turned, startled. Then, after her moment of wordless shock, she still had no words, only tears. She clung to him, the huge air, the life-giving sea, man's future history in the depths, the present towered town, the bearded man at the pinnacle, all shut out from the warmth of his presence, the closeness of his embrace. He became sea, sun, tower. The twins gurgled. There were still no words.

The wind rises . . . we must try to live. The immense air opens and closes my book. The wave, pulverized, dares to gush and spatter from the rocks. Fly away, dazzled, blinded pages. Break, waves. Break with joyful waters. . . .

PZ   Burgess, Anthony,
4   1917–
B953
Wan   The wanting seed
1976

DATE			
SEP 27 '85			
Oct 18 85			